The
Stellenbosch
MAFIA

Pieter du Toit

The
Stellenbosch
MAFIA

Inside the
BILLIONAIRES'
CLUB

JONATHAN BALL PUBLISHERS
JOHANNESBURG & CAPE TOWN

© Text Pieter du Toit (2019)
© Published edition Jonathan Ball Publishers (2019)

Originally published in South Africa in 2019 by
JONATHAN BALL PUBLISHERS
A division of Media24 (Pty) Ltd
PO Box 33977
Jeppestown
2043

ISBN 9781868429189
ebook 9781868429196

Every effort has been made to trace the copyright holders and to obtain their
permission for the use of copyright material. The publishers apologise for
any errors or omissions and would be grateful to be notified of any corrections
that should be incorporated in future editions of this book.

Twitter: www.twitter.com/JonathanBallPub
Facebook: www.facebook.com/JonathanBallPublishers
Blog: http://jonathanball.bookslive.co.za/

Photograph on back cover: Fairview Winery,
vineyards with Simonsberg, Paarl, S. Africa, Shutterstock
Cover by publicide
Design and typesetting by Martine Barker
Set in Minion Pro/Gill Sans

This book is dedicated to my family, who have supported me throughout the long days and longer nights of writing. Thank you Janetha, Schalk and Lukas.

CONTENTS

CAST OF CHARACTERS

1 Johann Rupert
Chairperson of Remgro, Richemont and Reinet Investments

2 Anton Rupert
Founder of the Rembrandt Group (later Remgro)

3 Julius Malema
Leader of the EFF and a critic of the 'Stellenbosch Mafia'

4 Andile Mngxitama
Leader of Black First Land First

5 Jannie Durand
CEO of Remgro

6 Edwin Hertzog
Chairperson of Mediclinic International

7 Jannie Mouton
Founder and former CEO of the PSG Group

8 Piet Mouton
Son of Jannie and CEO of the PSG Group

9 Christo Wiese
Former chairperson of Steinhoff and founder of Pepkor

CAST OF CHARACTERS

10 Whitey Basson
Former CEO of Shoprite

11 Markus Jooste
Former CEO of Steinhoff

12 Michiel le Roux
Former chairperson of
Capitec Bank

13 GT Ferreira
Former chairperson of
FirstRand

14 Nelson Mandela
Former president of
South Africa

15 Floyd Shivambu
Deputy president of the
EFF

16 Bruno Steinhoff
Founder of Steinhoff
International

17 Jurie Roux
CEO of SARU, former
senior director of finance at
University of Stellenbosch

18 Ben la Grange
Former Steinhoff CFO
and CEO of STAR

ACRONYMS AND ABBREVIATIONS

BAT   British American Tobacco
BLF   Black First Land First
CCRD   Centre for Competition, Regulation and
          Development
CEO   chief executive officer
Cosatu   Congress of South African Trade Unions
EFF   Economic Freedom Fighters
FNB   First National Bank
Iscor   Iron and Steel Corporation
JSE   Johannesburg Stock Exchange
NPA   National Prosecuting Authority
PwC   PricewaterhouseCoopers
RMB   Rand Merchant Bank
SACP   South African Communist Party
SARS   South African Revenue Service
SARU   South African Rugby Union
STAR   Steinhoff Africa Retail
TIB   Tegniese en Industriële Beleggings
TRC   Truth and Reconciliation Commission
UAE   United Arab Emirates
WMC   white monopoly capital

PREFACE

DE VOLKSKOMBUIS restaurant is opposite the Markötter Rugby Fields, which belong to Paul Roos Gymnasium, Stellenbosch's prestigious boys' school. Stellenbosch used to be a quaint village, known mainly for its university, rugby club and surrounding wine farms. Today, however, it's an exclusive, wealthy business centre, whose surrounding mountains create a kind of buffer zone seemingly keeping out the rest of South Africa. It's also the home of the so-called Stellenbosch Mafia.

De Volkskombuis, which had fallen on hard times, was refurbished by, depending on whom you listen to, either Johann Rupert himself or Remgro, the holding company founded by his father as a cigarette manufacturer called Rembrandt.

'Go there for lunch – it's a fantastic place,' Rupert said after an interview he gave me for this book. The restaurant is a Stellenbosch institution. It has been there for years and continues to serve local Boland fare, such as *waterblommetjiebredie* and a hearty oxtail. Since its revamp, the slightly run-down, rural look is gone, replaced by a modern kitchen and understated but expensive finishings, and it boasts a wine list populated by produce from the best estates in the area.

In April 2018, I attended a lunch event there organised by Jannie Durand, the CEO of Remgro. A colleague and I were to give a talk that evening about the political climate in the country, and the event was intended as an opportunity to talk with local businesspeople about South Africa and its problems. Besides the affable host, Durand, the lunch was attended by Jannie Mouton, the retired founder of the PSG Group, GT Ferreira, one of the driving forces behind Rand Merchant Bank, Edwin Hertzog, who built the Mediclinic private hospital group from scratch, Wim de Villiers, the vice chancellor of the university, Jean Engelbrecht, proprietor of Rust en Vrede, a pre-eminent Stellenbosch wine estate, lawyer

Arend de Waal, Ronnie van der Merwe, Mediclinic's CEO, and Nils Flaatten, a former CEO of Wesgro, the Western Cape government's economic development agency. The guests represented some of the country's biggest corporates and between them controlled billions of rands in investments, employed thousands of people and made enormous contributions to the fiscus. They considered themselves rainmakers, but, in some quarters, they stood accused of being the high priests of so-called white monopoly capital, a shapeless and faceless entity allegedly controlling the economy, exploiting workers and living off the fat of the land. If ever there were a Stellenbosch Mafia, this might well be it, I thought, as we took our seats and started exchanging pleasantries.

The Stellenbosch Mafia has been described as a grouping of influential white Afrikaner businessmen who use their clout informally to steer the economy and pull the strings of government from their Boland lair. The term, which got a lot of media air during the height of the Bell Pottinger-inspired defence of the state-capture network in 2017, has been around for many years but its definition has changed in recent times. Whereas a decade or more ago it was confined to business circles and used only in grudging respect when referring to a select few businessmen in Stellenbosch, it has now become a swear word and conjures up images of conspiracy and control, of back-room dealings and illegal influence. The Stellenbosch Mafia was an oddity, the term a quirk of business journalism and, for some, a badge of honour and amusement. But, in present-day South Africa, it has taken on a much more sinister image, with the Mafia being accused of manipulating the economy and even being in charge of the country and controlling society. And, in Johann Rupert, the Mafia had its don, a larger-than-life figure who controlled Stellenbosch and the country.

Of course, this Mafia is a fascinating subject to investigate, even more so after the scandalous demise of Steinhoff and its flamboyant chief executive, Markus Jooste, the quintessential *inkommer.*

Stellenbosch is a town of intrigue and gossip, power and influence, and constructed along class, if not racial, lines. The town's old money has always exerted influence beyond its borders, and in alliance with academia has helped forge a micro-society in which many believe themselves to be removed from the realities of present-day South Africa. This belief of living in a bubble has in some ways made research for this book easier, and in other ways much harder, compounded by the fact that the author spent his formative years at school and university in the town. Stellenbosch has always been awash with delicious tales of deceit and disaster, even before the Jooste debacle anecdotes of fast cars, fast women and fast money did the rounds. But, beyond Steinhoff, it was clear that the phenomenon that is Stellenbosch, a place of influence and fortune, had more to it than what had been reported up until now.

For someone who came of age in Stellenbosch, I found research for the book more difficult than I had anticipated – after-dinner talk about who lunches with whom and who lost how much on the JSE is hardly enough for a book, after all. There is some good and proper *skinder* in Stellenbosch, but not all of it could be verified. Townsfolk were by and large very guarded, even those I had known for decades. Some refused to talk, while others had to be persuaded over many months to firm up anecdotes, fables and legend.

At the Volkskombuis lunch, conversation ranged from state capture to the disastrous tenure of Jacob Zuma as head of state. Questions were posed about the state's capacity to effect change and the degree to which certain institutions, like the South African Revenue Service and the National Treasury, had been hollowed out under the previous government. And whether or not Cyril Ramaphosa, who was then still very much in his honeymoon period as head of state, had the political capital and will to make the necessary fundamental changes to party and state in order to repair the damage wrought by wilful neglect and graft.

Durand, a gracious host, kept our glasses filled with Stellenbosch's finest. Next to me, Mouton was restless, and I thought we might be boring the famous raconteur and billionaire to death. But, as the afternoon wore on and the main courses were served and cleared, he started listening more intently and engaging more often. Just before dessert was served he couldn't keep it in any more: 'Ja, ja, you guys have been telling me what's wrong with the country – but now tell me what's *right* with the country! Give me some hope!' he said. Mouton pointed out that he is a South African, and that there is nowhere else for him to go. There are enough good people in the country to help build a future, and that's what he wanted to do in his retirement. 'I'm off to speak to accounting graduates later; what should I tell them about our future?' Mouton animatedly demanded. Hertzog and Ferreira spoke about the responsibility of big business to 'stick its head above the parapet' and to play a meaningful role in society. Ferreira referred to a corporate clash with government in 2007 when his friend, colleague and fellow Stellenbosch old boy Paul Harris, was castigated by Essop Pahad, then President Thabo Mbeki's hatchet man, after FNB ran an advertising campaign highlighting the effects of crime. Business hasn't always covered itself in glory, I contended, preferring to protect its own interests and steering clear of active corporate citizenship.

Business, of course, has a different societal function from politics and activism, but surely it cannot isolate itself from society when political convulsions grip the country? Big business has tended to be pretty weak and lethargic when society has been grappling and fighting with change. In fact, it was only during the final years of apartheid that business decided to take the initiative, and then only because of the inevitability of political change. And in the immediate aftermath, during the rainbow years of democracy, it fell over its collective feet to ingratiate itself with the new order. State capture has again shown up the failings of the captains of capital. There seemed to be a wholesale reluctance to engage with the ANC and government while Zuma's project was in full swing, even though it became clear that the environment was not conducive to profitmaking.

Hertzog agreed. 'We don't like involving ourselves in politics. It's not what we do,' he said, adding that the era when business could retreat into boardrooms, leaving the country to sort itself out, was over.

Being at that event with Durand, Hertzog, Mouton et al. was fascinating. Whenever the Mafia had been attacked over the last few years, the comments had invariably been directed at these men I was having lunch with. This book is an attempt to draw the outlines of the so-called Stellenbosch Mafia: does it exist, who are they and what do they do? It will by no means be the definitive account of the Boland town, with its unusually high concentration of billionaires, and it cannot possibly do justice to the colourful array of characters who constitute the elaborate networks of contacts and schemers.

Stellenbosch is a unique town, steeped in Afrikaner political and cultural history. Its oak-lined streets and Cape Dutch architecture, girded by cobalt-blue mountains, certainly make it one of the prettiest towns in the country and an eminently desirable address. But it has in recent times become a smug little place, taken with its own sense of grandeur and importance, thanks in large part to the wealthy industrialists who have taken up residence there. Success in Stellenbosch often revolves around whom you know, which networks you are plugged into and where you come from. It is difficult to secure access to those networks if you are not part of its feeder system – the schools, the university and its halls of residence. Many of the most successful Stellenbosch enterprises have at their core relationships between people that stretch beyond company balance sheets – bonds between individuals who grew up together, went to school together and studied at university together. Of course, this interconnectedness does not always translate into acceptance within the broader network, nor does it guarantee success, as the case of Markus Jooste and Steinhoff illustrates.

The term 'mafia' connotes a criminal syndicate involved in various illegal activities. It recalls images of Italian crime families and New York mobsters who intimidate and racketeer their way to illicit riches. In the South African context, driven by political expediency, 'Stellenbosch Mafia' refers to a wealthy group of businessmen who have supposedly cynically exploited workers in order to make obscene profits while the divide between rich and poor grows wider every day. Not only are they seen by some to be the very embodiment of the worst excesses of capitalism, but they also reportedly wield influence over government and society, pulling the strings of the minister of finance or deciding who plays fly half for the Springboks. This group of businessmen, so the narrative goes, care about nothing but themselves and growing rich off the fat of the land. It is not an easy portrait to sketch.

I have been a beneficiary of those networks and school ties that are so reviled by many. The hallowed halls of school and university where many of these corporate captains were educated are the same institutions to which I owe allegiance. And many Stellenbosch friends and acquaintances have leveraged these networks to elevate themselves to the top tier of connected capitalists. But these networks have also afforded me access to some members of the so-called Mafia. Thanks to interviews I conducted in Stellenbosch, at their offices, homes and in social settings, and by retracing the steps of my youth, I have been able to piece together a narrative that, hopefully, gives the reader some insight into this fascinating town and its influential inhabitants.

A study like this one, incomplete as it undoubtedly is, cannot rely solely on anecdotes about liquid lunches at the Decameron restaurant or a billionaire importing luxury vehicles and giving them to friends. Nor can it only be about the vanity of Jooste and the inevitability of Steinhoff's demise. This book attempts to determine whether or not the Stellenbosch Mafia is real, who the members are and how they created their wealth.

Pieter du Toit
Johannesburg
June 2019

1. A POWERFUL ELITE, OUT OF TOUCH AND OUT OF REACH

'It is time ... that you guys have enough self-confidence ...
that [you realise when] we interact that there's no ...
not always ... ulterior motives.'

– Johann Rupert, during an interview
with Given Mkhari on PowerFM, 4 December 2018

JOHANN RUPERT was nervous before his interview on PowerFM, the Johannesburg talk-radio station established to give a voice to the growing black middle class and cohort of black professionals in Joburg. He had been stung by a PR campaign during the height of that project of grand corruption, state capture, that sought to position him as the high priest of so-called white monopoly capital, and now he wanted to put the record straight.

At the age of 68, South Africa's second-richest man was growing concerned about his legacy as the inheritor of the huge business empire that his father, Anton, had built. And he resented the repeated accusations that he was the Godfather-like leader of the 'Stellenbosch Mafia', a term coined by his detractors to collectively denote an amorphous set of rich, white tycoons from the designer Boland town, who, it was said, gerrymandered and manipulated the economy to their own selfish ends.

It had all grated on Rupert so much that, at the insistence of his family and friends, he had met a biographer to discuss the possibility of a tome about his life to sit alongside the one about his father. (The intended author allegedly didn't impress Rupert or his wife, Gaynor, and the project was shelved.)

The PowerFM interview had been brokered so that Rupert could speak directly to a demographic that he believed was hostile to him, his family, his business – and Afrikaners in general. He wanted to explain that he was not a modern-day incarnation of Hoggenheimer, that caricature of a stereotypical Jewish capitalist effectively used by Afrikaners in the 1930s and 1940s to whip up nationalist sentiment.

But the interview went awry almost immediately. Maybe it was his frayed nerves or perhaps it really was the hubris that often comes with great wealth, but, either way, Rupert proceeded to rile listeners with his combination of outdated racial epithets and anecdotes, his brusque manner and the way he engaged with Mkhari (who, admittedly, was all at sea, just like his interlocutor).

He repeatedly spoke about Shangaans – an ethnic group who, in many quarters, bear the disparaging connotation of tsotsi-like characters – and Vendas, and other African tribes. He referred to 'blacks' in a style that smacked of pre-constitutional South Africa. 'It's "black *people*", Mr Rupert,' Mkhari corrected him.

'Aah, you're part of the snowflake generation!' Rupert stumblingly replied, using the term now in vogue when referring to millennials who seem easily affronted by political incorrectness.

Iman Rappetti, a PowerFM presenter and senior journalist, was in the audience. She did not care about Rupert's legacy, his bumbling manner or his apparent detachment from race, society and blackness. As he spoke – and while the mostly black audience were lapping up his observations, lessons and tales – Rappetti bristled, increasingly irritated and disgusted by what she saw as a slight delivered to a sceptical but receptive black audience by a beneficiary of apartheid networks and injustices. 'He is so very arrogant,' she said under her breath as the conversation on stage continued. 'How dare he?' she asked.

Rupert went on to speak about his parents – how hard they had worked, studied and saved to get ahead in life. They wouldn't have hung around at Taboo (a Johannesburg nightclub famous for glamour and excess, and frequented by new black money), he said. He knew Steve Biko, and you would never have seen him there, he said. 'I look at your generation and I don't see leadership,' Rupert told Mkhari.

For many listening – and certainly for Rappetti – those comments encapsulated Rupert and his contemporaries' ignorance about history and society. Was he oblivious to the fact his parents had the distinct advantage of being white, with access to education and other gateways to opportunity? Did he not understand the grave offence caused by his gross generalisations about young black people hanging around clubs?

'Mr Rupert, you suffer from cognitive dissonance,' Rappetti said, before telling him that many would interpret his comments as racist. The chairperson of luxury-goods company Richemont, who had just concluded a lucrative agreement with Chinese online retail giant Alibaba, was taken aback. His friends, black and white, knew he wasn't racist, he protested. It was no good – the accusations came thick and fast: you fail to recognise your own privilege; you talk down to black people; what you say is racist…

'This was a mistake,' Rupert muttered after the interview, detaching the microphone from his lapel.

While black Twitter blew into a storm of criticism and Power-FM's telephone lines were jammed with indignant callers, the audience mobbed him, tugging at his sleeves to take a selfie, shaking his hand and hoping to exchange details. His team of supporters, including professional golfer and close friend Ernie Els, quickly exited the venue as the attendant staff of Johannesburg Stock Exchange (JSE) Top 40 company Remgro – the investment company Rupert chairs – tried to make sense of events. They couldn't understand the furore but acknowledged that Rupert could have been better prepared. They jetted back to Cape Town that night.

Mkhari, who had been outwardly deferential to Rupert during the interview, acknowledged afterwards that the reaction to the conversation showed that deep cleavages in South African society persist. 'A cursory glance at social media reveals that, to many, Rupert is a symbolic representation of white, and in particular Afrikaners' racial privilege, through which collective black disadvantage makes meaning,' he wrote in the *Sunday Times*.[1]

Journalist and editor Ferial Haffajee said the interview was 'cringeworthy' and that there are many other billionaires who 'practise' a much more ambitious and inclusive form of capitalism than Rupert does, citing reclusive insurance mogul Dick Enthoven, who owns, among other businesses, Spier wine estate, near Stellenbosch.[2] And Talk Radio 702's Eusebius McKaiser said that even though Rupert did provide some salient lessons for black people, the messenger 'does matter', and Rupert was not the right one to deliver it.[3] The Economic Freedom Fighters (EFF), the party that is one of Rupert and the Stellenbosch Mafia's most ardent critics, labelled him the 'president of whites' and said his comments exposed him as the 'face of white privilege'. Rupert, the EFF said, is 'an arrogant white Afrikaner who sees nothing beyond his selfish racist white capitalist interests'.[4]

The Rupert family is not alone when it comes to this kind of criticism. That disastrous radio interview came shortly after a high-profile and much-publicised court case involving former Minister of Public Enterprises Malusi Gigaba and the Oppenheimers' private aviation company, Fireblade.

The dispute centred on promises made by Gigaba while he was Minister of Home Affairs to the effect that Fireblade would be granted assistance and resources to establish a private international terminal at OR Tambo International Airport. The courts found in the Oppenheimers' favour and declared Gigaba to have lied under oath when he denied giving the country's richest family a number of undertakings. But this case was about more than just perjury. South Africans were repulsed by the audacity of the super-rich seeking the luxury of their own international terminal, bypassing a regular port of entry that we common citizens must use. And why should government help the Oppenheimers with resources from Home Affairs in the form of border-control and customs staff?

Wealth has always been contested: who has it, how did they acquire it and what do they do with it? But the Oppenheimer saga and the Rupert interview seem to have underscored what many already believed – that the very rich benefit from a different set of rules from those that the rest of society must conform to. Because they are rich, the Oppenheimers can have their own terminal, staffed by public servants; because he is rich, Rupert can get away with tribalistic slurs.

---*---

There is no clarity on exactly where the phrase 'Stellenbosch Mafia' originated, but the first recorded references were apparently in an interview Alec Hogg did with market analyst David Shapiro in January 2003, referring to the birthday of a Remgro heavy, Pietie Beyers.[5] Nevertheless, it's clear that it now denotes the existence – in the minds of many – of a grouping of influential and wealthy millionaire and billionaire businessmen, who use the Western Cape town as a base from where they control hundreds of enterprises. These businesses generate enormous amounts of revenue for their shareholders and founders, which, they argue, gives them leverage over society: a food retailer, Shoprite, controls the prices of basic goods; a trading company, PEP, influences what clothes you wear; and Mediclinic, a private hospital group, decides who receives medical treatment. The super-rich owners of these companies, through their economic clout, influence behaviour not only in society, but also in politics, as they are able to call upon the powerful and connected, and make demands ordinary South Africans cannot. Or so the theory goes.

The Stellenbosch mafia control everything, Julius Malema told an election rally in March 2014. 'They control the judiciary, they control the economy, they control the land, they control the chain stores, they control the mines, they control the banks.' And, then, just to emphasise the outsized influence of the Mafia, he added: 'If the Stellenbosch boys don't want you to be anything, you will never become something in life.'[6]

Malema, the populist leader of the EFF, has been one of the most vocal proponents of the notion of a Stellenbosch Mafia, as well as its most strident critic. Ever since the party's formation in 2013, Malema and the EFF have campaigned on economic issues, attacking 'white capital' and regularly invoking the 'Rupert' name as a catch-all for everything capitalist, anything that might indicate that workers are being exploited or as a collective name for big business and big money. He told students in 2016 that white monopoly capital was the biggest impediment to justice in South Africa, and fingered the Ruperts and the Oppenheimers as the faces of 'WMC' and 'the enemy'. He said black South Africans must take back their land and stop being slaves in the country of their birth.[7] But, as we shall see later, one of Malema's closest confidantes, Floyd Shivambu, had no qualms about reaching out to Rupert and 'the Mafia' when he wanted help.

Andile Mngxitama, leader of anarchist black-consciousness movement Black First Land First (BLF) has also targeted the Mafia. The organisation has attempted to occupy property and farms belonging to Rupert – which earned it court interdicts. When a fire broke out on farms belonging to Rupert in February 2018, BLF said: 'We are excited by the news that fire has broken out in some of the farms currently illegally owned by the Rupert family. Black First Land First believes that the fire is the retribution by our black God. The fire is just and welcomed.'[8] After Rupert's PowerFM interview, Mngxitama threatened violence, telling an election rally in Potchefstroom that five white people would be killed for every black person murdered.[9] He also said that Rupert admitted that he had his own private army in the form of taxi associations, and that BLF would retaliate in response.

But, for some, it may go even further than capital and ownership.

Mngxitama and his fellow travellers, like former *Sunday Times* columnist Pinky Khoabane, believe that the Mafia – with Rupert as its nominal head – are in charge of the ANC government and that they have the power to order, for example, the head of state to replace the minister of finance with one who is more to Stellenbosch's liking.

The BLF and EFF's criticism of the Mafia, and almost exclusively of Rupert, is largely unsophisticated, however. Both groups venture deeply into territory reserved for conspiracy theorists and race-baiters, and often make sweeping statements and grand accusations without offering much evidence of their claims. Towards the end of 2018, for example, Malema hosted a press conference in his party's spartan Braamfontein headquarters and said he was told that the Stellenbosch Mafia would sort out his tax affairs, presumably because they are all-powerful and control the South African Revenue Service (SARS). 'Never,' he said. He would never bow down to Rupert and his friends. Yet he offered no evidence that the Mafia were in control of tax administration.

The South African Communist Party (SACP), however, takes a more measured line and locates the Mafia, with Rupert and Naspers chairperson Koos Bekker named as prominent members, within the context of rabid global capitalism. It believes the Mafia is an example of 'corporate capture' – not unlike state capture – and that, as representatives of capital, such individuals seek to undermine the post-apartheid order. But, the party believes (in contrast to the EFF and Mngxitama), 'simply treating corporate capture as a monolithic plot hatched by global (white) capital … leaves us strategically and tactically disarmed'.[10]

The SACP believes that not only did Rupert inherit his business empire, but its creation in the first place during apartheid was thanks to Anton Rupert's position and skin colour:[11]

It is an empire that does not depend on South African government tenders. Johann Rupert can leave the schmoozing of ministers to others. He can leave the bullying of the South African government, the heavy lifting to 'market sentiment', to the ratings agencies, while he enjoys a weekly family meal at the Ruperts-only reserved table in his favourite Stellenbosch restaurant when he is not on holiday in one of the family's properties in the Seychelles or in Onrus.

Although people like Rupert and Bekker show some form of loyalty to South Africa, the SACP believes them to be not far removed from the Guptas (the Guptas are a family that were deeply involved in the corruption of the state during the presidency of Jacob Zuma), and that there are no 'good capitalists' and 'bad capitalists': they are all part of the same system of global exploitation.[12]

Rupert, and many other former bankers, chief executive officers, venture capitalists and entrepreneurs who call Stellenbosch home (Rupert does not), detest being labelled as part of the so-called Mafia. Rupert is not averse to the odd ribbing or sniping comment, but Malema's constant badgering of him as the embodiment of the exploitation of workers and ultimate representative of white capital started to chafe in the latter part of 2016. The EFF leader had blamed Rupert for his woes with SARS, publicly stating that the businessman had ordered an investigation into his affairs.[13] Rupert decided he'd had enough and sent Malema a message through a mutual acquaintance, telling the EFF's 'commander-in-chief' that if he did not stop lying about him, he would tell the world that the EFF was funded by Rupert's money.

But this hasn't stopped Malema from hounding Rupert and the Mafia. In 2017 the EFF leader referred to Rupert in a speech in which he spoke about the problem of 'whiteness', saying Rupert had never challenged him in court for his statements.[14] In 2018 he went further, calling President Cyril Ramaphosa 'a product of the Ruperts', saying that Ramaphosa was a 'cleaner' in Stellenbosch and that the newly appointed chairperson of the Eskom board, Jabu Mabuza, belonged to the same WhatsApp group as Rupert and Ramaphosa.[15] And, shortly before Ramaphosa was elected head of state in 2018, he lashed out again, implying that the ANC leader was being 'handled' by Rupert.[16]

But, beyond the populist and often rabid form of politics espoused by Malema, the idea of the Mafia persists in other quarters. Shortly after the spectacular crash of the opaque behemoth Steinhoff in December 2017, the Mafia was described in *City Press* as 'the Afrikaner-industrial complex', which included Rupert, Jannie Durand (CEO of Remgro), Dr Edwin Hertzog (Mediclinic International), Jannie Mouton (PSG), Christo Wiese and Whitey Basson (Shoprite and Pepkor), and disgraced Steinhoff CEO Markus Jooste.[17] A former employee of a Steinhoff subsidiary described the Mafia in as far as it refers to Steinhoff, as a group of Stellenbosch University graduates and friends who instilled a 'domineering, patriarchal, misogynist and racist culture in which no human emotion was spared when it came to those all-powerful aphrodisiacs: profit and money'.[18] And financial news service Bloomberg, attempting to make sense of the Steinhoff debacle, explained that Jooste and Wiese are part of the Mafia, 'the close-knit group of wealthy businessmen who have owned vineyards in the exclusive hills around Cape Town'.[19]

---*✶*---

The term 'Stellenbosch Mafia' has been part of the South African political and economic lexicon for more than a decade, and, although nobody seriously believes that the grouping exists formally, it cannot be denied that there are networks and back channels among the Boland-based businessmen. Back in 2003, Shapiro referred to VenFin, which merged into Remgro, as 'very, very secretive',[20] while financial journalist Jana Marais in 2014 attempted to figure out who the Mafia was, arguing that many of its alleged members actually trace their roots back to Johannesburg, where people like

Mouton, Jooste and GT Ferreira (from the Rand Merchant Bank orbit) spent a chunk of their professional careers.[21]

There is no doubt that the phrase gained currency in the wake of the Steinhoff crash, with politicians – as is their wont – slating big business as corrupt, and blaming the Steinhoff scandal on the greed and criminality of the Mafia. Jan Mahlangu, trade-union federation Cosatu's coordinator for pension funds and a trustee of the Government Employees Pension Fund, said in the aftermath of the Steinhoff crash that it represented 'corruption at its worst',[22] and that the federation declared that it wanted 'the criminals responsible to be prosecuted and their assets seized. These so-called irregularities are nothing but naked corruption and they are proof that the South African private sector is rotten to the core.'[23]

Bloomberg reported that Steinhoff's fall 'cracked open the Stellenbosch Mafia'; meanwhile, the *Financial Mail* published a cover with a mock-up of *The Godfather* movie with the headline 'The fall of a Stellenbosch don'.[24]

Such reports and commentary have done enormous damage to the town and its reputation, and have served to solidify the perception that the Stellenbosch boys aren't a force for good, but rather capitalist evil incarnate. In an era of fake news and Twitter bots, the Mafia narrative has seen social media run rampant, with allegations of incestuous business relationships, members of the Mafia 'buying' journalists, and politicians being at the beck and call of the Stellenbosch elite.

Christo Wiese, one half of the suave partnership behind the Pepkor and Shoprite empires (the other half being Whitey Basson), acknowledges the negative impact of the Steinhoff implosion on Stellenbosch and big business, but argues that just because there are 'a few bad apples' doesn't mean everyone is bent. 'This [Steinhoff scandal] wasn't only bad for corporate South Africa, but especially [bad] for segments that were impacted, like Stellenbosch, the so-called "Stellenbosch Mafia" and Afrikaners,' he told *Finweek's* Marcia Klein in July 2018.

Rupert acknowledges the existence of a lunch club that meets at the Decameron – an eatery apparently favoured by Stellenbosch top executives – and Wiese says Steinhoff did damage to the Mafia. But a functioning, formal network? That doesn't exist, say many who are considered to be part of it.

'Do businesses that operate from Stellenbosch really control the country? No way. It really is a narrative that must be laid to rest. Sure, we exert influence in our sectors of the economy, but, then again, every business does that to certain degrees. But, we cannot even control the sector we operate in: the person in charge of regulating private hospitals from the Department of Health even believes the word "profit" is a swear word!' laments Hertzog, former CEO of one of Stellenbosch's big success stories, Mediclinic International, during an interview in his private office just off Dorp Street, across the road from Distell Corporation (another Stellenbosch corporate institution and part of the Rupert orbit).[25]

Hertzog, whose father helped Rupert's father found the Rembrandt Group – forerunner of Remgro – says it is a fallacy and a myth that there is a grouping, formal or informal, that could be termed a 'mafia'. 'Besides, a mafia refers to a gang that is involved in criminal activities. And also, who belongs to this Mafia? I certainly know many of the wealthy and successful businesspeople in Stellenbosch, but that does not mean I do business or deals with them, or that I know them particularly well,' he says.[26]

Yet there's no denying that the town has become something of a South African cross between Silicon Valley and the Hamptons in the United States, a hotbed of innovation and entrepreneurship as well as home to some of the richest corporate titans of our time, with wine estates, Cape Dutch mansions and modern, cubist architectural wonders serving as family homes dotted around the town.

Besides Rupert's Remgro, with its associated companies and multimillionaire executives, Stellenbosch is also where a host of current and former Rand Merchant Bank (RMB) chiefs have their homes, including Ferreira, who is still chairperson of Rand Merchant Investments, Michael Jordaan, the former rock-star CEO of First National Bank, and Paul Harris, the former chief executive of FirstRand. (Harris's base is in Johannesburg, but he owns properties in town and his son Kevin manages his business interests from Stellenbosch.) Rupert was the founder of RMB. Beyond the RMB stable, Capitec, the country's coolest and most effective young bank, catering for the unbanked with its no-frills approach, also had its origins in Stellenbosch. It was conceptualised and conceived by the trio of Michiel le Roux, Riaan Stassen and Jannie Mouton. Founder of the PSG Group and an investment dynamo, Mouton has his personal and corporate base in Stellenbosch. (PSG is now run by his son, Piet.)

The town is also home to the head office of the country's leading private hospital group, Mediclinic, founded by Hertzog, with seed capital provided by Rembrandt. Basson, the country's most successful grocer, has been producing wine on his private estate just outside of town for years while taking the short commute to Shoprite's headquarters, twenty minutes away in Brackenfell. And while Wiese, the Pepkor patriarch, has never lived in Stellenbosch, he completed his law degree at the university and maintains a strong connection with the town through the various boards on which he used to hold directorships. Koos Bekker, chairman of Naspers (which was founded in Stellenbosch), and owner of Babylonstoren wine estate, is also regularly lumped together with this group. Not to mention Jooste and his Steinhoff friends, many of whom not only studied at Stellenbosch and settled there, but stayed in the same university residence, Wilgenhof, where South African rugby's patriarch, Dr Danie Craven, ruled the roost for many years. And almost all of their children either went to the same high schools in town or attended university there.

The size and reach of the companies either founded or controlled by these businessmen from Stellenbosch are enormous. Between them, they have major or direct stakes in no fewer than 16 of the JSE's top 100 companies. This includes three among the top 10, seven among the top 30 and nine in the prestigious Top 40 Index. All have their roots in, or demonstrably strong ties with, Stellenbosch.

Naspers, where Bekker now serves as non-executive chairman after many years as chief executive, is the biggest of the bunch, with a market capitalisation in excess of R1.5 trillion. Rupert's Richemont comes in at number six, with R607 billion, and FirstRand, born after Rupert sold his bank to Harris, Ferreira and Laurie Dippenaar, is at number eight (R385 billion). Shoprite is at number 18 (R130 billion) and Rupert's Remgro at number 22 (R108 billion), followed by Rand Merchant Bank Holdings at number 23 (R106 billion). Capitec sits at number 24 (R100 billion), Hertzog's Mediclinic at number 32 (R70 billion – almost as big as its major competitors, Netcare and Life Health, combined) and Steinhoff Africa Retail (or STAR, Steinhoff's South African operations, previously Pepkor) at number 39 (R57 billion). Other notable Stellenbosch-linked companies listed on the JSE's Top 100 include Rand Merchant Holdings (#40), Mouton's PSG Group (#43) and PSG Konsult (#99), Rupert's Reinet Investments (#47), the Distell Group (a merger between Rembrandt's Distillers Corporation and the Stellenbosch Farmers' Winery at #66) and Wiese's Brait (#79).[27]

These companies' interests encompass almost the entire spectrum of the South African economy and, given the fact that the Top 40 Index represents almost 80% of listed shares on the JSE, they carry some clout. From media and technology to banking interests, healthcare, finance, consumables and retail, the members of the so-called Mafia continue to manage a diverse portfolio of money-spinning interests. Not only do many of these companies hold interests in one another (the PSG–Steinhoff relationship is the best known), but many members also sit on one another's boards, such as Ferreira and Harris, who sit on Rupert's Remgro board (and both also sit on the First Rand/Rand Merchant Bank boards); Capitec's

Stassen sits on the PSG board (and PSG holds a major stake in Capitec); Remgro's Durand sits on the Mediclinic board, while Mediclinic's non-executive chairman, Hertzog, serves as Rupert's deputy on the Remgro board.

It is these close relationships that provide conspiracy theorists with fodder. Despite the Stellenbosch elite's denials of the existence of a beast such as the Mafia as a grouping, whether formal or informal, of influential capitalists and financiers who have the capability to direct both governments and market forces, like the Randlords of old, suspicions abound and animosity remains.

This seems to be largely due to the stupendous wealth that many of the town's most prominent residents enjoy. Beyond the obvious cast of characters – the old money in the Remgro stable and the new money in the PSG–Steinhoff orbit – there is a tier of equally wealthy investors, fund managers and entrepreneurs flying under the radar. They gather at restaurants in town to exchange ideas and capital, strike property deals worth millions over chilled glasses of wine and jump on private jets for weekend golfing getaways at private and exclusive estates. And the networks overlap with old school ties, or bonds formed in university halls of residence and often through shared experiences in the cauldron of Johannesburg's corporate cut and thrust. The concentric circles of these networks increasingly include the next generation, too, with the progeny of many millionaires (and billionaires) leveraging their industrialist fathers' contacts as they build their own empires.

Some of the offspring's projects succeed; others don't. But there always seems to be enough capital, and chutzpah, to tackle the next. Take National Braai Day, for example. It's run by a guy called Jan Braai – real name Jan Scannell – whose efforts are funded by the Millennium Trust. The trust, by all accounts a billion rand or more strong, is a foundation run by Michiel le Roux, one of the founders of Capitec, and managed from Stellenbosch. Scannell, whose father was CEO of Distell, is married to the daughter of Claas Daun, one of the drivers behind Steinhoff. And Jan Braai is paid to organise braais and social-media campaigns to usurp Heritage Day in favour of Braai Day. Not a bad living, especially if it's funded as lavishly as this one.

Wealth is clearly on display among the Stellenbosch elite. One 'inkommer' in Jonkershoek Road, one of the most expensive and exclusive streets in town, built a grey aluminium-and-granite block-house, with a see-through garage door of Perspex so that passers-by can view the owner's luxury cars.

But a particularly conspicuous display, legend has it, occurred in 2015 when one of the town's richest men, owner of a splendid wine estate on the Helshoogte Pass, was enticed by one of his children to purchase a Mercedes-Benz G63 AMG 6x6. The G63, with six wheels, is a monster of a truck and costs in excess of R13 million. When the model was spotted on South African roads in 2015, the retired banker allegedly contacted the manufacturer but was told there weren't any right-hand-drive vehicles available for the South African market. Not to be put off, he contacted no less than the Mercedes-Benz CEO in Germany, Dieter Zetsche, and enquired about a G63 for his son. A deal was struck in which Mercedes agreed to deliver right-hand-drive vehicles at around $1 million each – but the minimum order had to be ten trucks. The banker managed to fill up the rest of the order among his fellow moguls in town, keeping two for himself. The G63s have been spotted in Stellenbosch, driven by some of the most glamorous of the town's young folk.

The most delicious part of this tale, and it has been told many a time in town, is that the banker gave one of the trucks to a fellow billionaire as a gift (the two are close, and had worked together in the past), but asked the recipient to pay the import duties. Lore has it that the vehicle was returned to sender with a note saying that gifts don't normally come with a price tag, thank you very much. (The actors in this vignette are known to the author and the story has been confirmed by more than one source. The protagonists, however, did not want to comment on the matter.)

But the story about the Friday lunch club is perhaps the quintessential anecdote about how the Mafia operates. The venue can be any one of the many exclusive eateries around town, but legend has it that Decameron, a 1970s-style Italian institution in Plein Street, is the club's favourite haunt. Diners have seemingly included Mouton and Ferreira, and allegedly Wiese, as well as less-known hangers-on. Rupert has denied being part of the lunch club, while some of the younger generation claim to have been summoned to languid and liquid lunches, often leaving with instructions or ideas – or capital investment. The Mafia's critics have latched onto this, claiming these exclusive Italian lunches are where plans are hatched and schemes cooked up, with accumulation and exploitation the main objectives.

---***---

The fact that the alleged Mafiosi are all of the same hue, white – and mainly Afrikaans – adds to the conspiracy theorists' narrative, as does the fact that apartheid brought them economic advantage. These are held up as explanations for how this group have been able to not only hang on to their seemingly ill-gotten gains, but increase their wealth many times over.

But the reason why the theory and idea of a secret and all-powerful Mafia controlling the country has gained broad traction lies in poverty and politics. South Africa is considered an upper-middle-income country, but the high levels of poverty and unemployment make it one of the most unequal societies on earth. South Africans have become used to these economic statistics being bandied about, but it remains instructive to note that the country in which these powerful companies and individuals mentioned earlier operate is still caught in the clutches of transferred, chronic and extreme poverty.

A report by the World Bank[28] released in March 2018 makes

alarming reading, especially for those who refuse to acknowledge South Africa's deep crisis of economic and social development. High unemployment – in the 30%-40% range, according to the broader definition – a widening wealth gap and extraordinarily high rates of poverty mean South Africa is the most unequal society in the world. The Mafia's clutch on big business and their wine-quaffing and Mercedes-flaunting lifestyle are keeping the poor in their place, their enemies proclaim.

Many members of the Mafia dispute this, though, and argue that enterprising capitalism creates jobs and generates wealth. The country's ruling elite, however, do not see the success of capital, never mind Afrikaner capital, in the same light. Many in the ANC have taken an adversarial position to enterprises that seek to create profit and wealth. The party itself has adopted an official position that identifies 'monopoly capital, made up of local and foreign corporations controlling large chunks of the economy', as the primary enemy of the national democratic revolution'.[29] The governing party has always had a fraught relationship with its faux socialist character, but the emergence from within its own ranks of the bellicose Malema,[30] who has openly and consistently attacked big business and corporates, seems to have forced the ANC into a more reactionary position.

Although the party nominally says it supports free-market enterprise, it has made doing business in the country exceedingly difficult. Hertzog says the private-hospital industry is regarded more as an adversary than as an asset by government. The SACP, the ANC's alliance partner and often regarded as the intellectual nerve centre of the ANC, says capital remains the enemy. 'The Ruperts and the Bekkers, part of the so-called Stellenbosch Mafia, appear to have some degree of commitment to South Africa, presumably both for wealth preservation and sentimental cultural reasons,' the SACP says. The party believes, however, that the scourge of state capture must not serve 'as a diversion from confronting monopoly capital, as personified by the Ruperts and the Bekkers'.[31]

And Stellenbosch is considered the epicentre of the capitalist project, a town steeped in Afrikaner history, the home of old money and new, originals and *inkommers*, where the Rupert empire had its beginnings and where the Steinhoff dream is buried. But does that mean there is a Mafia controlling the country, from Stellenbosch? 'I don't think so,' says Durand. 'We're normal people who just happen to run big businesses. I still drive an old bakkie and there's nothing I enjoy more than to go and watch my children play sport in the afternoon.'

Rupert concedes, though, that the town is over the top:

> Some of it is too much. But it isn't only the Afrikaners in Stellenbosch – Afrikaners across the country sometimes have the tendency to go over the top, so Stellenbosch isn't unique. It's the peer pressure ... if you drive a Maybach, then I want a Maybach II. Nobody there would have been like that had my father still been alive. It just wasn't done. Certainly no Remgro, Farmer's [Stellenbosch Farmer's Winery] or Distell people would have been like that. But, now it's seemingly become a competition who can build the most vulgar house.[32]

Stellenbosch is a university town, said to be standing for 'an idea'. It is now transformed into a designer enclave, seemingly the home of a Mafia.

2. STELLENBOSCH: LIFE IN THE BUBBLE

'Employees of the big corporates are clogging our streets … the bosses of these enterprises grew up here, in Stellenbosch, and studied here too. I don't understand how they can place their own, egocentric and capitalist interests above the preservation of a unique town and environment!'

– Anonymous letter to *Eikestadnuus*,
the local Stellenbosch newspaper, 4 June 2018

PAUL ROOS GYMNASIUM is a grand old boys' school on the banks of the Eerste River in Stellenbosch. The school hall is inspired by Roman architecture, its extensive grounds include aquatic facilities built by old boy Johann Rupert, and its well-manicured sports fields have produced many a national player.

Founded in 1866, with Scottish theologians serving as the first three headmasters, the institution was first known as the Stellenbosch Gymnasium and later as Stellenbosch Boys' High, before being re-christened after Paul Roos, a strict Calvinist Latin teacher, who served as the school's rector from 1910 to 1940. Roos was also the captain of the first Springbok rugby team to tour Europe, in 1906.

The school, along with the university that grew from it, is very much a Stellenbosch institution, having produced leaders in politics, business, academia, sport and the arts through its storied history. Its most famous old boys are arguably also its most controversial, with the first apartheid premier, DF Malan, having written his matriculation exams there. And before him, Jan Smuts and JBM Hertzog, two of the three Boer generals who dominated South African politics in the first half of the 20th century, did the same.

Roos stood as National Party candidate for Stellenbosch in 1948 and was elected to Parliament under Malan, who proceeded to implement the party's apartheid policies.

Unusually, for an Afrikaans-dominated school, there is a fair contingent of English-speakers among its alumni – its honours boards list past students who died during the anti-apartheid struggle, including Anton Lubowski, the Afrikaner Swapo activist who was assassinated in 1989.

In March 2002 Nelson Mandela spoke at this incubator of the Afrikaner and Stellenbosch elite when he delivered a speech to mark the opening of the school's new assembly hall. In prison Mandela had realised the importance of understanding the Afrikaners' psychological make-up, and made an in-depth study of Afrikaans history, politics and literature. As president, he considered reconciling with the erstwhile oppressor class one of his main tasks.

It was a poignant and ironic moment: a black former president addressing a largely white, exclusive school that had produced some of the main architects of the country's segregationist policies. The rector, Jock de Jager, and the students' representative council listened in awe as Mandela spoke.

In his speech, Mandela acknowledged the contributions that the school's political triumvirate of Malan, Smuts and Hertzog had made to the country's history, but observed that times change and institutions adapt: 'Amidst all of this, there are those values that remain valid through all the changes, such as self-discipline, respect for others, sense of duty, application and responsibility,' he told the mesmerised assembly of maroon-blazered children and their parents. 'Three prime ministers [were] schooled here ... With some of the policies of those men we might have differed deeply and taken grave issue. That they were leaders of great significance in the history of our country none can dispute.'[1]

Mandela's address to the posh school (arguably the Afrikaner equivalent of Eton or Harrow)[2] may have been a first for Stellenbosch, yet, around that time, the country's new black political leaders had in fact long been curious to understand the town and the role it occupied in Afrikaner society. Earlier, Mandela's successor, Thabo Mbeki, had visited Stellenbosch to pay tribute to Marinus Daling, a former chief executive and chairman of Sanlam, after his death. At a memorial service held at the Dutch Reformed Church, also attended by the then finance minister, Trevor Manuel, as well as Johann Rupert and Christo Wiese, Mbeki described Daling as 'a great South African' and 'one of the fathers of the new South Africa'.[3]

The ANC and its leaders went to Stellenbosch, arguably, to extend a hand of friendship, to pay homage to its best and brightest. And, in 2002, the party's executive chose the town as the venue for its elective conference, its third after being unbanned in 1990. The first two were held in Durban and Mahikeng, and the Stellenbosch conference was seen by many in the party as a show of force, demonstrating that it could go anywhere – including the cradle of Afrikanerdom, where apartheid theology was founded. But, for others, it was also meant as a way of embracing the whole of the country, including the erstwhile oppressor class.

The new political class's engagements with Stellenbosch are by no means insignificant gestures. But, more recently, other actors in the political sphere have not shown this level of political diplomacy across the racial divide, instead stoking the fires of the country's structural divisions for political ends. This has been evident in the anti-Stellenbosch-mafia narrative promulgated by Malema and others.

A brief history of Afrikaner capitalism will go some way towards explaining this animosity towards the Mafia, espoused in the political arena by Malema and the EFF, and by radical fringe actors like the Gupta-sponsored and militant Mngxitama.

In his opus about the Afrikaners, eminent historian Hermann Giliomee explains that in the early 20th century, Afrikaners controlled or managed no major industrial enterprise – no commercial bank or company on the JSE – even though they had come to dominate in South Africa's political arena. They played almost no part in the emerging and modernising economy, and the social crisis of the 'poor white' was largely an Afrikaner one.

Nationalist fervour, coupled with political self-confidence, had led to the establishment of a few landmark Afrikaner businesses, including Nasionale Pers (now Naspers), a media house founded with the mission of promulgating the message of Afrikaner nationalism. In 1918, insurance company Sanlam was founded and Santam followed shortly after. Both companies marketed themselves as 'genuine Afrikaner people's institutions'.[4] In 1924 the establishment of KWV, a wine producers' cooperative, sought to band together a group of successful Western Cape wine farmers. And, later, the management of publicly owned enterprises, including the Iron and Steel Corporation (Iscor) and the Electricity Supply Commission (Eskom), became the province of Afrikaner management. But, according to Giliomee, these Afrikaner-owned businesses were modest undertakings: 'Driving them was not profit alone, but the determination that Afrikaners could succeed in the world of business, which was considered the domain of English or Jewish South Africans.'[5]

However, the desire among Afrikaners to conquer the business world became a major driving force behind the nationalist movement of the time, and the establishment of Volkskas (a forerunner of today's Absa) in 1933 was the result of a decision by the Broederbond (League of Brothers), a secretive society of influential Afrikaners, to create its own Afrikaner bank.

The irony is that Afrikaners were inherently suspicious of business and had reservations about the capitalist system. Major Afrikaner-owned businesses established before 1948 were not constructed along classic capitalist lines. Nasionale Pers, for example, printed newspapers at a loss, its mission being to propagate nationalist ideology. Meanwhile, the government regularly threatened nationalisation.[6]

Both Afrikaner and African nationalists were suspicious of

capital because they weren't naturally part of the capitalist class. Both, however, exploited it to its fullest once they were admitted. The First Economic Congress of the People, held in 1939, charted a collective course whereby Afrikaners were empowered to seize control of a larger share of the economy. The solution to the 'poor white' problem was now seen to be private Afrikaner enterprise.[7] The outcome of the congress and the theory of *volkskapitalisme* (people's capitalism) saw the founding of key institutions, including a finance house, the Federale Volksbeleggings (Federal People's Investments), whose function was to provide venture capital. In 1943 the bank extended a loan to Anton Rupert to establish Voorbrand Tobacco Company, the forerunner of Rembrandt and eventually today's Remgro.[8] A decade later, Rupert once again turned to Afrikaner capital to allow him to make his company's biggest purchase – one that would create enormous wealth for the family in the decades to come. With it, he acquired British cigarette manufacturer Rothmans. The capital was provided in the form of loans from Afrikaner financial institutions willed into existence by nationalism and necessity.[9]

Later, the apartheid era saw the Afrikaner business world flourish, with the state creating a protected environment for white enterprise to grow. But the advent of democracy turned the tables again, and the new government's policies of transformation and black economic empowerment meant that Afrikaner businesses had to adapt to new political and social constraints. Perhaps counterintuitively, they managed this with aplomb. According to Giliomee, apartheid-era Afrikaner businesses were eager to shed their ethnic character so as to attract customers from across the racial and language spectrum in the new democratic environment, and by the end of the 20th century they were making great strides in terms of both growth and racial diversification.

It is perhaps ironic that Afrikaner capital – which in certain political spheres later became known as 'white capital' or 'white monopoly capital' – flourished after it was unshackled from apartheid. Naspers boomed, Sanlam grew exponentially, and new enterprises, like PSG, emerged. Scenario planner and author Clem Sunter provides an explanation for this newfound buoyancy, arguing that Afrikaners were the real beneficiaries of the democratic dispensation: when democracy came to South Africa in 1994 and Afrikaners suddenly lost their privileged position in society, they were forced to fend for themselves, no longer able to rely on the state and its networks to succeed. And they did so 'fantastically well', according to Sunter, who cites spectacular growth of Afrikaner-owned companies on the JSE and entrepreneurialism that flourished across the region. He calls this phenomenon the 'great trek into business' – a collective consciousness that created a successful commercial network among Afrikaners. 'The Afrikaners were liberated by the creation of a level playing field. Necessity is indeed the mother of invention. Entitlement shackles it,' Sunter said.[10]

Anton Rupert rapidly became part of the firmament of the new South Africa. Mandela saw a friend in Rupert and once advised his finance minister, Trevor Manuel, to consult Rupert to help the fledgling democracy find a way out of the economic dead end it had found itself in.[11] Mandela described Rupert as a 'super heavyweight industrialist' and believed he had vision and a social conscience. 'As long as there are people of Dr Rupert's calibre and commitment, South Africa will never be a land without hope,' he said.[12]

Sentiment has changed, however, since the ANC held that landmark elective conference in Stellenbosch in 2002. Today, many among the new order do not see the success of capital in the same light. Some have branded many prominent white businessmen, like the Ruperts, who grew their corporate empires from the seeds of Afrikaner capital, as land-grabbing thieves and agents of Western imperialism who have exploited the black majority for generations.

Johann Rupert was excoriated after his interview on PowerFM

for his lack of social, political and historical awareness, and his condescending attitude. His thoughts and views on entrepreneurship and success, and the fact that his businesses help grow the pensions of workers and contribute billions in taxes were simply lost amid the noise of the outrage the broadcast engendered.[13]

But, as with most contentious arguments in South Africa, there is a grain of truth in the populist criticism of the country's business barons and the Stellenbosch Mafia. The country's labour regime was built on a supply of cheap black labour, with the mining industry especially drawing enormous benefits from worker exploitation. Coupled with job reservation, Bantu education and influx control, an economic environment was created that, by the mid-1960s, had made white South Africans one of the richest groups in the world. In 1966, *Time* magazine said South Africa was experiencing a massive boom; the *Rand Daily Mail* declared that the country was 'experiencing a surfeit of prosperity'; and the *Financial Mail* called the period between 1961 and 1966 'the fabulous years'.[14]

All this as black South Africans were not only shut out from wealth creation and economic development, but denied political rights. All this hasn't been forgotten.

---◆---

Besides being home since 1994 to a disproportionately large number of big Afrikaner-owned corporates, Stellenbosch has always occupied a unique place in Afrikaner lore. It was the town where the identity of 'Afrikaner' was first recorded;[15] and the place that gave birth to the university that would deliver much of the intellectual and statutory scaffolding on which racial segregation was constructed. The university produced a succession of apartheid premiers, including its chief architect, Hendrik Verwoerd, and, today, it is still the university of choice for many of the country's well-heeled elite.

But, for many South Africans, Stellenbosch merely evokes an

idea of white, Afrikaner privilege, stoked by populist politics in which the Twitter phrase 'white privilege' is closely associated with 'white monopoly capital'.

Stellenbosch has always been at the centre of Afrikaners' political and cultural life; it was the incubator for apartheid as an ideology and the embodiment of Afrikaners' desire for Afrikaans mother-tongue education. Malan led the fight to retain Victoria College (the forerunner of today's Stellenbosch University) as an institution of higher learning, which had been threatened as the Union government forged ahead with plans for the University of Cape Town. Malan had been co-author of a manifesto drawn up by a committee constituted by Afrikaner representatives from across the country, which was tasked with ensuring the continued existence of Victoria College. Their manifesto contained the now famous phrase that Stellenbosch 'stood for an idea' ('*Zij staat voor een idee!*').[16] That 'idea' became the town's ideological touchstone.

After the South African War of 1899 to 1902, Afrikaners were a defeated people. Stellenbosch emerged as the centre of a newfound defiance in the south. The town was held up as the breeding ground for Afrikaner nationalism, and as a way to isolate the Afrikaner youth from the influence of the English.[17]

Stellenbosch was also the focal point of the struggle for recognition of the Afrikaans language, which played a big part in the political and cultural life of the time.[18] With efforts by the British administration after the South African War gathering pace to anglicise the whole of South Africa, the town became the symbolic centre of a rising Afrikaner political and linguistic nationalism.

If the victory of Afrikaner nationalism was to be achieved, an education institute and a national voice were key, and Stellenbosch was at the epicentre of those efforts. But the capital to put these aims into practice was also needed. Enter Jan Henoch Marais, possibly the first South African tycoon to hail from the Boland town. After matriculating from the school that would be later renamed

the Paul Roos Gymnasium in 1870, Marais set out for the dia-
mond fields of Kimberley, and returned to the Cape 21 years later
a wealthy man. Marais co-founded the fiercely nationalistic daily
newspaper *De Burger*, published by De Nasionale Pers Beperkt.
The prime movers behind what is today Naspers were a group of
influential Stellenbosch businessmen, politicians and farmers who
were all in some way or other related, either through business or
marriage,[19] possibly the first iteration of what today is known as
the Mafia.

When Marais died in 1915, he bequeathed 100 000 pounds
sterling (equivalent to more than R100 million today) from his
estate to the university through a trust that still carries his name.
This endowment enabled the college's management to resist efforts
by the government to incorporate it into the new university in
Cape Town because it now had financial independence. Marais's
statue still stands proudly in the university campus. His trust, Het
Jan Marais Nationale Fonds, is also still in existence. Its mission,
as laid down by Marais in his last will and testament, is to 'advance
the national interest on any terrain of the Afrikaans-speaking part
of the population of South Africa anywhere in the country, but
with preference to the town and the district of Stellenbosch'. In
2016 the fund's capital stood at a healthy R1.29 billion, slightly
down from the previous year's R1.39 billion, and all in service of
the Afrikaans cause. 'This university has Jan Marais to thank for
its existence; this town's adornments were created thanks to Jan
Marais; one of the country's economic giants, Naspers, would not
have existed without Jan Marais and this country and town would
culturally and socially have been much poorer without Jan Marais,' Professor Andreas van Wyk, chairperson of Het Jan Marais
Nationale Fonds, said in 2015.

The University of Stellenbosch is inextricably linked to the for-
mulation and fleshing out of apartheid's ideology. Its academics
played a major role in establishing a theoretical framework within

which the system could be justified, they argued, and function in practice. The university also give content to Afrikaner nationalism, primarily through strengthening the use of Afrikaans as the language of academia and commerce. The burgeoning university therefore gave succour to a generation of Afrikaners who were beginning to escape the domination of English-speaking South Africans in the country's political and economic life.

One of the university's brightest young minds, Verwoerd became professor of sociology at the age of 31 – in the words of his biographer, Henry Kenney, a remarkable ascent for this 'brilliant student and powerful personality'.[20] According to Kenney, Verwoerd's years in Stellenbosch were decisive in shaping his intellectual outlook.[21] Verwoerd did not have an extended academic career, but he used it as a springboard to enter the national stage as a policymaker. He came to prominence in 1934 when he delivered a paper at the Volkskongres in Kimberley on the issue of poverty among whites. In his address, Verwoerd revealed the thinking that would later define him as an ideologically determined minister of native affairs and prime minister. His arguments were unashamedly sectarian, supporting racial discrimination that favoured Afrikaners.[22]

Around that time, nationalists were trying to construct the theory of apartheid, attracting interventions both from those among them who wanted absolute segregation and those who believed that black people's human dignity should be recognised. While the National Party was struggling to develop a coherent apartheid policy, academics from Stellenbosch proposed founding an institute (as a counterbalance to the liberalist South African Institute of Race Relations) to investigate and research apartheid solutions. The South African Bureau of Racial Affairs, or SABRA, was established for this purpose, with considerable support from the Broederbond, to which most leading Afrikaners belonged.

Since democracy, and increasingly in recent times, the university has attempted to shed its image as a bastion of Afrikanerdom, and claims that it has tried to inculcate a more inclusive, all-embracing culture. But Giliomee, a former lecturer at Stellenbosch, believes that the university's attempts to shed its Afrikaans and Afrikaner character will lead to the death of the language. He says it's a 'cruel irony' that English will in future probably be the medium of instruction at an institution established to escape the yoke of the British. And he believes Stellenbosch need not try to appease the race and language ideologues in present-day South Africa, arguing that by the 1990s the Afrikaans language was 'no longer the instrument of chauvinistic Afrikaner nationalism'.[23]

Stellenbosch's vice chancellor, Dr Wim de Villiers, does not share Giliomee's position on the policy of parallel media of instruction and believes the university will continue to teach in Afrikaans only if the demand exists. At the university's centenary celebrations in March 2018, De Villiers said that the idea for which Stellenbosch stood was upliftment through education – but emphasised that this should not be only for a few. 'This idea was clearly too narrow. It was an exclusionary and inward-looking approach instead of an inclusive outreach ... To argue that the idea of a *"volksuniversiteit"* is too narrow does not mean we are against Afrikaans. There is a misperception that the university is aiding the demise of Afrikaans. The opposite is true,' De Villiers said.[24]

There is no doubt that the Afrikaner as a clearly defined homogeneous political and cultural entity no longer exists as it did during the years of Afrikaner nationalism. In the south, and in Stellenbosch, the character of the Afrikaner has taken on a hue of independence and self-sufficiency, content with the political order as it stands and seemingly unperturbed by the realpolitik of African statehood.

But Afrikaners, and especially those seemingly part of the so-called Mafia, no longer owe their allegiance to any artificial construct of a nation or 'volk', as that brand of nationalism, which wreaked such havoc in South Africa, demanded for generations.

This form of nationalism required unquestioning loyalty to people and language, with disastrous consequences.

Democracy unshackled the Afrikaner, with many not only discarding their tribal bent, but disavowing it altogether. With the weight of apartheid illegitimacy lifted from their shoulders, Afrikaners have flourished in democratic South Africa, and the majority have taken to racial integration and multiculturalism. And intergenerational wealth and opportunity have made them possibly the most mobile and skilled group in the country.

With the civil service becoming the preserve of the ANC's policy of cadre deployment and transformation, many Afrikaners were forced into leaving the tight – and false – embrace of the state for the uncertainty of entrepreneurship and private enterprise. This they seem to have done with success. Only 7.1% of white South Africans are unemployed, compared to the national figure of 27.5% and black unemployment of 31.1% in 2018.[25]

Networks, bonds and friendships (real or otherwise) established during formative or schooling years are often a prerequisite for gaining entry to some big corporate boardrooms. And although times have changed and so-called 'school ties' don't open the doors they used to, there are some demonstrably strong links between many individuals and companies that are accused of being part of the Stellenbosch Mafia. These networks generate contacts, opportunity and often capital, with a safety net provided by social position and standing.

····✱····

In Stellenbosch today, the next generation of dealmakers and entrepreneurs take great delight in referring to the town as 'the Bubble', a place that is cosseted and removed from the reality of increasing poverty and a governing party at war with itself.

Like most South African towns, Stellenbosch still exhibits the stark spatial divisions of apartheid. The town, founded in 1679 by Dutch governor Simon van der Stel (who promptly named it after himself), is still very much divided along colour demarcations, the result of forced removals, with white residents living in the old town and luxurious new developments; Coloured people in Ida's Valley, Cloetesville and Jamestown; and black people in Kayamandi.

According to the Stellenbosch Heritage Foundation, a non-profit organisation that is concerned with the preservation of the town's character and architecture, this delineated layout is 'partly the result of historical patterns of race- and class-based develop-ment; partly the result of specific planning frameworks that have been implemented over the decades; and partly the result of ad hoc decisions driven mainly by profit-seeking property developers or desperate homeless households that have invaded land'.[26]

In terms of its topography, the town is cut off to an extent by the mountains that surround it, but the notion of 'the Bubble' derives not only from the fact that it is isolated by mountainous terrain, but also from the way in which it has been able to isolate itself econom-ically from the rest of South Africa. The term has come to denote a sense of self-protected wealth or opportunity, confined within the town's boundaries, with generations of Stellenbosch old boys returning to the place that spawned them.

With its whitewashed Cape Dutch gables and restored slave lodges, towering oaks lining the streets, and faux European cafés and restaurants, adjacent to investment firms and venture-capital start-ups, Stellenbosch is simply far removed from the smog and grime and mismanagement of the rest of South Africa, some inhabitants believe.

The old town, which includes the original 17th-century precincts, university campus and schools, remains an area of af-fluence and influence. Neighbourhoods like Dalsig (view of the dell), Paradyskloof (paradise valley), Die Boord (the vineyard), Uniepark (union park), Brandwacht (the sentinel) and Mosterts-drift (Mostert's crossing) now sit next to exclusive lifestyle estates among ancient vines and on dramatic mountain passes overlooking the jewel in the Boland's crown.

Markus Jooste holds court with some of his closest friends on a private estate called Jonkersdrift. GT Ferreira can lay claim to having one of the most spectacular wine estates of them all, atop the Helshoogte Pass, called Tokara (named for his children, Thomas and Kara), while the Ruperts' original family home, in Thibault Street in Mostertsdrift, still has the original features from when Remgro patriarch Anton bought it in the early 1950s. (Johann Rupert no longer lives at the family home in Stellenbosch; he lives in Somerset West.)

Unsurprisingly, the town today is awash with developers trying to get in on the action. Property prices have skyrocketed – the lure of the Stellenbosch lifestyle attracting *inkommers* from Johannesburg, Pretoria and, increasingly, Durban. With demand far outstripping supply, the place has become one of the most sought-after addresses in the country. According to the South Africa Wealth Report 2018,[27] Stellenbosch has 90 residential properties valued at more than R20 million. It has also attracted a big influx of dollar millionaires over the last ten years. The Bubble counts no fewer than 3 200 residents with an estimated personal value of more than a million dollars, and 150 with a personal wealth of $10 million or more.[28] And the townsfolk's alma mater, the University of Stellenbosch, has produced the third-highest proportion of the country's high-net-worth individuals (12%), behind the Universities of the Witwatersrand (22%) and Cape Town (19%).

Developers have bought up large tracts of land around the town, made deals with wine farmers to develop parts of their vineyards into estates and acquired portions of agricultural land that stretch for miles beyond the town's boundaries. According to some sources, the goal of such land development is to preserve the exclusivity of the Bubble by creating a buffer around the town. According to Mark Swilling, an academic at the university, the new exclusive developments around the town have 'created a patchwork of disconnected, privatised elite enclaves of urban consumption, which have contributed nothing to the building of an integrated and sustainable urban culture'.[29]

And yet Stellenbosch has been changing and can no longer be considered the Afrikaner and whites-only exclusive address it was in the past, no matter how hard some want to keep it that way – or how hard its detractors want to paint it as such. According to the 2011 census, the black population was the fastest-growing demographic segment in the town: there was a 40% increase in the number of black people living in the town between 2001 and 2011. Kayamandi, a black township outside of the town, is today home to more than 40 000 people.[30] And if one examines the statistics, Stellenbosch has more than double the number of informal dwellings and shacks (34.1%) than the provincial average (16.5%); it registers an employment rate (50.6%) that is on par with the provincial statistics; and has an annual average household income (R29 400), which is the same as the provincial median.[31]

In fact, by some estimates, black and Coloured South Africans each make up 44% of Stellenbosch's population, meaning that only 12% of the town's inhabitants are white.[32] The in-migration of black people means isiXhosa is now the second most spoken language (39%) in town, though it still lags behind Afrikaans, which, at 51%, is still the most spoken tongue. And although the town may still revolve around the university, English seems to dominate in today's lecture rooms and meetings. These days, the Afrikaner character of the place seems to reside more in the suburban culture of its residential complexes than its centres of education.

The reality is that despite its disproportionate concentration of wealth and prosperity, Stellenbosch has not been able to escape the fact that it is a town that is part of a broader nation in transition. Crime, inequality and unemployment afflict the most affluent parts of the country, and even the Bubble.

Many of the Stellenbosch elite aren't blind to this, nor to the privilege they enjoy and the acute developmental needs of a country beset by poverty, unemployment and increased contestation for scarce resources. Rupert doesn't want to shed light on his own philanthropic endeavours, but acquaintances believe he spends close to a billion rands a year on various projects. GT Ferreira has invested billions in a trust for his farm workers while Capitec's Michiel le Roux has committed a large chunk of his wealth to support civil society organisations fighting corruption.

Wealth might buy freedom but it doesn't necessarily buy trust, however. The Mafia's critics believe that accumulating riches thanks to individuals' social and cultural capital and the networks that flow from it makes the Mafia not much different from the Broederbond, to which they're often compared. The Bond used networks to advance their own secretive causes, and the Mafia – as well as the broader moneyed class – is doing exactly the same thing, some argue. And, like the Bond, only to their own narrow benefit.

But that's how business and politics work: they are built on relationships and trust, which aren't mutually exclusive. When Jannie Mouton moved to Stellenbosch, his business really took off. And when Jooste started to construct the edifice that became Steinhoff, it was Stellenbosch to which he looked for validation – and capital. Mouton is now fabulously rich. Jooste is still rich, even though thousands of people lost their fortunes in the process, thanks to his questionable business practices.

The Bond was a detested organisation because of its secrecy and malevolence. The Mafia is believed to be made of the same social fabric, and just as influential as the Bond.

3. THE WHITE MONOPOLY CAPITALIST

'He [Zuma] drove a campaign against me because he couldn't control me. He did everything to get dirt on me: got people to watch me, investigators overseas, set up immigration officials against me, SARS, the Hawks, the NPA ... all of them looked at my affairs. What can they do to me? Nothing.'

– Johann Rupert, interview with the author, 22 August 2018

WHEN ZUMA dismissed his finance minister, Nhlanhla Nene, in December 2015 and replaced him with a state-capture deployee, the international markets reacted with shock.

The country had already taken collective note of the corrosive effect of grand corruption under Zuma and his patronage networks, and the markets wanted to know what Nene's dismissal signified. It soon became clear the market was rejecting Zuma's decision and that when the Nikkei opened in Tokyo on the Monday after Nene's dismissal, it would be a bloodbath. If drastic action weren't taken, there would be a massive sell-off of government bonds, stock in the country's banks would be dumped and the currency was set to plummet.

Johann Rupert has always maintained relations with some of the biggest institutional investors, as well as the biggest lenders, in the world. His reputation in Europe, where his luxury-goods conglomerate Richemont is based, is well established and his links to some of the biggest bankers and investors on Wall Street – many of them keen golfers, like him – span decades.

So when Zuma replaced Nene, many of them didn't need to call analysts in Johannesburg or London, emerging-market desks at investment banks or even the National Treasury. They called

Rupert, who was at his home in Somerset West at the time.

One particular investor and hedge-fund manager, believed by many to be the most prolific and astute investor of his generation, called Rupert and asked him if he should short the rand. 'No! Please don't do it!' Rupert replied, well aware that his friend, a golf buddy from the exclusive Seminole Country Club in Florida, would make a ton of money from South Africa's misfortune. He convinced the Wall Street operator that it wouldn't be worth his while and that the South African government would soon come to its senses.

Rupert detests being called part of the Stellenbosch Mafia. For starters, he says, he doesn't even live in Stellenbosch. And, besides, he grumbles, 'I wasn't part of the establishment in the old order, and I'm not part of the establishment in the new order either. Even if there were a "Stellenbosch Mafia", I would probably not be invited anyway.'[1]

There is no denying, however, that Rupert, arguably the best-travelled of South Africa's top executives, carries some serious clout in the salons and rosewood-panelled boardrooms of influence and high finance in Europe and the United States. He has used this influence to help further his own business interests, but he says he has also used it in the country's best interests – although he concedes that it is becoming increasingly hard to do the latter.

In July 2018 the British High Commissioner to South Africa, Nigel Casey, and the American Chief of Mission, Jessye Lapenn, went to see Rupert to enlist his help because they could not seem to get an audience with Ramaphosa. Rupert told them he couldn't help, but, to him, it was clear what was happening: the ANC government was still actively eschewing its friends in the West and pivoting towards the East.

When Ramaphosa went on a global drive in 2018 to secure $100 million in new investments in South Africa, one of the president's advisers called to ask for advice. They were about to visit the Middle East and wanted to get Rupert's take. Rupert is friendly with

Mohammed bin Zayed Al Nahyan (known as MBZ), the crown prince of Abu Dhabi (known as MBZ) and one of the most influential leaders in the region. Mohammed has called on Rupert for favours (he calls him 'the Sheik from South Africa'), and Rupert has enjoyed watching sports events with the prince. 'Do you realise it's summer in the UAE [United Arab Emirates] and that all the influencers are in Europe or on yachts somewhere? It's too hot, they aren't going to be there,' Rupert told Ramaphosa's man.

But Ramaphosa and his team went ahead with their trip nevertheless and returned with promises of $20 billion worth of investments after meeting with, among others, MBZ, who did remain behind while the rest of the emirate elites decamped to cooler climes. These investments weren't going to be in hard cash, however, and the hosts were driving a hard bargain. The South African government was going to have to provide opportunities for Emirates business, and if these were going to be in the form of local partnerships, proper due diligence would have to be done. For example, a hugely successful Middle Eastern airline was interested in SAA, the corruption-plagued national carrier – but they insisted on control. Their overtures again came to naught after earlier efforts had already been derailed because some SAA bosses had allegedly insisted on kickbacks.

Then Rupert was called by his friends in Abu Dhabi: should they get involved with South African investments? Should they look for partners? And if the South African government were to bring investment opportunities to the emirs, would Rupert help vet them? Because they didn't trust the South Africans. 'Guys,' Rupert replied. 'I love my country, I'm not going to get involved. I'll help you with analysts who can tell you, and I'll even invest alongside you, but I normally don't get involved in this sort of thing.'

A month after the South African visit to the UAE, Rupert received an SOS from the selfsame Ramaphosa adviser: the promised investments weren't materialising. Could he help? 'What am I supposed to do?' he replied. 'You didn't tell me what you were planning at the time. You purposefully kept me out of the loop!'

What the South Africans had failed to understand with their investment foray in the Gulf, Rupert says, is that Ramaphosa's government will struggle to make friends with the UAE and Saudi Arabia if it continues to vilify the US, Britain and Israel. 'James Mattis [then US Secretary of Defense] is like MBZ's godfather. MBZ and Mattis talk almost daily. Without the US's protection, the UAE is nothing. They know that. So they work together with Saudi, Israel and the US against Iran. And now we go cap in hand to ask for money, while we treat the US and Britain like we do? We won't get any money. And the South African government doesn't understand that,' Rupert says.

Sometimes Rupert uses his influence to get messages across to government in a roundabout way. In late 2018, he was in London finalising a deal that would see Richemont become a supplier of luxury goods to Chinese online retail giant Alibaba – a massive coup for a company battling it out with rival LVMH Moët Hennessy – Louis Vuitton (the world's largest luxury-goods company) for prime position in that lucrative market.

After concluding the details with presumptive Alibaba CEO Daniel Zhang, he flew to China for the official announcement and met with Jack Ma, the legendary Alibaba founder, who told him of his invitation by Ramaphosa to speak at the South African government's investment summit. 'What would be your advice?' Ma asked the South African. 'You need to tell the president that he needs to make allies of business, he needs to embrace entrepreneurs,' Rupert told him.

Later, delivering the keynote address in Johannesburg, Ma told the audience and Ramaphosa: 'For a country to develop, there are three basic things that have to be done that are important. The first is education; it's always good to invest in education. Investing in people is the best investment in the whole world. And the second thing is trust; build and support entrepreneurs. Make entrepreneurs the heroes. At the top of this is a good and clean government.'[2]

And Ramaphosa's response? 'We should treat our entrepreneurs as heroes and move away from what we have been fed, where we treated our businesspeople like enemies, called them white monopoly capital and all that. That must end today. Let us see our business people as heroes.'[3]

Christine Lagarde, the managing director of the International Monetary Fund, is considered a good friend of Rupert's and nominated him to receive the Légion d'honneur, France's highest civilian order. He also has a direct line to Steven Mnuchin, a former Wall Street fund manager and Trump's Secretary of the Treasury. Rupert's network covers the US, Europe, the Middle East and the Far East, including hundreds of relationships with high-level government officials and businessmen in the economic powerhouses of the world.

But, at least to his detractors, Rupert is the leader of the Stellenbosch Mafia, manipulating government and in control of the levers and the commanding heights of the economy. Malema has often led the charge, accusing Rupert of being the vanguard of a Western conspiracy to subjugate and recolonise South Africa. In October 2018, Malema said he refused advice that he should 'go to Stellenbosch' so that Rupert could sort out his tax woes.[4] And at an EFF black-tie event in January 2019, with wines from the estate of Rupert & Rothschild on the tables, Malema again attacked Rupert, saying he had rebuffed an offer 'from a sister of Rupert' for a meeting that could 'benefit' both. The spokesperson for the EFF said, 'Can you please tell the Ruperts that at least there must be one party in South Africa which they do not control. And let that party be the EFF. Because the likelihood is that the Ruperts have got everyone except the EFF. We run the risk of all parties in South Africa being owned by the likes of Rupert who have the money to buy everything that moves in this country.'[5]

Interestingly, though, Malema's public statements about Rupert haven't deterred his deputy, Floyd Shivambu, from cultivating a relationship with the ultimate so-called white monopoly capitalist. During the ANC's brutal presidential election in 2017, Shivambu was one of Rupert's go-to men in his informal intelligence network, sometimes explaining the inner workings of the governing party's processes and procedures – and often giving Rupert a heads-up before major developments in the party. (During the height of the contest, Shivambu told Rupert that Ramaphosa would win the leadership race.)

And while his party leader was attacking Rupert on any platform and ranting about white monopoly capital, Shivambu advised Rupert to set the record straight in public and suggested ways he might achieve that: 'Believe it if you will,' said Rupert, 'but Floyd Shivambu advised me to do the PowerFM interview. Once he got to know me, when he realised what I was actually doing, that I was opposed to apartheid and who I knew [during the struggle], he said: "But nobody knows this. You've got to go on Given Mkhari's show and do the Chairman's Conversation [with Mkhari]."'

Shivambu, who also asked Rupert for help with a personal project he was planning, seemed concerned that the public and political image created of the Remgro chairperson was unfair and harsh, and felt that by engaging Mkhari (who had done a similar interview with Mbeki), Rupert could change that narrative. The interview was promptly organised and Rupert had his opportunity to put the record straight – thanks to Shivambu's prodding.

But before that, Shivambu and another EFF colleague went to see Rupert and Ferreira in Stellenbosch. 'He and a colleague – I can't remember the man's name – came to see us to ask for help. We had lunch together at Tokara, Ferreira's wine estate on the Helshoogte Pass. They wanted to build a hospital in Limpopo and asked if we could help. They wanted expertise. They had two businessmen that already built a couple of Spar supermarkets and wanted to work with Mediclinic. I told them we couldn't but maybe the people from Mediclinic could. Jannie then took them to Fleur du Cap, the farm my father bought and that is now owned by Remgro. I was concerned that they might think that all white people live like that, because they already believe we bathe in champagne,' Rupert recalls.

It is ironic that, as Malema was setting up Rupert as the white, capitalist bogeyman, off which the EFF could construct their populist support base, Shivambu was not only attempting to enlist Rupert's support for his own projects, but actively advising him on public relations to counter the message. For Rupert, it was a functional relationship, but he grew tired and disappointed when the personal attacks from Malema did not abate. (Shivambu has denied all of this, including meeting Rupert, and advising him or receiving any help from him.[6])

···✶···

The Rupert seat in Somerset West, about twenty minutes from Stellenbosch, is in the suburb of Parel Vallei, on the slopes of the Helderberg. Across from the property's main entrance is a cluster housing development, and the house is surrounded by unassuming, middle-class family houses. Somerset West's main thoroughfare, with its takeaway shops and taxi stops, is minutes away. The security gate is barely noticeable from street level. (Steinhoff's Markus Jooste, in contrast, lived in a fortified private-security estate in the Jonkershoek Valley.)

A winding road from the gate through thick brush underneath a canopy of trees opens up to a large clearing where the Cape Dutch-style house with its magnificent gables and large windows sits alongside whitewashed old stables and farm outbuildings. The estate, Parel Vallei, after which the suburb is named, can trace its roots back to the 1600s, when the property was granted to a free burgher from the Dutch colony at the Cape.[7]

Security guards show visitors where to park, while a lawn extends from the gravel road at the back of the house past the outbuildings in the direction of the high-school sports fields opposite. In the garage, one car is parked, a black sports utility vehicle (which looks like a Lexus). Rupert arrives a little later driving an oldish-looking black BMW X5.

He waves me in while he parks the car and talks to one of his staff. A large old Dutch colonial front door, with the top half ajar, swings open into a warm and spacious drawing room. The colour scheme is in keeping with the tasteful surroundings: brown and caramel colours dominate the comfortable couches and large chairs. Antique sideboards, tables and chairs dot the room, while a bronze sculpture of what looks like a leopard adorns a sideboard. A fire is roaring away in an oversized fireplace with fine powder-blue and white Delft china tiling along the edges. Finely chopped pieces of wood (possibly old vines) keep it going.

The staff are friendly and welcoming; they say that 'meneer Johann' will be with me shortly. The sounds of activity become clearer as Rupert strides towards the room from the garage and staff greet one of South Africa's most respected business leaders.

Rupert, dressed casually in slacks without socks (and trailed by two farting grey Weimeraners), apologises for being a couple of minutes late. He had been to Kayamandi, where residents were taking part in a protest march. 'Nobody could tell me what it was about, so I decided to go there myself and talk to the people about what their problems are. I went to see for myself what conditions those people are living in. I'm not scared, no, they know me there and they aren't unwilling to talk to me,' Rupert explained.

A few days earlier, a group of people from Hermanus, where violence had erupted, had come to ask him for help. 'We can't keep on treating people like this.'[8]

Rupert tends to overpower his interlocutors and takes ownership of most spaces he enters, an imposing figure who knows how to use silence effectively during conversations. He is rarely deflected, and, once his course is set, it is difficult – if not impossible – to interject. Business and leadership, gossip and anecdotes, sport and politics are his staple, not necessarily in that order. There aren't many heavy-hitters in those disciplines in the world whom he doesn't know, or isn't friendly with, and he ever so often reminds you of that fact.

The conversation veers from capital and politics to rugby and golf, Steinhoff and other companies. Suddenly Rupert stands up and walks to the door, where he hugs a staff member in the doorway. He has come to say goodbye to Rupert, who explains that the worker has been with the Rupert family for almost 30 years and that he always takes a month's leave in the middle of the year to visit his family in KwaZulu-Natal. 'Where are you staying over?' Rupert asks him, before advising him to break the journey in Colesberg rather than drive through the night.

He grins and explains that his father 'suckered' him into buying the old house and that although it is a magnificent home, its ancient beams and decaying walls have meant that he has had to spend a lot of money on its upkeep. 'It's been thirty years of work in progress. I want to move to the farm.' They have farms in Franschhoek and Graaff-Reinet – but Gaynor, his wife, says, 'No, we're not moving, this is where the children grew up.' 'When we got here, it was a disaster. The grass was standing hip high and the insurers declared it a fire hazard. The house has no proper foundations, and in winter the walls draw in moisture from the clay earth.'

He talks easily, much of it off the record, some of it not, and all the while smoking Rembrandt van Rijn cigarettes. He grew up in Stellenbosch with his brother, Antonij, and sister, Hanneli. His family home, 17 Thibault Street, still has the same dusty pink sheen it had in the 1950s and still belongs to the family. Asked if he will ever let the house go, 'Heavens, no, the moment I sell it they will knock it down and build another monstrosity in its place,' he says.

The house had three bedrooms; an Aga stove in the kitchen is an abiding memory, as is cycling to school. 'Stellenbosch back then wasn't what it is today. We stayed in the same house all those years and never moved. It took my father's business thirty years to become cash-flow positive. He didn't care that much for money, it wasn't what motivated him. For example, the first new car my mother got was in 1968, when I was given her old second-hand Mercedes-Benz, a 190 diesel. My dad had a deal with every child: stay off a motorcycle and you can get a car at 18. It was a good deal. My mother got a new car after thirty years of his being in business.'

Rupert reveres his father and admires his resilience. 'You know, in 1948 there were 200 members of the Johannesburg Afrikaans Chamber of Commerce, by 1968 there were only two left: my father and Albert Wessels [who brought Toyota to South Africa]. So he [Anton Rupert] was motivated by something other than money,' says Rupert.

Rupert wasn't too keen on joining his father's business, so he left Stellenbosch to seek his own fortune overseas in the 1970s. In fact, Anton Rupert and Dirk Hertzog, the two Rembrandt founders, agreed that it was not ideal to have family and children join the business, even though Anton Rupert's two brothers were senior executives in the group.[9] Rupert headed off to New York after being offered a position at Chase Manhattan Bank, where his father's friend David Rockefeller was the proprietor. He later worked at the financial advisory firm of Lazard Frères before he returned to Johannesburg in 1979 where he helped found Rand Merchant Bank.

When he finally joined Rembrandt in 1984, it was because his father was having trouble with his partners at Rothmans International in London, and Rupert junior wasn't going to have any of it. 'I didn't go to Rembrandt with the idea that I wanted to make lots of money: I went because my father was starting to lose control of the company,' he says. By that time, PW Botha was at the height of his ideology of 'total strategy' and South Africa was in the grip of widespread violence. Sanctions had started to bite. Rothmans, which had ascended to near the top of the international cigarette industry, thanks in large part to the Ruperts and Rembrandt, decided that the company's representatives were no longer welcome at board meetings because of their nationality and South Africa's apartheid policies.

The Ruperts' opponents on the board were concerned about politics. But, for Rupert, the problem was personal. As he told Anton Rupert's biographer, he couldn't stand his father being treated in such a way by board members, many of whom he had brought into the Rothmans fold.[10] Through a series of strong-arm tactics and boardroom skirmishes and by calling on ancient relationships, Rupert was able to take control of the Rothmans board and force out those board members who opposed him and his father.

Rupert says they came out on top because they fought harder. 'We were always the smallest: Rand Merchant Bank was the smallest, and even Rothmans and BAT [British American Tobacco, in which the Ruperts had a large stake] was smaller than Philip Morris [the large American cigarette and tobacco manufacturer]. Again, now with Richemont, we're smaller than LVMH. It's like having a grocery store in the Karoo – everyone thinks you're huge, but you're not. In South Africa we weren't that big; in global terms we were nothing. We tried to be faster than the rest, we tried to work harder. That was what set us apart,' he says.

Rupert doesn't suffer fools. Colleagues say he was as hands-on as they come when he was running Rembrandt. Whitey Basson took notice when he heard that Rupert once went behind the counter in one of his stores to check for dust on the top shelf of the cigarette counter. 'It's the oldest trick in retail: check for dust, because it tells you whether the rep has been doing his job. At Rembrandt we inculcated a culture of attention to detail.'

Once, in Johannesburg while driving to Rembrandt's offices, he noticed a vehicle belonging to a company rep parked outside the office. He peered in and noticed the car was littered with rubbish like empty Coke cans and food packets. He left an anonymous note on the windscreen: 'Sir, please look after this car a little better and clean it up.' A week later, the car was still in the same state. 'So I went into the office and let the rep have it … the story quickly spread throughout the country. A company has to pay attention to its culture, because the little things can make or break it. A PowerPoint presentation doesn't mean a thing; culture is everything,' he says.

Rupert's real achievement in his early days at Rembrandt was to safeguard the company's future by restructuring the organisation and consolidating its overseas interests in a separate company, Richemont, which was dually listed in Switzerland and Johannesburg. Richemont became the vehicle in which many of Rembrandt's most successful investments were housed, including Cartier and other luxury brands, and has become a powerhouse holding company in its own right.

The Rupert family has ultimate control over Richemont through their European vehicle, Compagnie Financière Rupert, which controls 50% of voting rights. When he was confronted by Cyril Ramaphosa in 1990 about Richemont and the decision to concentrate the family and Rembrandt's overseas interests in a separate, foreign entity, Rupert replied: 'Cyril, it's actually very simple, and you can tell that to your stakeholders: I have to protect the assets of my stakeholders, the shareholders, against your stakeholders, so that if they want to steal stuff, they won't be able to. No capital has left the country, no capital will ever leave the country and all the revenue still returns to South Africa … over the years we have not taken out a single penny.'

Rupert and Ramaphosa, according to Anton Rupert's biographer, became good friends, with Ramaphosa serving as a board member of his Peace Parks Foundation, the transfrontier national parks initiative.

···✳···

In November 2016, Rupert received a text message from a contact in the ANC. The message confirmed to him something that he had long suspected: there was an orchestrated campaign afoot to discredit him, his family and his companies. 'They're coming for you. The Guptas have hired Bell Pottinger to push the "state capture" story onto you. They'll earn R24 million, plus expenses, for their work. It will be paid by an intermediary,' the text message read.

It went further: 'It seems to also be slightly personal, about Edward Zuma and the cigarette trade. They also believe you are funding Maria [Ramos, then Absa's chief executive], Trevor [Manuel, married to Ramos], Pravin and [Mcebisi] Jonas [then deputy minister of finance]. Apparently Zuma is on the front foot against Thuli and massive cabinet changes coming. Bell Pottinger [are the] brains behind the attack on you …'[11]

Less than two weeks later, Richemont's contract with Bell Pottinger, a London public-relations firm that had been contracted to the company for more than 18 years, was terminated by Rupert. At Remgro's annual general meeting he railed against the firm, disgusted by a company he had long trusted. 'Whilst they were still in the employment of Richemont, they started working for the Guptas.' Their task, he explained, was to deflect attention from state capture allegations involving the Guptas and target Rupert – a client of theirs![12]

Rupert denied that Remgro unduly influenced the media or that he was involved with state capture. 'We have never done business with the state … ever. Firstly, I didn't trust the previous bunch, and I don't trust these guys. We have zero influence on the media or the media companies we are invested in.' He says that has never been to the offices of eNCA, a company in which Remgro has a stake, and he doesn't even know where the offices of Caxton, in which the company also has a stake, are. During apartheid he was branded a 'verraaier' ('traitor' in Afrikaans). 'The attacks used to come from the right, now they come from the left. It's not fun … and it's steered by Bell Pottinger. I'm saying this publicly now. It is well known in the press about how well this campaign is orchestrated to protect a certain family and a certain individual.'

By that time, Rupert had been the target of a sustained and vitriolic social-media campaign – run by Bell Pottinger, it would later emerge. The company had been contracted by the Guptas and Zuma's son Duduzane, to counter the rolling coverage in the media of the Indian family's apparent undue influence on the head of state, the ANC and government.

Rupert's image was regularly satirised by the army of anonymous users on Twitter, many of them part of the network and narrative spawned by Bell Pottinger. The Rupert name was used with the hashtag 'WMC', or 'white monopoly capital', and gained traction as the family was positioned as the torchbearers of exploitation and capitalism. One Twitter account, created by Bell Pottinger, published an image of fat, rich, white people gorging themselves while emaciated black people ate crumbs off the floor. One of the fat, rich people resembled Rupert.[13]

Rupert initially merely expressed concern that Bell Pottinger was aiding the state-capturing family and communicated it to the company. But Bell Pottinger's Victoria Geoghegan, who ran the lucrative campaign, wasn't to be swayed. 'As we have known from the start, we are in the middle of a civil war, with the Guptas and allies on one side, and Johann Rupert and others on the other side,' she wrote in an email to the company's bosses. 'More mud will inevitably be thrown. However, it is difficult to turn down such a large retainer.'[14] Lord Tim Bell, one of the company's founders, said he had been opposed to the contract. 'It was the wrong thing to do. Johann Rupert was a client. And I wasn't sure why we were doing something against his interests. I instructed everyone to stop working for the Guptas, and they completely ignored me,' he claimed.[15]

Zuma sat behind it all – Rupert's vilification and that of his name and his family – Rupert believes. 'He drove a campaign against me because he couldn't control me. He did everything to get dirt on me: got people to watch me, investigators overseas, set up immigration officials against me, SARS, the Hawks, the NPA [National

Prosecuting Authority] ... all of them looked at my affairs,' he says. 'What can they do to me? Nothing ... In the old days, you could take a factory, but today it's all about intellectual property rights. And they can't take that.'

The Bell Pottinger campaign and subsequent assault on him and his name – the association with white monopoly capital – have hurt his family. He says it was a relief the day he turned on the television to find that the Guptas' news channel, ANN7, was no longer on the air.[16]

----✦----

Rupert, who has always been vocal about his loyalty to South Africa (his private plane bears the national springbok symbol), has started to doubt the country's future. His children live in England – he thinks it's better that way. 'When they are here [in South Africa] we don't sleep. When they were here, they couldn't go out into public without being insulted. It affected my family.'

The self-styled Afro-optimist doesn't believe he'll stay in the country if things don't change drastically. 'I've told some in government and the ANC in private as much: if SARS ever again tries to sabotage me ... I have been by far the highest individual taxpayer in this country for the last twenty years. Our family companies are the biggest payers of dividends from outside into the country, more than what the rest of the JSE does combined. We have never taken money out of the country, I promised Dr Gerhard de Kock [a past governor of the South African Reserve Bank] that if he allowed me to build Richemont overseas, I wouldn't take money out. The value Remgro and Richemont created through BAT is immense.'

He's angry at being considered the face of white monopoly capital and says that former president Thabo Mbeki understood his family businesses. Mbeki, Rupert says, explained that the government (thanks to investments by the Public Investment Corporation) owned twice as much stock in Rupert businesses as the family itself did. And he adds that he's given away his salary since 2005. (With his estimated personal wealth of $5.9 billion,[17] he can surely afford it.)

'At the age of 69 I'm therefore working for the state and third parties … and I'm going to stop, I've had it up to here. I am not going to be taxed three times for the same earnings. I pay tax overseas, I pay tax here, and they [SARS] want to argue over rubbish while, in actual fact, they owe me money!'

Rupert believes his phone has been tapped for years because his enemies are convinced he controls the currency. He doesn't, he says. But if he wanted to, he could cause some damage. 'I have been protecting the currency, not weakening it. Investors from the US call me and ask whether they should short the rand, and I always say no. I don't control the currency, but if I did decide to encourage people to short the rand, it will have an impact.' He had hoped that the ANC leadership that was elected in December 2017 would be an improvement, but he has lost faith in the party. He believes the country has already reached a point of no return, and that the proximity of David Mabuza, the deputy president, to the top job is too close for comfort.

Rupert loves South Africa, but is dismayed at what has become of the country over the last decade. He was a friend of FW de Klerk and they were in contact while he was president. He also had a close relationship with Mandela, whom he revered as a father figure. He often spoke with Mbeki. But never to Zuma, and he has had no contact with Ramaphosa since he became ANC president and head of state. There's no inclination in the Ramaphosa government to involve Rupert in discussions about business or the economy. Or, it seems, to leverage his global network in favour of economic development. Rupert is persona non grata, it seems. 'I'd like to have contact with Ramaphosa, but I'm not going to force myself on him.'

Rupert will never again put his head above the parapet in public as he has done over the last couple of decades. He rarely grants interviews and almost never agrees to receive awards, to which he made a notable exception in September 2018, when he agreed to an award presented to him in New York in recognition of his business and philanthropic work.[18] He was nominated by former US Secretary of State Henry Kissinger, who argued Rupert 'always stood up for what was right, from the 1980s up until today'.[19]

He says that his expansive network of contacts and acquaintances all over the world could be put to use to advance the country's prospects. But the powers that be have no desire to engage with him. 'What has happened over the last couple of years has been like Chinese torture: drip, drip, drip ... white monopoly capital ... drip, drip, drip ... Naspers attacks ... drip, drip, drip ... he's a rich bastard. You reach a certain point where you ask yourself why you should care. The French gave me the Légion d'honneur; I've created job opportunities; I pay my taxes; I give away money. You'd think people would say "thank you", not "eff-you". I'm sick and tired, and Afrikaners aren't better than Bell Pottinger, mind you. My heart is here, but my body will be overseas. I don't want to hear day and night about what we, the Rupert family, allegedly did wrong. That's the main reason [for wanting to leave].'

For Rupert, South Africa has also dropped off the world's radar. He doesn't get the same level of interest in his country as he used to when he travels in Europe and the US, and he feels the goodwill the country had enjoyed under Mandela and Mbeki dissipated under Zuma. And he cannot understand why South Africa does not leverage its position as a potential bridge between East and West. He believes the country's debt position is untenable and that the cross-guarantees which keep most state-owned enterprises afloat could be disastrous.

'I think we'll be at the IMF in a year's time. [The governing party] don't know what's awaiting. We'll either have an Arab Spring-type event, or Ramaphosa must restructure everything. And he cannot do it. The IMF will, however, force you to restructure, and if you think about it, isn't that the best thing that could happen to the country? Halve the public service, clean up the state-owned enterprises … Look, the Nationalists were rotten, but they didn't steal everything. These people are incompetent *and* they steal.

'The IMF will be a bloody fiasco, I don't know how many companies will be able to manage interest rates of 25%, 30% – but what's the alternative? I've asked Remgro and Rand Merchant Bank to come up with disaster scenarios. Every company should do it. Paul Harris [an RMB board member] says the IMF is a black swan … I told him, "No it's not: it's a serious possibility."'

Rupert, who had a close bond with Ramaphosa in the 1990s, is disappointed in his leadership of the country and the governing party. And he sees the regular instances of violence that break out because of service-delivery frustrations as evidence of poor leadership and emotions reaching boiling point. 'Ramaphosa is going to have to take the bit in his teeth. I think he should do something similar to the fireside chats Reagan had … where he calmly explains to the country what he is going to do.'

Rupert does not want to talk about his philanthropic initiatives, although Remgro CEO Durand says in 2017 he spent hundreds of millions of rands of his own money on poverty-alleviation projects. He invests heavily in his father's home town of Graaff-Reinet, where he has refurbished almost all of the historical old buildings in town. He funds a hospitality academy that annually trains hundreds of young people from disadvantaged backgrounds for a career in the tourism industry, supports local schools with the upgrading of infrastructure and provides daily meals to hundreds.

He also supports the Free Market Foundation, with which he has partnered to secure title deeds for people without property in Stellenbosch and Graaff-Reinet. And he provided the impetus and capital to start non-profit organisation Freedom Under Law.

'I told my wife at one stage that I'm done with collecting art, I'm going to give all my money away. I'm richer than I ever thought I would be and I take pleasure in giving it away while I'm still living ... but I'm doing it quietly. When we recently gave a title deed to an old lady from Kylemore [a Coloured area outside Stellenbosch], she told my wife, "Now I'll have something to leave to my grandchildren."

···✦···

In Stellenbosch, Rupert is often spoken of in hushed but reverential tones, his fiery temper and domineering personality universally acknowledged characteristics of the so-called don of the Winelands Mafia. Whether he wants to acknowledge it or not, Rupert is the personification of Stellenbosch: affluent, elitist and influential. That is the way he is seen not only by his political and ideological opponents, but also by many well-disposed residents of the town, too.

As a friend, he is known to be loyal, but not blind to associates' faults, and honest to the point of being brutal. He is unafraid to speak his mind – sometimes to his own detriment – and gets frustrated when others don't conform to his views. He readily shares intelligence and information but can be prickly if the outcome is not closely aligned to his desires and objectives – or if his interlocutors disagree with him in any way.

He has managed to take his father's company and not only consolidate its wealth and reach, but reconfigure and repurpose it to ensure its sustainability and profitability, to the point that it scarcely resembles the organisation from the early 1990s. The Rupert family ethos and culture permeate Remgro, and its principals remain aware of the chairperson of the board's demands and involvement. There is a reluctance to defy or challenge Rupert, and a deference to his way and convictions. When the disastrous PowerFM interview concluded, his staff were reluctant to tell him how badly it had been received, and Remgro people in Stellenbosch will never say anything that could be construed as remotely critical of the chair of the board.

With great wealth comes great distance from ordinary life, and Rupert is no exception. Besides the standard-issue private aircraft, exclusive homes and public friendships with popular sport stars, he sometimes comes across as frustrated in his inability to direct narratives or effect societal change. His attempt at shaping his legacy among the black elite by agreeing to the Shivambu-advised interview on PowerFM is a case in point. He was convinced that was the correct route to take and that his approach would be vindicated. It was not, and he departed the stage angry and disappointed. His support staff were equally bewildered, taken aback by the reaction and too wary to dissect events for their boss.

My interactions with Rupert, however, have revealed a human side to the caricature, someone who clearly cares for those he considers close, who speaks fondly of others and is deeply concerned about the future of his land of birth. He carries his name and wealth with a guarded grace and doesn't flaunt it, although that doesn't quite fit with the image his detractors portray.

Rupert's identity is closely linked to his heritage as an Afrikaner, his love of his culture and his language. He once withdrew Richemont's advertising from a luxury European magazine because it called Afrikaans one of the ugliest languages in the world, and he is helping to finance the reconstruction of the Afrikaans Western Cape town of Wupperthal, destroyed by fire in late 2018.

Perhaps it's that heritage, and his unashamed espousing of it, that has riled his enemies. The Ruperts did become tycoons during apartheid, after all.

4. THE FIRST AFRIKANER BUSINESSMAN

'Verwoerd never wanted to hear anything good about Rupert again.'

– Paul Sauer, a senior member of Hendrik Verwoerd's cabinet, after the umpteenth time that Anton Rupert and South Africa's then prime minister had clashed about the National Party government's apartheid policies.[1]

NO NAME in post-apartheid South Africa – with the possible exception of Oppenheimer – is more closely associated with the narrative of white monopoly capital or the construct that has become the Stellenbosch Mafia than Rupert. The campaigns to vilify the Rupert name found fertile ground in a society riven by racial division and where the disparities between the wealthy and the poor are still characterised by levels of pigmentation. The Ruperts, the clan that alongside the Oppenheimers became the wealthiest of all South Africans, are an easy target for populists and certain politicians.

By all accounts, Rupert is either the richest or second richest man in South Africa; some sources put him at number one on the list of wealthiest South Africans. According to Forbes, though, one of the more reliable trackers of private wealth, Rupert in 2018 commanded a family fortune of $6.6 billion, which equates to roughly R87 billion[2] and puts him at number two in the country.[3] South Africa's richest man is Nicky Oppenheimer, the scion of the Anglo American and De Beers empires – now mostly spun off – whose family sits on assets worth $7.7 billion, or R102 billion, according to Forbes.[4] (Aliko Dangote, a Nigerian cement magnate, is Africa's richest man, with a private wealth of $12.2 billion, or R167 billion.[5])

The Rupert wealth is centred on interests in South African

diversified investments firm Remgro, luxury-goods holding company Richemont and international investment vehicle Reinet, named after the Karoo town of Graaff-Reinet, from where Anton Rupert hailed.

The Ruperts are regularly caricatured as the archetype of Afrikaner capitalists: brash, arrogant and oblivious to the political system under which they accumulated their vast fortunes. When Johann Rupert criticised the ANC's rhetoric about radical economic transformation, a phrase that had gained much exposure in the messy build-up to the party's elective conference in 2017, he was pilloried by the ruling political class. 'Radical economic transformation is just a code word for theft ... They're raiding the state's coffers. And it's public knowledge,' he said, adding that the Bell Pottinger campaign had been launched to deflect attention from the corruption in government.[6]

Rupert also said it was known that the state was being 'robbed blind' but that his comments must not be misconstrued: 'It doesn't matter what your political orientation is, the fact remains that it's close to midnight for South Africa ... we're facing a fiscal cliff thanks to maladministration and corruption. We're all going to have to work together, business, civil society and government.'[7]

The ANC, radical-transformation theorists and reactionaries exploded, with the common theme being that a white capitalist of Rupert's repute has no standing to comment on the government's policies or to speak of corruption (which was nevertheless rampant). Zizi Kodwa, the ANC's spin doctor, was first out of the blocks, saying Rupert 'and his ilk' continue to benefit from an unequal society and its resultant monopolies. Kodwa, in a wordy statement defending the ANC's policy of broad societal transformation, called Rupert 'disingenuous', 'extremely opportunistic', 'a beneficiary of apartheid's exclusionary policies', 'arrogant' and a 'naysayer' – and 'advised' him to refrain from making public comments because it was based on his 'innate inclination to preserve privilege and prosperity for a few'.[8]

Thami Mazwai, an adviser to Lindiwe Zulu, the firebrand minister of small-business development and a big proponent of 'RET', called Rupert's remarks 'a kick in the teeth of blacks' and added that the family had 'benefited substantially from apartheid, despite the objections it had'.[9]

Edna Molewa, a minister in Zuma's government, accused Rupert and his family of being beneficiaries of the erstwhile National Party government's favouring of Afrikaner business. 'It is regrettable that his scathing critique of the black majority government came from a beneficiary of the largesse of the interventionist apartheid state. Rupert can thank what historian Dan O'Meara called "*volkskapitalisme*" for the stellar fortunes of his late father's and his impressive empire,' Molewa wrote in *Business Day*.[10]

Not exactly true, retorted Tim Cohen, editor of *Business Day*, a week later, explaining that just because apartheid was 'fundamentally evil' does not mean 'historical accuracy' should be jettisoned by Molewa and the enemies of capital and private enterprise in the ANC. Cohen agreed that many Afrikaner businesses were indeed given preferential treatment by the government of the day through economic interventionism, but argued that it did not happen to the same extent as is seen in present-day South Africa: 'There was never anything close to the huge gobs of legislation forcing firms to give up equity, buy from designated groups, or do training for one group only that we see today.'[11]

Cohen argues that *volkskapitalisme* was never intended to force so-called English business to give up ownership and shares through 'fiat and bullying': 'The idea was exactly the opposite: it was to go into direct competition with English business by fully owned Afrikaner businesses. The underlying notion was to leverage Afrikaner agricultural wealth into formal businesses that would be "ours", in the idiom of Afrikaner leaders of the time.'[12]

In his appearance before the Truth and Reconciliation Commission (TRC) in 1997 – he was one of only a handful of businessmen who chose to do testify – Rupert dismissed the notion that the Rembrandt Group was a favourite of the apartheid establishment and enjoyed special privilege. In fact, he said, Rembrandt and its founders were not close to the establishment at all – Anton Rupert's feud with apartheid premier Hendrik Verwoerd was well known; meanwhile, his efforts to convince PW Botha to dismantle apartheid were rejected time and again.

Rembrandt, Rupert told the TRC, was a company that had contributed to society and continued to do so. It has created wealth for its shareholders, both locally and abroad, and provided security for its employees.

Indeed, the TRC – increasingly criticised in later years because either it did not delve deeply enough or was too lenient on apartheid criminals – had to make sense of Rupert and others' argument that business was limited in its scope of influence during apartheid. It found that 'most businesses benefited from operating in a racially structured context' and cited the influence of laws and regulations that enforced job reservation, influx control, wages, access to resources, migrant labour and the hostel system.[13]

---*---

In democratic South Africa, it is nigh on impossible to talk about politics without considering the economy. And when the economy is the topic for discussion, the conversation will inevitably hinge on the role of capital and the private sector in alleviating the country's most pressing problems: unemployment, inequality and sluggish economic growth. The ANC seems to have an almost visceral distrust of the profit motive, although the party, in all its guises and at all levels, slavishly adheres to the material abundance that capital investment, economic growth and private enterprise can provide. Economic centralism – with the state both as generator of opportunity and regulator of the trade environment – remains the ANC's ideology.

When Anton Rupert established his first business in the 1940s, he did so in an environment that, as mentioned in Chapter 2, was not only hostile to Afrikaners, but in which Afrikaners distrusted capital. The trail of destruction the South African War had left in its wake led to the awakening of both Afrikaner and African nationalism, with the country's racial and segregation policies allowing the former to flourish and the latter to flounder. The South African National Native Congress was founded in 1912 to foster black aspirations, while the establishment of the National Party a year later was to become the prime vehicle for Afrikaner nationalism.

Even though, under the Union, South Africa had become an independent country within the British Commonwealth, and there was a succession of Afrikaner prime ministers, the Afrikaner remained on the fringes of the economy of the 1920s and 1930s. Afrikaner ideologues were wary of industry and commerce, which were dominated by English-speakers and Jews, and Afrikaans newspapers, such as *Die Burger*, founded in 1915 to advance the Nationalist cause, created caricatures of that capitalist anglophone class.

'Many of the Afrikaner workers had deep reservations about the capitalist system with its apparently rampant individualism and greed. Afrikaner nationalists deplored the class divisions the system fostered and the exploitation suffered by the unskilled and semi-skilled Afrikaner workers. Their feelings were most intense in Johannesburg, a city built, as they saw it, on crude materialism, exploitation, corruption, vice and almost all other forms of human degradation,' Giliomee says,[14] arguing that this sentiment provided fertile ground for the rise of communism. Indeed, communists agreed that they must use the discontent among Afrikaner workers to win Afrikanerdom for their side.

Prominent Afrikaner communist Daan du Plessis wrote that it wasn't Parliament or Cabinet that wielded real power, it was the capitalists, who fomented racial hatred among workers: in its relentless pursuit of profit, the low wages the system paid black workers suppressed the wage levels of all workers. Du Plessis called on workers to unite and 'overthrow the existing system and turn it over to communism'.[15]

Much of the frustration felt by Afrikaners about their lack of inclusion in enterprise was defused by the government's establishment of state-owned companies, such as Iscor, which were largely managed by Afrikaners. Afrikaner governments of the day also never followed through on their threats to nationalise capital. Giliomee argues that these threats were nullified, thanks to English-speaking South Africans gaining large chunks of shares in companies dominated by foreign investors ahead of World War II.

But the Nationalists were hell-bent on advancing the Afrikaner cause in the economy, and even though they periodically threatened to nationalise the mines and banks, they tried hard to overcome the Afrikaners' general aversion to capital. Afrikaners were reluctant to entrust their savings to anyone beyond immediate family, and most farmers invested their profits back into their farms, leaving very little in terms of capital to be leveraged.

In 1939 Verwoerd helped to organise the Eerste Ekonomiese Volkskongres, or the First Economic Congress of the People, where Afrikaners were encouraged to band together to raise capital for their economic upliftment. Verwoerd, in his stride as a granite-hard nationalist, implored Afrikaners to organise themselves and to use their purchasing power as a counterpoint to the interests of organised retail and producers.[16]

As mentioned, one of the first loans granted by the finance house that was created by the First Economic Congress of the People was to Anton Rupert, with wine and tobacco farmers being the primary shareholders of his business, the forerunner of Rembrandt. The purpose of his new company, he said, was 'to further our nation's progress and help Afrikaners to gain their rightful place in industry and their future as employers and employees'. His partner, Dirk Hertzog, said: 'Our overriding concern was to prove that, by standing together, we [i.e. Afrikaners] could take our place in the business world with dignity and honour.'[17]

It was the start of an empire that today has interests around the globe, and is still a dominant player on the JSE.

----*----

Anton Rupert, the eldest of three sons, was born on 4 October 1916 in Graaff-Reinet into a politically active family. His father, John, a lawyer, was a member of the National Party and his mother, Hester, became chairperson of the local women's branch of the party.

Rupert wanted to study medicine, but his parents could not afford the tuition and he instead enrolled for a science degree at the newly established University of Pretoria in 1934. He graduated in 1936 with chemistry as his major, supplemented with courses in physics and mathematics. He continued his studies as a postgraduate and found employment as a lecturer at the Pretoria Technical College, teaching pharmaceutical students.

In 1937 he was offered a job on the staff of the *Transvaler* newspaper, where Verwoerd was editor. Because the work would mean that he would have to study part time, he turned down the offer. And he was not impressed by Verwoerd, whom he described as 'restless, rather autocratic and opinionated' during his interview.[18]

As was the case with most Afrikaners during those flourishing years of nationalism, Rupert was deeply involved in his people's cause, and played active political roles at the University of Pretoria as well as during the centenary celebrations of the Great Trek in 1938. He was a vehement opponent of then premier Jan Smuts's decision to enter World War II on the side of Great Britain, and went to seek advice about whether he should pursue a career in politics from retired General Barry Hertzog, who had been deposed by Smuts as prime minister on the back of Parliament's decision to declare war on Germany. But he was dissuaded from entering politics after a discussion with neo-Nazi minister Oswald Pirow's sister, who told him not to mingle with her brother's type because the Nationalists were 'grooming' him to become 'a leader in our party'. After the meeting, Rupert told his wife, Huberte: 'If that's what politics is like, I want nothing to do with it. I'm through with politics.'[19]

Rupert's business career was launched inauspiciously when he and two partners, Dirk Hertzog and Nico Diederichs (the latter would later become a minister of finance and ultimately ceremonial state president), established a dry-cleaning business in Pretoria. Rupert was lecturing at the technical college but this first foray into commerce was in line with the nationalist thrust at the time that Afrikaners needed to force themselves onto the business world, hitherto dominated by English-speaking South Africans.

In 1940 Rupert abandoned his doctoral studies in chemistry to join the Reddingsdaadbond (Rescue Action League), one of the organisations brought to life in the wake of the First Economic Congress of the People to advance the cause of poor and destitute Afrikaners. His task was to head the small-business section of the organisation in Johannesburg, and to help assess and award loans to deserving small enterprises. Thousands of small businesses were incubated with small loans granted by the Reddingsdaadbond, although many failed.

According to his biographer, Ebbe Dommisse, this exposure to entrepreneurship 'made him aware of the tantalising possibilities' that business held. The organisation did yeoman work to convince Afrikaners of what could be achieved if capital was collectively leveraged and that it could be put to use serving their interests.

At the time, even though Afrikaners had been the dominant political grouping in the country for almost thirty years, there were very few established Afrikaner businesses in the country, with the exception of Nasionale Pers, Sanlam, Santam, Volkskas and a northern newspaper house, Voortrekkerpers. According to Dommisse, at the end of the 1930s Afrikaner capital accounted for only 5%

of the country's total turnover in trade, industry and finance.[20]

While Rupert was attempting to broaden the pool of Afrikaner industrialists and entrepreneurs at the Reddingsdaadbond, he came across a bankrupt tobacco company in Paarl, Voorbrand, and proceeded to raise enough money – including ten pounds of his own – to buy the venture. His partners included Diederichs and Dr AJ Stals, who was later to become a member of DF Malan's first Nationalist Cabinet in 1948. Voorbrand – from which Rembrandt and Remgro later grew – had a tough time in a strictly regulated market already dominated by big players.

According to Dommisse, Rupert saw an opportunity for stronger competition in the market, in no small way driven by resentment among tobacco farmers that they weren't getting their fair share. The company unashamedly marketed itself as an 'Afrikaner factory' under control of 'Afrikaner capital', with products manufactured by 'Afrikaner hands'.[21] But board minutes indicate that Rupert was not convinced that this strategy was working and believed that the inherent inferiority complex that many Afrikaners suffered from prevented them from buying from kith and kin.

The answer, he believed, lay in better marketing, and he soon developed the marketing nous for which he was to become renowned. Michiel le Roux, one of the founders of Capitec Bank, recalls how Rupert insisted on approving every new marketing campaign or brand design whenever the Stellenbosch-based Distillers Corporation planned to launch a new product into the market. 'We could traverse the country from east to west, visit every pub and shebeen. But inevitably when we went to Dr Rupert to get his input, he would make changes to design – and it always worked.'[22]

----*----

In 1942 Rupert launched his first investment vehicle, Tegniese en Industriële Beleggings Beperk, or TIB (Technical and Industrial

Investments Limited), to help raise capital for Voorbrand after some investors threatened to pull the plug on the struggling company. TIB was established with the sale of the dry-cleaning business and would provide the vehicle for his entry into a range of industries, including the liquor business. Hertzog also joined the Voorbrand board of directors.

The Rupert empire then started to expand rapidly when the constraints Voorbrand had to operate under compelled Rupert to look wider than the tobacco industry. He entered the liquor trade after TIB acquired two businesses, including a bankrupt Stellenbosch company, along with its equipment and facilities on the outskirts of town. This new company became the Distillers Corporation and is now known as Distell. TIB's new ventures were heavily supported by Western Cape farmers, who bought large chunks of shares on offer.

Distillers was listed on the Johannesburg Stock Exchange in June 1945 – the first Afrikaans company to gain a listing.[23] The company's focus was to promote and market South African estate wines, at a time when imported wines were still the preferred tipple for upmarket wine drinkers because they were regarded as more sophisticated than locally produced wines. It also saw the opportunity in the local spirits market, particularly the production of high-quality brandy, including Oude Meester and Richelieu. Later Rupert came up with the Amarula brand of cream liqueur, which would become a worldwide favourite.

When the Rembrandt Tobacco Manufacturing Corporation[24] was established in 1946, it served to house all of the group's tobacco and liquor interests. Rupert, who considered himself a child of the depression era, 'cynically' remained convinced that those two industries were more resilient than most, and that when times were tough people never stopped smoking and drank even more.[25] Most of Rembrandt's shareholders were wine and tobacco farmers, and it made sense for the company to try to establish itself as the industries' champion.

Rembrandt produced its first cigarettes in June 1948, hitting the market a week after Malan's National Party won the 1948 election. The launch came three years after Rupert had met Sydney Rothman in London and secured the rights to manufacture and sell products from the famous London company Rothmans of Pall Mall.

The company relied on technical support from Rothmans, but it really hit its straps when Rupert started focusing on marketing. The company didn't have enough money to pay for traditional advertising, so it used company vehicles, painted in corporate colours, as moving advertisements, and erected billboards in strategic places. Rembrandt earned a reputation as a small company that put quality control first. A sign at its Paarl factory implored its workers to remember that every cigarette must be 'a masterpiece', in the style of the paintings by the company's namesake Dutch artist.

In its first year of operation, Rembrandt suffered a loss of £63 000, but by the following year it had turned a profit of £104 000. In 1950 it paid its first dividend to investors, which Rupert regarded as a 'giant breakthrough'.[26]

In 1953 the company started making strides internationally, when it bought Rothmans. This was one of the most revered tobacconists in the UK and boasted the royal seal of approval as supplier to the Court of St James.

Rothman, a friend of Rupert, was about to sell his family business to a competitor, but Rupert and Rembrandt intervened, offering £750 000 pounds for the enterprise. The offer was accepted, but Rupert was short of some £700 000. The deal was eventually financed after he addressed the boards of Sanlam and Volkskas, two major Afrikaner businesses, which agreed to a loan.

The acquisition of Rothmans gave Rupert and Rembrandt an international foothold and a base from which to expand overseas. Rembrandt by that time had become known for innovation. It was the first company locally, and one of the first internationally, to introduce so-called 'king size' filters on its cigarettes.

The company launched its international flagship, the Peter Stuyvesant brand, in August 1954 after Rupert acquired the rights to manufacture a new, modern cigarette filter. It was to become one of the world's biggest-selling international brands. Rupert derived the brand name from a Dutch governor of New York in the 1600s. His marketing vision of the cigarette – 'youthful, dynamic … for a new, young international product' – was supported by an international campaign.

It worked: supply struggled to keep up with demand. Dommisse writes that Rupert even helped pack cigarettes at night at the plant to keep the cigarettes rolling off the production line.

Peter Stuyvesant sales skyrocketed by more than 4 700% within the first year.[27] His company made rapid international progress, exporting to Canada and Australia. Rothmans was served well by board members, who included Pierre Trudeau (later to become Canadian prime minister) and Francis de Guingand, who served as chief of staff to British war hero Field Marshal Bernard Montgomery.

Rembrandt also expanded into the United States, and Peter Stuyvesant later became a favourite in Germany too, when that country's biggest cigarette manufacturer acquired the rights to distribute the brand in Germany. Peter Stuyvesant commercials became legendary, with the tag line 'your international passport to smoking pleasure' and images of global playgrounds of the rich and famous, such as St Tropez and Florida, featuring good-looking men and women skiing and diving before enjoying a drag.

Rupert's business philosophy was about creating successful partnerships. Once Rembrandt acquired a company, it would set out to assist the local management team with expertise and advice, and once the business was stable and functioning according to the mother company's standards and protocols, it was left to its own devices, with Rembrandt fading into the background.[28]

Rupert and Rembrandt's second big British acquisition came in 1958, when it took control of established manufacturer Carreras, owner of the Dunhill brand of luxury goods, including the cigarette brand. The deal was sealed after Rupert inveigled London financier Edmund de Rothschild into persuading the controlling shareholders of Carreras to sell out to Rupert. He proceeded to revamp the whole company, closed down inefficient factories and moved the Carreras and Rothmans operations to a sleek, modern new plant, which was opened by Prince Philip.[29]

Rupert expanded his business empire across the globe, with additional interests in Australia and New Zealand, Indonesia, Singapore, Jamaica, Zimbabwe, Malawi, Zambia, Switzerland, Ireland and the Netherlands. In 1972 he told students at the University of Pretoria, his alma mater, that Rembrandt built the Rothmans business in Britain: 'Today we control more than two-thirds of all cigarette imports from the British Isles and we are the biggest exporters of cigarettes in the world. Young South Africans did the groundwork, the planning, and the product design. And it was done at Stellenbosch. In the 1930s and 1940s our aim was to prove that Afrikaners also had a foothold. In the 1950s our aim was to prove that South Africans could compete anywhere in the world.'[30]

···✳···

Rupert was the inspiration for a generation of Afrikaner businessmen who came to believe that they could succeed in the English- and Jewish-dominated world of business. He showed that Afrikaners' place in society wasn't necessarily limited to the public service or farms.

One of those who looked up to Rupert as a child, and who later worked for him, is Capitec's Le Roux. 'Rupert was a big figure,' he said. 'He was someone that came from the *platteland* and begged a couple of *ooms* to invest, and proceeded to build an international company. That made me think, "Heavens, if Anton Rupert can do it, so can I!"'

Rupert's success inspired him and gave him confidence as a young Afrikaner (Le Roux prefers the term 'Afrikaans speaker'). In later years, Le Roux moved to Stellenbosch and became part of his empire at Distillers.[31]

Rupert was the first internationally acclaimed Afrikaner businessman, and Stellenbosch remained his and his company's base. He was recognised as a master marketer, who knew how to design a product and then how to sell it. 'Rupert was unique. He was an expert on advertising and branding. We had to present every new liquor label to him before it was finalised – the same with all the cigarette brands. I don't think he ever set foot inside a shebeen, but he instinctively knew better than us, even after loads of research, what a young black consumer would want. We would make a proposal about branding, or whatever, and he would come with something else. And it worked.'[32]

It worked well. Rembrandt became the byword for Afrikaner achievement in business in the 1970s and 1980s, but the company prospered in a skewed political environment. It is difficult to engage Johann Rupert about the company's relationship with apartheid. But he maintains the company always adhered to ethical business principles – a view corroborated by Remgro's CEO Durand. If anything, Rembrandt suffered because of his father's opposition to Verwoerd, and later PW Botha, Rupert insists.

Apartheid caused everyone, black or white, rich or poor, to become an activist in service of one cause or another – even if they didn't realise it. And the Ruperts were no exception.

5. MAKING MONEY DURING APARTHEID

*'I told him that if I were a black man I would also be a
Pan-Africanist, I would also be a member of the
PAC, not the ANC.'*

– Johann Rupert to Steve Biko in 1973.[1]

THE RUPERT FAMILY have never been formally involved in politics. Like his father, Johann Rupert has never stood for public office,
as Harry Oppenheimer did, and he has never openly declared his
support for any political party.

Because of Anton Rupert's stature in the old South Africa, however, and Johann Rupert's wealth in the new, they have also never
been politically neutral either. Both became involved in various
political imbroglios in their careers and both moved close to the
political ruling class of the day, with Johann perhaps less close in
present-day South Africa than his father was in the South Africa
of his time.

As is the case in most societies, the wealthy in South Africa
always have access to the politically powerful. There is simultane-
ously a symbiosis between business and politics and a consistent
tension, with the one dependent on the other. The former needs
politicians to create an environment in which capital can thrive and
grow; the latter needs business to help it perform to its utmost, so
that it has a good story to tell to the electorate. The relationship has
never been equal, though, with business loath to involve itself too
much in the vagaries of political governance. Politicians know this
too well. And when business oversteps the mark, politics snaps back –
regulation, taxation, victimisation.

The Ruperts have maintained ties to most South African
heads of government and state, and their networks. Anton Rupert

was part of the elite in the 1940s when political power shifted to Afrikaner nationalism, with his original business partners all connected and politically influential (one later became ceremonial state president). Johann Rupert played golf with FW de Klerk and calls him 'a pal'. Both became close to Mandela after he was released from prison; Mandela believed Rupert Snr to be a remarkable man and Rupert Jnr considered the first democratic president to be a father figure.

Johann Rupert has known Ramaphosa since the early 1990s, cementing a relationship with the former trade unionist during a working session at the presidency in Pretoria, where the two took part in discussions around a new labour regime. While Mandela was leading the dialogue, they were keeping an eye on a Formula One race, with Ramaphosa particularly distracted by events on the track. Today, Rupert no longer has direct contact with President Ramaphosa.

He has in recent years become increasingly vocal about the state of South Africa, state capture and corruption. A misfiring and collapsing state are issues he has raised in public, and repeatedly got flak for. He has also been at pains to tell anyone who would listen that he and his family were excommunicated from the ruling Afrikaner political establishment before 1994, and that the post-1994 order was not well disposed to the family and their interests either.

But he's also no shrinking violet, as many in the Remgro stable can attest, and he is one of the few senior business leaders who has chosen to stand up and criticise government. In 2015, shortly after Zuma fired Nene, Rupert publicly declared that Zuma must go – 'for the sake of our children!' This came after Zuma told a meeting of the ANC's top brass how Rupert had flown from London to drum up a plot for Gordhan to return to the National Treasury. Not so, Rupert said, pointing out that it would have been impossible for him to fly from Britain because he was in Stellenbosch at the time officiating at a graduation ceremony at the university.

----✦----

Although Anton Rupert never entered politics, it was impossible to escape the Afrikaner nationalist cause in the 1940s and 1950s, and he was no exception. He was very much part of the national project, working for fledgling institutions, such as the Reddingsdaadbond, and he became a member of the Broederbond, the shadowy and secretive organisation that promoted Afrikaner interests and was said to be the power behind the National Party government. Between 1945 and 1947, Rupert took part in Broederbond discussions about a future economic structure for South Africa, and it was during these dialogues that the debate between socialism and free-market principles was decided in favour of the latter. According to his biographer, Ebbe Dommisse, it seems that he never really felt comfortable in the organisation, however, and eventually let his membership lapse.[2]

Despite his involvement in the burgeoning nationalist Afrikaner system, in 1951 Rupert proposed that private capital be invested in black areas and that Afrikaners should establish a Bantu Development Corporation to assist black entrepreneurs.[3] His proposal was never acted upon. Shortly afterwards, during a secret conference of the Broederbond, he rejected the idea of quotas for Afrikaners when doing business with the state.[4] The Broederbond's executive council was seemingly not enthusiastic about a quota system in favour of fledgling Afrikaner businesses, and the idea was dropped shortly after.

Rupert drifted away from the Broederbond and its activities, saying it had become 'an absurdity' and 'counterproductive'. Rembrandt also rejected criticism that it had been 'founded' by the Broederbond. Rupert's partner, Dirk Hertzog, said in an internal memorandum that the company might have had support from the organisation in its early days when Afrikaners were trying to break into business, but it did not have the Broederbond to thank for its existence.[5]

During his career, Anton Rupert clashed with two of apartheid's strongmen, Verwoerd and PW Botha, the former the rigid, headstrong and dismissive architect of apartheid, and the latter the isolationist and militant enforcer of apartheid doctrines. Rembrandt's central philosophy, espoused by Rupert, was that partnerships between people and 'groups' were a prerequisite for success and peace. But when he proposed that private capital be allowed to invest in the homelands, or Bantustans, it was met with acid rejection by Verwoerd, who developed a 'permanent enmity' for the Afrikaner tycoon.[6] Verwoerd's biographer, Henry Kenney, argues that Rupert should have been the pride and joy of the Nationalists because of his demonstrable international success and the elevation of the Afrikaner to the top table in the business world, but that Verwoerd never forgave him for the fact that he wanted to invest in black industry. Verwoerd tolerated capital inasmuch as it enabled the state to suppress insurrection without outside interference. Rupert and capital (preferably without Jewish influence) had to know their place.

In 1959 Rupert met Verwoerd at his office to inform him of Rembrandt's intentions to establish a partnership with a group of Coloured South Africans in Paarl. His plan was that this new company would be managed by Coloured people. Verwoerd was having none of it and rejected the idea after Rupert confirmed that Coloured people would serve on the new company's board and white people would report to them. 'To my utter dismay, he said if that is the case he would close the factory down,' Rupert recalled.[7]

It was a heavy blow for Rupert, who described his relationship with government and the ruling class as one of 'loyal resistance': he would criticise harmful policies domestically but would defend the country overseas.

The following year, after the Sharpeville massacre, he met Verwoerd again to implore him to change tack. The meeting was a disaster, with Rupert attempting to convince the immovable object that was Verwoerd that black South Africans must be allowed to own property. He first proposed a 99-year leasehold in 'white' cities for black people, and when Verwoerd shot the idea down, he floated a 30-year leasehold option instead. Finally, he told Verwoerd the government had to sell houses at discount prices to black people because a title deed provided security and was the basis upon which wealth could be built. Verwoerd again rejected Rupert's proposals and the two men never spoke to each other again.[8]

Rupert enjoyed a more cordial relationship with Botha, although it was no less fruitless than the one he had with Verwoerd. During the 1970s and 1980s, when big business increasingly started engaging with government, Rupert came into more regular contact with the political leaders of the day and, as he had with Verwoerd, he tried to establish a working relationship with Botha. This culminated in two incidents that had the same effect as his run-ins with Verwoerd.

In 1986 an exasperated Anton Rupert, by then acutely aware of the destructive road down which the country had been travelling, wrote a personal letter to the head of state imploring him to em-bark on political reforms and flagging the realities of the country's dire state to the cantankerous and irascible president. Apartheid, Rupert wrote, 'does not represent the cornerstone of white survival in South Africa'.

'It is a myth that apartheid guarantees the white man's survival. As a matter of fact it jeopardises his survival. Apartheid is seen by too many as a transgression against humanity, the neo-Nazism of a *Herrenvolk*. Reaffirm your rejection of apartheid. It is crucifying us, it is destroying our language, it is degrading for a once heroic nation to be the lepers of the world. Remove the burden of the curse of a transgression against mankind from the backs of our children and their children. Should you fail in this God-given task, then one day we will surely end up with a Nuremberg.'[9]

Botha responded curtly: 'I gladly listen to advice from good friends. But I tend to ignore advice that does not sound genuine to me.'[10]

Two years later, Rupert wrote to Botha again, this time to inter-vene in the death sentence of the so-called Sharpeville Six, who had been sentenced to death after an apparent necklacing south of Johannesburg. Townships were burning, the army was on night patrols and violence was part of the country's news staple. Rupert asked Botha to show mercy to prevent six 'Jopie Fouries'.[11] Botha replied, but his main thrust was that he objected to the compari-son between the condemned and Fourie. The six were eventually released in 1991.[12]

Anton Rupert and Rembrandt did a number of other things of political consequence that were innovative for the time: they intro-duced a minimum wage for all their workers, attempted to build the first regional development bank, helped establish the Lesotho Industrial Development Corporation, managed an air ambulance out of Maseru for more than a decade, established the Small Busi-ness Development Corporation and played a leading role in the Urban Foundation (chaired by Oppenheimer and Rupert), which sought to improve the socio-economic conditions of black South Africans. During the company's involvement in Lesotho, Rupert, when answering critics who felt he should not involve himself in the landlocked state's internal affairs, memorably said: 'We won't sleep if our neighbours don't eat.' Rupert was asked by Leabua Jonathan, Lesotho's prime minister, to help his government with development.

Establishing a development bank, the Development Bank for Equatorial and Southern Africa, was a noble effort to try to encour-age entrepreneurship in southern Africa. It existed for a number of years and helped hundreds of small businesses but was eventually just too hamstrung because the South African government refused to allow it to be managed from the country. It meant the bank, which relied on European and local donors for its founding capital, had to be managed from Zurich, but with a regional office in Mbabane, Eswatini (then Swaziland), which was never conducive to effective operations.

----*----

Anton Rupert was a product of his era. He was born in a time of political tumult when Afrikaners were starting to embark on the apartheid project driven by the fanning of nationalist sentiment in the first decades after the South African War. He was consumed by his people's plight and took advantage of the environment created by the ascendancy of Afrikaner politicians in the 1930s and 1940s to build a multibillion-rand empire. This is clearly illustrated by the fact that influential and politically connected Afrikaners of the time were intimately involved in the early days of Rembrandt and also acted as mentors for the young upstart. Rupert also played a significant role in the broader social and political movement to uplift Afrikaners.

He wasn't entirely convinced by universal franchise, and in the 1960s explained as much in a speech in the United States, in which – in the era of *uhuru*, African independence and the civil-rights movement – he warned against 'one man, one vote, once'. He reportedly argued that before the extension of voting rights to non-whites could occur, social and economic development should be on a sound footing. Without those foundations, he believed, democracy could not survive.[13]

In 1978 he repeated this theme in a speech in Maseru when in his prepared remarks he reiterated that too much emphasis was placed on 'one man, one vote', instead of 'one man, one job'. He was warned beforehand that this would not be well received and decided to leave it out, but by then the written text had been distributed.[14]

It seems, however, that Rupert, even though he benefited from the statutory and governance framework constructed by the policies of separate development, was never an apartheid ideologue. His biographer argues that Rupert had come to understand as early as 1947 that racial segregation could not be the long-term solution to the country's social and developmental problems.

Rupert and Rembrandt's business philosophy of mutually benefi-
cial partnerships also seemed to stem from his political views, in
that although he apparently wasn't wholeheartedly committed to
liberal democracy for a long period of time, he did understand that
the subjugation of an entire people would destroy both business
and society.

He clearly had an antipathy to Verwoerd and, according to an
interview with his biographer, believed the Dutch-born hard-line
apartheid premier to be 'the same kind of catastrophic outsider that
Hitler had been to the Germans'.

In 1966 he was interviewed by journalist Allen Drury in Stellenbosch and said that the fortunes of white and black people in South
Africa were interwoven, that 'if the African doesn't eat, we don't
sleep … if he doesn't succeed, we won't, and if we don't succeed,
he won't'.[15]

As his business empire grew and his interests beyond South
Africa's borders expanded, Rupert took on a more public role, and
became increasingly vocal about apartheid, describing it as a system
founded on white fears, which he felt was unsustainable.

But, could Rupert – and Rembrandt – have done more to expedite
the end of apartheid? Yes, Rupert's son Johann believes.

----◆----

Johann Rupert had always considered himself an opponent of apartheid and was ejected from officers' training in the navy during his
military conscription when it came to light that he had taken part
in producing an anti-apartheid edition of the student newspaper at
Stellenbosch.

'After we published the newspaper, the *Cape Times* ran a front-
page headline: "Anton Rupert's son turns against apartheid",' he
recalls.[16] That was in October 1970. In 1973 he struck up a relationship with Black Consciousness leader Steve Biko. 'Biko was in

Stellenbosch to attend a conference of the South African Students' Organisation. I wanted to meet him and talk about his convictions and beliefs. We met one day and we continued talking until very late. I told him that if I were a black man I would also be a Pan-Africanist, I would also be a member of the PAC, not the ANC. We agreed that there could be no peace in the country unless there was a deal between white nationalists and black nationalists.'

Rupert's dislike of politicians and the apartheid government intensified during the time he worked at Chase Manhattan Bank in 1974. David Rockefeller called him into his office one day to ask what was happening on the border between South West Africa and Angola. 'Did the [South African] army invade Angola?' he asked. To find out what the situation was, Rupert called his father, who, in turn, asked Hilgard Muller, then minister of foreign affairs. Muller assured Anton Rupert that South Africa was not 'in' Angola. When he relayed the message to his son, so that he could pacify Rockefeller (Chase Manhattan was one of South Africa's largest creditors), Rupert said, 'But, Dad, looking at the images on television here, it sure looks like we are. I know what our soldiers and armaments look like.'

The National Party government and the intransigent ideological bent of apartheid politicians repulsed Rupert. 'I didn't know black people when I was young and living in Stellenbosch – back then, there were something like 10 000 black people in the whole of the Western Cape. I became an opponent of apartheid because of what the government did to Coloured people. I never went to the Transvaal, but I did see what the Group Areas Act was doing in Stellenbosch, where it forced out all the Coloured inhabitants of Andringa Street. Trevor Manuel's surrogate father used to live there. He used to do plumbing work for my mother, and always bought her tea,' he says.[17] 'Apartheid was an immoral system, and I told Botha as much when they moved on District Six.'

When Rupert returned from his stint in international banking in 1979, he settled in Johannesburg and launched Rand Merchant

Bank. He had struck up a friendship with Brian Gule, a black South African studying in New York and they decided to test the regulatory environment back home by starting a joint venture. 'We opened a hair salon in the Carlton Centre, Black Wave, because back then there were no black hair salons in the city. And when we opened our doors it was the only black business in the whole of Johannesburg. But then the Group Areas Act came looking for us. Because we were in a partnership, the property owners of our premises, Anglo American, were good to us. They said they couldn't eject us purely on the basis of the law. The clientele we drew were the young black professionals of the time: doctors and their wives, for example.'

He tells of his visits to Soweto with a black friend, Lucky Michaels, who introduced him to the Pelican Jazz Club. 'I went there on Fridays to listen to jazz ... up until 1983, at which point Lucky told me it was becoming too dangerous.'

The black community increasingly asked Rupert for loans from Rand Merchant Bank to start businesses, but because of the nature of merchant banking he couldn't help. 'We said: "Boys, this is a problem. Something major is wrong. What can a black guy do when he wants to start a business? What options does a black entrepreneur have?" I thought of my black friends in New York – guys like Reggie Jackson and Ahmad Rashad – and I thought, "*Nee, donner, so kan dit nie werk nie.*"' ('No, darn it, it cannot work like that.')

Rupert approached his father and persuaded him to provide capital, so they could buy industrial properties around Johannesburg, close to the townships, and give 99-year leases to aspiring black businessmen. 'This enabled them to borrow from banks. Black people could not hold title deeds – they couldn't even own their homes, so they couldn't start building up capital. We started the Small Business Development Corporation and one of the first properties we bought was Basil Landau's old Leyland factory.' Then they issued leases and the state couldn't do anything about it, he explained.

'Part of the first round of leases was issued to a group who repaired taxis, and I became friendly with them, and I still am to this day. They remember what we did to help them back then. We created 70 000 jobs through the Small Business Development Corporation, and all that they needed was title deeds. Do you have any idea how creative you had to be when you were a black entrepreneur without capital? They traded on their wits because they had no assets against which they could borrow, but they were natural businessmen.'

---***---

In the late 1980s, Rupert attended an event of the South Africa Foundation, an organisation set up to promote the country's image overseas, and became embroiled in an altercation with Magnus Malan, then minister of defence. Malan boasted about who the real power brokers in Cabinet were and remarked disdainfully that the minister of finance, Barend du Plessis, simply did as he was told. At one stage during the exchange, Malan said the Oppenheimers' Anglo American was a big company, and whatever Harry Oppenheimer said wouldn't cost the National Party votes, but that Rembrandt was small and could be easily broken.

'Politics is a cut-throat business ... and I mean that literally,' he said menacingly to Rupert, who was later warned by Gavin Relly, Anglo's chairperson, that he needed to take heed of Malan's threat. 'I wasn't aware of things such as hit squads. Gavin told me to be careful. When I told my wife about the threat, she gave me sage advice: she said the only way to protect myself was to tell the story to as many people as possible in order to expose him, and that's exactly what I did.'

Rupert appeared before of the TRC's special hearing about the role of business and labour during apartheid in November 1997. He was the main act on the second day of hearings, which saw only a handful of South Africa's major corporations take the opportunity to try to put their activities during apartheid into context.

Besides Rupert and his father's submission, on behalf of Rembrandt, companies that did appear in front of Archbishop Desmond Tutu, his deputy, Alex Boraine, and the rest of the commissioners were Anglo American, BMW, mining house Gencor, Hulett Aluminium, Mercedes-Benz, Nampak, Old Mutual, South African Breweries, Sanlam, Tongaat Hulett and Toyota. Mike Rosholt appeared on behalf of the then Barlow Rand Group. But, generally, South African business appeared to be reluctant to account for its role in apartheid, or at the very least explain it.

At the TRC, Anton Rupert recalled his fraught relationship with Verwoerd and the prime minister's rejection of his proposed partnership with Coloured business, as well as his meeting with the PAC leader, Philip Kgosana, and explained Rembrandt's relationship with the apartheid government: 'We have never done any business with any government, have not received favours from government, nor has any prime minister or president asked my advice in the period under review,' Rupert senior told the commission.[18]

Johann Rupert was his usual strident self at the TRC hearings, acknowledging that Rembrandt had operated in an unjust and unfair society, but rejected the suggestion that the company had explicitly benefited from apartheid. 'It is well known ... that both my father and I have been and were outspoken opponents of apartheid. We viewed the system as an immoral, oppressive attempt at social engineering,' he told the TRC.[19]

His testimony was 'from the heart', he said, and proceeded to explain that he and his father believed that Rembrandt, although it did not do enough for affirmative action, treated their employees fairly, paid decent wages over the years and invested heavily in their training. More broadly, Rembrandt also created value for the country in terms of taxes and capital investments, he told the TRC. Rembrandt had a certain loyalty to South Africa: 'Had the founders of the company emigrated, they would have had far superior returns on their investment. South Africa however, would have lost jobs, taxes and foreign exchange.'[20]

The company's growth wasn't achieved by exporting raw materials or finished goods, nor was it built 'on the sweat of black workers'. Rembrandt was a South African company with shares held by South Africans. 'Now, I'm immensely proud of those achievements. It shows what could be achieved by a few people, from the southern tip of Africa who believed in miracles and set out to make them happen. However, for over 40 years in South Africa, we've operated in an unjust society,' he said.[21]

Rupert admitted that white people had benefited unjustly from apartheid and that certain companies had too. However, he seemed to struggle to reconcile himself to the fact that, generally, business, dominated as it was by white people, by extension had benefited from the system of segregation, subjugation and a supply of cheap labour: 'I think the first question we must ask, is, did the private sector benefit from this unjust and inhumane system of social engineering? And I think that's an [unclear] point. I'm not going to debate it, I think that's a debate that can be held over weeks.'[22]

He told the commission that Rembrandt had had no sweetheart deals from government and never dealt with the state, except once in the democratic era when it had helped union pension funds get a slice of mobile telephone deals. Rembrandt had been financed by Afrikaner money and its first shareholders were farmers because, he argued, 'frankly, nobody wanted to invest'.[23]

The family's opposition to apartheid led to them being threatened and insulted by the Afrikaner community, and he was labelled a communist, he told the commission.

After Rupert had concluded his testimony, Boraine lauded Rupert's father and his philosophy around social and economic justice. He was also moved by his father's letter to Botha, in which he had asked the then president to dismantle apartheid, saying that such a sentiment in some way allayed fears that business was engaged in nothing other than profit and public relations. At the same time, however, Boraine observed that Rembrandt, according to research, had remained close the National Party and asked, had it not made 'heavy financial contributions' to the party?

'When I joined the company,' replied Rupert, 'I started by going through all the records ... I certainly didn't find any contributions to the National Party. There might have been some, but I can guarantee you, they had no money to give. The company was not in the position to give money to anybody,' he said.

Rupert explained that from a very young age he had understood that the family wasn't 'with' the National Party and that the mutual animosity that defined his father and Verwoerd's relationship would have prevented Rembrandt from providing support to the party. The party only rose in his esteem when De Klerk embarked on political reforms knowing full well that he would be crucified by his own people.

When one commissioner asked about a speech that his father had given at the Second Economic Congress of the People in 1950 in which Anton Rupert had referred to the Afrikaners' need to take responsibility for the white man's mastership (as opposed to the native's 'followership'), he defended his father, explaining that the ruling ideology of the time was based on concern for survival and that there was a genuine belief that separate development would safeguard the white man's future: 'Now, it soon became apparent that it was not going to be equal, if one minority group had all the assets. Therefore it was going to be separate, but unequal. And then it became not only immoral, but practically not implementable.'[24]

But the TRC didn't agree with the argument put forward by many corporates that they had struggled in an artificial and highly regulated environment. The notion that apartheid had been a burden to them by raising the cost of doing business and eroding the skills base was rejected. Critics of business, notably the ANC, argued that, on the contrary, business had achieved wealth, power and access through 'discrimination and oppression of the black majority'.[25]

This was echoed by Stellenbosch professor Sampie Terreblanche, who said, 'Business should acknowledge explicitly, and without reservation, that the power structures underpinning white supremacy and racial capitalism for 100 years were of such a nature that whites have been undeservedly enriched and people other than whites undeservedly impoverished.' Terreblanche argued that this entailed collusion between different sectors in society 'to create a context that leads to the systematic execution of gross human rights violations. It contributes to the emergence of an economic and political structure, a culture and system which gives rise to and condones certain patterns of behaviour.'[26]

This was illustrated even more starkly by apartheid's so-called 'superspy', Craig Williamson, who had earlier told the hearing on the armed forces:

> Our weapons, ammunition, uniforms, vehicles, radios and other equipment were all developed and provided by industry. Our finances and banking were done by bankers who even gave us covert credit cards for covert operations. Our chaplains prayed for our victory and our universities educated us in war. Our propaganda was carried by the media and our political masters were voted back into power time after time with ever increasing majorities. [27]

The TRC ranked the categories of corporate culpability into first-, second- and third-order involvement. It classified mining houses as examples of first-order involvement in apartheid because that sector had helped formulate and implement apartheid policies (such as labour legislation, for example). In the second order were banks providing services to the state in the knowledge that those services aided and abetted repression. Third-order involvement included businesses that did not trade with the state but operated in the 'racially structured context of an apartheid society'.[28]

But the TRC report found that not all businesses could be tarred with the same brush because many funded opposition parties as well as resistance movements against apartheid:

> The issue of third-order involvement does, however, highlight the fact that the current distribution of wealth (which is substantially concentrated in white hands) is a product of business activity that took place under an apartheid system that favoured whites. This acts as a counterbalance to statements by business that apartheid harmed them, a reminder that white business accumulated (sometimes vast amounts of) wealth in spite of this alleged harm.[29]

The TRC concluded that there did indeed exist a special relationship between business and government, and various submissions argued that Afrikaner business particularly enjoyed access. A few companies had 'overwhelming economic power' concentrated in them and 'huge bargaining power' with the state, which they could have used more aggressively for reform.

English-owned corporates told the TRC that they were often treated with hostility by the National Party government, with both Anglo American and South African Breweries saying they were victims of the system.

Insurer Sanlam, considered an Afrikaner business, acknowledged that its origins could have contributed to its relationship with the government after 1948. Terreblanche argued that Afrikaner favouritism was gradually replaced with a system of patronage, particularly when business was co-opted into the military-industrial complex.

During the TRC hearings, the ANC directly accused Rembrandt, along with Sanlam and Volkskas Bank (later Absa) of being 'key players in the Broederbond' and of being close confidants to and advisers of 'political leaders of the apartheid state'.

Although not all businesses benefited in equal measure from

apartheid, it was 'difficult not to conclude that, between 1910 and 1994, government and business (despite periodic differences and conflicts between them) co-operated in the building of an economy that benefited whites,' the TRC found. Business promoted white power, privilege and wealth, while helping maintain the structures of black deprivation, discrimination, exploitation and poverty. 'Business was part of the mindset of white South Africa,' said the TRC report.[30]

Could business have done more to resist apartheid and bring about political change? After Rupert's testimony, Rosholt's and a number of other submissions to the TRC attempted to answer that question. Several businesses acknowledged that more could have been done. Rosholt, however, added: 'To claim this today is to apply the perfect vision of hindsight, a privilege not available to one at the actual time.'

The TRC grappled with two opposing views when it tried to answer the vexed question, did business have a moral role that extended beyond its normal activities to encompass certain social responsibilities?

In its submission, Sanlam said no:

> Any notion that business could have acted as a watchdog of the government as far as human rights violations are concerned is totally unrealistic and should be dispelled. Business was unable to act in that way in the past and will not be able to do so in the future ... government is so powerful and dominant that a business organisation will seriously jeopardise its prospects of success by crossing swords with politicians.[31]

Economist Ann Bernstein agreed and said that business, at its core, is not a moral being and cannot be expected to act as such:

> Corporations are not institutions established for moral purposes. They are functional institutions created to perform an

economic task (production of goods and services and so on). This is their primary purpose. They are not institutions designed to promote some or other form of morality in the world. Other institutions exist to fulfil these purposes. This does not of course absolve individuals within companies from moral choices, but that is a different matter.[32]

Life, Bernstein explained, 'is not a morality play' and added that business accommodated itself in the South Africa of the time and provided jobs, created infrastructure, unwittingly unleashed democratising pressures and helped create a platform for post-1994 growth.

But, in its final analysis, the TRC disagreed and found that business played a central role in sustaining the South African state during apartheid: 'Certain businesses, especially the mining industry, were involved in helping to design and implement apartheid policies. Other businesses benefited from co-operating with the security structures of the former state. Most businesses benefited from operating in a racially structured context.'

In 2017 Hennie van Vuuren, director of NGO Open Secrets, found that many big conglomerates in the country lent the National Party financial support, including Anton Rupert's. He found in a letter from then minister Hendrik Schoeman in August 1989 marked 'private and confidential' evidence of 'at least one' donation from Rupert. In the letter De Klerk thanked Rupert for a donation of R20 000: 'Please be assured that we place this delightful gesture in high regard. It is highly appreciated. We are aware that you do not wish to give any publicity to this donation and will handle it in a confidential manner.'[33]

The Rupert empire was conceived in an era when Afrikaner nationalism was taking root and the *volk* was beginning to shed its social inferiority complex. The success of Rembrandt was symbolic of Afrikaner success, and notwithstanding the testy relationships

Anton Rupert had with various National Party leaders, it is clear that he was part of the Afrikaner project. His business came about thanks to the intervention of Afrikaner institutions and networks, and his businesses grew thanks to investments made every bit as much for political as for financial reasons.

In a country where politics, not the economy, has been the biggest driver of social change, proximity to power is non-negotiable for big business. Both Ruperts have managed to do this without being beholden to power, which has given them space to criticise the government of the day when they have felt the need to, Anton challenging Verwoerd, and Johann the ANC.

Both Ruperts were products of their eras: one from a period of segregation and subjugation, the other from a period of transition and reckoning. But their fortunes and businesses survive.

6. OLD MONEY AND THE STELLENBOSCH ORIGINALS

'I find it troublesome that everyone in town is being tarred with the same brush, as if we are all part of the so-called mafia and as if everyone is from Steinhoff.'

– Edwin Hertzog, chairperson of the Mediclinic board[1]

REMGRO'S UNDERSTATED corporate head office is at the end of Stellentia Road, nestled between the Eerste River, which flows through Stellenbosch on one side, and Adam Tas Road on the other.

As you turn into Stellentia Road, the magnificent Rupert Art Museum appears on the left-hand side. Surrounded by green vineyards, the building was designed by famed architect Hannes Meiring and is a perfect example of Boland country-style architecture, with high beams and a whitewashed structure. It houses one of the most renowned private art collections in the country, including part of the extensive Rupert collection. Anton and and his wife, Huberte Rupert were keen patrons of the arts. The museum was opened in 2005 and has a good collection of the works of some of the country's most celebrated painters and sculptors – Maggie Laubser, Irma Stern, Anton van Wouw, William Kentridge, Walter Battiss and JH Pierneef – which populate the walls and open spaces in the museum, alongside one of the few copies of Auguste Rodin's sculpture *The Kiss*.

Across the road from the art gallery, and next to Remgro's offices, are the headquarters of Steinhoff International.

In retirement Anton Rupert used to run the Peace Parks Foundation from Millennia Park next door to Steinhoff, but the building has for a number of years now been where Remgro is headquartered. The premises are neat, almost clinical, and the reception is sober but warm, with cream-coloured flooring leading to the reception area, a bronze sculpture on a plinth and the Dr AE Rupert Auditorium beyond that.

The corner office of Jannie Durand, the Remgro CEO, is on the second floor. It is surrounded by the offices of Remgro's senior executive team and on a sideboard is another bronze sculpture, this one of a raging bull with a plaque that reads: 'From the Blue Bulls Rugby Union: Thank you for the support.'

A smaller boardroom next to the CEO's office has a sign on the door: '*Stiptelik!*' (literally, 'promptly!'). On a coffee table in between four wingback chairs is a Richemont annual report; on another table there is a leather-bound publication, *Paul Roos Gymnasium 150*, a book celebrating the 150th anniversary of Rupert and Durand's high school.

Durand's office – it used to be Anton Rupert's – is comfortable, if a little cramped. The furniture is the sort you would find in a doctor's waiting room, certainly not as plush as one would expect in the office of someone in charge of billions of rands in investments (although Durand does have his own private bathroom and toilet).

The company's culture is directed and shaped by the Rupert family, Durand explains. Being the anchor shareholder and the backbone of Remgro, everyone takes their lead from the chairperson. And it is patently clear that even though 'the big man', as some in Stellenbosch refer to him, isn't at the Stellentia HQ daily, he's the personality that lurks in and hovers over Remgro.

Nobody takes shortcuts at Remgro, Durand declares: Rupert would never stand for it. If people make mistakes, they need to own up, and own up quickly. And they never accept freebies. Ever. 'If he uses the company jet for personal purposes he immediately pays for it ... and if his family fly on the plane he pays for them too, including the dogs. That's the Remgro culture.'[2]

Outside in the car park is Durand's mud-caked Ford Ranger. He regularly ducks out in the afternoons to go and watch his children play sport, he says. And although he went to Paul Roos, Stellenbosch University and Oxford (and played rugby), he has never considered himself Afrikaner royalty. 'Our family was chased from the Dutch Reformed Church and I was baptised in the [Coloured] Rhenish Mission Church. I married my wife there,' he says.[3]

----*----

Remgro is arguably the leading enterprise in town and, with its vast interests in many industries, it is considered the most successful of any holding and investment company in the country.

One if its most valuable offspring, Mediclinic, has its corporate head office in an old Rupert building in Du Toit Street, and Remgro retains a share of 44.6% in the private hospital group. Today Mediclinic is the most valuable private hospital group on the JSE, with a total market capitalisation of more than R76 billion.[4]

Distell is the other Stellenbosch original, founded in 2000 after the merger of the Rupert-controlled Distillers Corporation and Stellenbosch Farmers' Winery. Today Remgro holds an interest of 31.8% in the company.

Edwin Hertzog, founder of Mediclinic and deputy chairperson of the Remgro board, is a Remgro blue blood. He was drafted into the company before Johann Rupert, and the Hertzog family trust was one of the founding shareholders in Richemont before it was bought out by Rupert. Hertzog spearheaded the establishment of the successful and profitable Mediclinic, which today owns and operates 53 hospitals in South Africa and has major interests in the Middle East, Switzerland and Britain.

The Remgro network is intricate and wide: those that are part of it are extremely successful and the bonds between executives and board members as old as the surrounding mountains. Yet both Hertzog and Durand say stories about a Stellenbosch Mafia are overblown. 'I find it troublesome that everyone in town is being tarred with the same brush, as if we are all part of the so-called mafia and as if everyone is from Steinhoff,' Hertzog, the non-executive chairman of Mediclinic, says.[5]

'It just simply isn't true. I've met Jooste and I know Danie van der Merwe [Steinhoff's former chief operating officer] because he is a member at Leopard Creek.[6] You'd walk past them in town and you'd greet them. But this story about the Stellenbosch Mafia acting with the Steinhoff people ... and the rest of us being lumped together really grates. Nothing that we at Mediclinic have ever done has a whiff of being a deed in the dark or done in a shady manner.'

Durand, who used to be at Distell, agrees with Hertzog. 'If a mafia existed, I wouldn't know about it. There are networks, however, with bonds that stretch back into the past. Yes, some of us do socialise together and we sit on each other's boards.' Durand says there is an understandable wariness about Stellenbosch, given the Steinhoff 'explosion'.

Both Durand and Hertzog are aware of the famous Friday lunches at Decameron, an old Italian restaurant atop Plein Street, close to the town hall, where prominent members of the Mafia allegedly meet to plot and scheme. Decameron has undergone few changes over the last couple of decades and, apart from some new decor and the addition of prints on the walls, remains exactly the same as it was in yesteryear. Including its famous calzone pizza.

'I know about the lunches, but neither I nor the Remgro people were ever invited or attended. There's many stories about the lunches, what was being said ... but we never bothered,' Durand says. 'I would guess their turnover has doubled over the last few years, with all the gossip to be had on Fridays ...'

Hertzog says the lunches are anything but sinister. 'It's ad hoc ... you'd bump into someone, ask if he's free for lunch. But I'm not part of that lunch club of Jannie Mouton, GT Ferreira, Chris Otto, Johan Schoeman and some others. I don't know, maybe I'm too busy.'[7]

When those in the know talk about the Decameron lunch club,

Mouton and Ferreira's names always crop up, but also those of prominent local lawyers and property developers.

Hertzog feels that the associated narrative that dubs white people in Stellenbosch fat cats, thieves and exploiters is problematic. 'We hear Julius Malema say these things [about the Mafia] and, on the one hand, you understand it because it's politics, but, on the other hand, it really irritates you because always being cast in the role of the villain isn't fair either.'

Both Durand and Hertzog find it understandable that, because of the remarkable concentration of high net worth individuals in town, as well as the number of prominent corporate headquarters there, the Mafia narrative took root. 'Stellenbosch has always had some corporate head offices. But I suppose the reason why it has recently become so popular is because of its location. It is an attractive town, close to Cape Town and the airport,' Hertzog says, but feels that too much is being made of the town as the seat of South African capital. With a few exceptions, he says, 'the big ones are still in Johannesburg'.

Durand believes the character of Stellenbosch, once a rustic, university town, has changed with the influx of money and, with it, power – and the arrival of Steinhoff. 'Those types of *inkommers* irritate Johann. The culture changed. It became flashy, which is certainly not part of the Remgro culture. I don't drive a sportscar – my children would be embarrassed – but [with the arrival of Steinhoff], suddenly there were Ferraris everywhere.'

The old guard in town, many related to Remgro, the paterfamilias of Stellenbosch capital, all have bonds in one way or another, and not least the location of their personal and corporate offices.

Hertzog has his personal office in one of the town's old historic homes in Dorp Street, across the road from Distell. Ferreira is ensconced in the Old College Building in Church Street – the same building where Mouton's PSG have their headquarters. And Basson also rents office space in the building.

Less than a hundred metres up the road, on the corner of Church and Van Ryneveld streets, sits Devonshire House. On the first floor are the offices of Michiel le Roux, one of the founders of Capitec and the patron of the Millennium Trust, which funds various projects, including investigative journalism unit amaBhungane. And on the ground floor are the offices of George Steyn, a former managing director at Basson's Pepkor and board member of Remgro's RCL Foods. Near Devonshire House is Concorde, an old retro apartment building, where it is said that Jooste owns the whole penthouse floor.

Everyone within walking distance of each other. And everyone a stone's throw from Decameron.

···✳···

Remgro has been labelled conservative by many an investment analyst, but the company has been providing good returns on investment for decades now.

'After the arrival of Steinhoff and PSG in Stellenbosch, we at Remgro were considered too conservative, we invested in old busi-nesses; we weren't aggressive enough, was the gossip. We didn't go on these nice overseas trips, like some others did ... we didn't do all these exotic deals. The new crowd was just much more fun ... they drive Ferraris, everyone has their homes in De Zalze ... the gap between us and them just grew bigger and bigger. And now, all of a sudden, after the Steinhoff crash, everyone is talking about us again ... sentiment just turned. So I'm somewhat sceptical of the town,' says Durand.

The office of Remgro's CEO faces the back of Steinhoff's head of-fice, some fifty or sixty metres away, from where Jooste constructed a convoluted and ultimately doomed international pyramid. Well, Durand, adds, lucky for Remgro the company stayed its course. Remgro is as blue chip as they come. It has an estimated market capitalisation of R105-billion, sits high up on the JSE's Top 40 index and has interests in healthcare, banking, consumer products, infrastructure, media and sport.

Alongside South Africa-based Remgro sits Swiss-based Richemont, the luxury goods firm initially established to house the old Rembrandt's overseas interests and Reinet Investments, later set up to house the group's tobacco business. And at the centre of this multibillion-rand empire is Rupert, non-executive chairperson of Remgro, executive chairperson of Richemont and executive chairperson of Reinet.

'Our culture and direction are determined from the top, by the example set by the Rupert family,' says Durand. 'We have stability and sustainability thanks to them as anchor shareholder and we share the same values. Johann always says everything that we do must be of such a nature that we wouldn't be embarrassed if it landed on the front page of a Sunday newspaper.'

Hertzog agrees: 'You can have visions and missions, and the like, in companies; you can have pretty and flowery language about what the company is about, but without a certain set of values it won't work. And Remgro's values are such that there's nothing that my father, Anton Rupert and Daan Hoogenhout[8] did of which I'm not proud.'

'We've invested in Vodacom and in Vumatel, which surely is going to be worth R30 billion in future. If there's criticism, it's that maybe we're not always as entrepreneurial as we should be.' Durand says that Remgro has a culture of co-responsibility among employees and loyalty. 'We believe in responsibility and accountability. Our staff annual turnover is pretty much zero,' Durand says.

Then he looks across to the Steinhoff building, where Jooste's bruised and battered company is trying to survive and manage the fallout of what many are calling South Africa's biggest corporate scandal ever. 'There has never been a moment when I was not proud of this company ... I don't think they can say the same,' he says gesturing towards Steinhoff.

'If someone at Remgro makes a mistake, we always try to correct it as soon as we can. Johann's instruction is: "Good news by surface mail, bad news by fax." When you've made a mistake in this environment, it needs to be reported immediately and acted on at once. Yes, we're conservative. The guys at Mediclinic mock us and say we turn over every five cents about twenty times before we spend it. But it works for us.'

----*----

If it weren't for Remgro's deep pockets and patience, Mediclinic would not have survived, Hertzog says.

The company was established in 1983 after Hertzog, an anaesthetist who wrote matric at Paul Roos, studied medicine at Stellenbosch and won a Rhodes bursary to Oxford, was commissioned by Rembrandt's board to investigate the viability of private hospitals.

Back then, there were only a handful of private clinics, which dealt mostly with procedures that medical aid did not cover, like cosmetic surgery or private birthing rooms for prospective parents. 'We became a listed company in 1986 and from then on we had to account for our financial position every six months. But all we could do was to explain why we were making losses,' Hertzog recalls.

'We started turning an operating profit only in year seven and Remgro held its breath for a long time after that. We just continued to tell them: "We have a fighting chance, we'll make it."'

When the company devised its business model, it had hoped to entice life-insurance companies and pension funds to buy the properties where the hospitals would be built, so that Mediclinic could rent space from them at a reasonable rate. But it was deemed too risky an investment, and Mediclinic and its primary investor, Rembrandt, had to carry all the risk themselves.

Mediclinic's first hospital was in Panorama in Cape Town; it opened its second in Mitchells Plain, a Coloured area on the Cape Flats. 'Our research indicated that there was a sizeable market there, seeing that many civil servants with medical aid lived there, and although they didn't have the best medical plans available, there seemed to be a demand for basic hospital services, labour wards and smaller operations. So we built a hospital with 220 beds, but it was never profitable,' Hertzog says. He blames the politics of the day as the reason why specialists weren't willing to set up shop at the hospital.

The Mitchells Plain hospital was eventually sold to the University of the Western Cape, which located its dentistry school there. With the demise of apartheid, Hertzog says demand increased as the democratised public healthcare sector came under increasing strain. 'Specialists used to ply their trade at academic hospitals and whites received a fair standard of medical care at those hospitals. The end of apartheid drew patients and doctors towards the private healthcare sector and there was a proliferation of medical aids, some 230 of them, although many were nothing more than smoke and mirrors. Private hospitals were regulated from the beginning, and we had to comply with strict health-and-safety standards,' he says.

Today, the company has 55 hospitals, of which the company owns 53 properties. 'We were dealt a heavy blow in Mitchells Plain, but you just have to make a plan to keep head above water. When we captured 25% of the market, the Competition Commission said that's it – no more. So we had to diversify or look overseas, and that's what we did. When a number of specialists told us that they were earning a lot of money in the Middle East but that healthcare management was poor there, we invested in Abu Dhabi in 2005. And two years after that we expanded to Switzerland,' he says.

It also owns 30% of Spire, the second biggest private-healthcare group in Britain. The Swiss deal, however, was a make-or-break transaction, according to Hertzog. 'We bought into a company there for 3.4 billion Swiss francs. If it hadn't worked, it would have sunk us: the South African operation would not have been able to subsidise the investment.'

Mediclinic survived its first couple of years because it was agile and disciplined, says Hertzog. 'We were also cost-effective. We couldn't just dip into our investors' money whenever we felt like it, or go to a minister and ask for a R100 million or R1 billion. When we failed, like we did, we had to sell the building and tell our employees it wasn't working.'

----✦----

Johann Rupert was appointed deputy chairperson of Rembrandt's board in 1989 and chairperson in 1991. Shortly after that, he completed the establishment of Richemont, which holds the controlling interests in European luxury icons such as Cartier, Mont Blanc and Alfred Dunhill. It also held Rembrandt's original share in cigarette company Rothmans International.

After taking the company's reins as chairperson, he proceeded to position Rembrandt – by then the pre-eminent company in Stellenbosch, almost the Steinhoff of its time – for future growth two years later by investing in Vodacom, then a fledgling cellular service provider. Two years later, Rupert spearheaded the consolidation of Rembrandt and Richemont's local and international tobacco holdings into one vehicle, R&R Holdings, in Luxembourg.

In 2000 the Rembrandt corporate structure, as it had existed since its founding in 1941, was flattened, and the company became Remgro (the brand name derived from a conflation of 'Rembrandt' and 'Group'). It established a new listed company, Venfin, which looked after the telecommunications and technology interests, while the group's other investments – including tobacco – were held by Remgro.

The era that had started with Voorbrand Tobacco finally came to an end when Remgro split its interests in BAT from the parent company. (When Rembrandt's tobacco interests were absorbed by BAT, many Rembrandt employees were angry and disappointed, with some regarding their relationship with the company and its founder as almost sacred.[9])

Remgro and Richemont never made any public announcement about the company's positioning in an era of growing concerns and public awareness about the link between smoking and health, but there was some speculation at the time that the family had come to terms with the idea that investments in tobacco carried ethical baggage and should ultimately be disposed of.[10]

In 2009 Remgro and Venfin merged again, with the latter's investments in media and technology added to Remgro's principal investments. Today the company holds major interests in healthcare through Mediclinic, and banking and financial interests through its suite of investments in Rand Merchant Bank Holdings and First-Rand (FNB), as well as Rand Merchant Investments (Outsurance). It also holds investments in RCL Foods (which owns brands such as Bobtail, Ouma Rusks and Selati Sugar).

It disposed of its stake in Vodacom, but still invests heavily in technology: in 2018 a Remgro subsidiary bought a 35% share in Vumatel, one of the country's fastest-growing data fibre providers.

The company also indulges many of its senior executives' passion for sport, including that of its chairman. Through its subsidiary Remgro Sport Investments, Remgro held a 50% stake in English Premiership rugby club Saracens for nine years. (Many of South Africa's top players have played for the London club.) It has also invested in the Stellenbosch Academy of Sport, a multi-million-rand, high-performance sports centre funded by Remgro and used by some of the country's top sportsmen and women, which provides a permanent base for the Springbok Sevens rugby team (and which, until 2018, was sponsored by Steinhoff), and the first-division soccer club Stellenbosch United, which Remgro bought in 2018.

In 2015 the Centre for Competition, Regulation and Development (CCRD) at the University of Johannesburg found in a study that Remgro's investments gave it influence over firms with a total market capitalisation of R1.3 trillion, equivalent to 12% of the total capitalisation of the JSE. Remgro maintains 'extensive and continued' influence over the economy thanks to long-term investments in several sectors of the economy. 'The value of Remgro's highly diversified interests held over a long period of time position it in the top tier of South African conglomerate groups, and it is most likely the largest of the conglomerate groups given the unbundling and decline in value and holdings of large mining groups such as Anglo American in particular', the study found.[11]

Although Rupert serves as non-executive chairman, he retains control of Remgro through the family's Rembrandt Trust (Pty) Ltd, which is entitled to 42.5% of the votes in the company.[12] Rupert is also chairperson of two vitally important board committees: the investment committee and the remuneration and nominations committee. The CCRD regards this as evidence of the huge influence Rupert still wields over the company: 'Both committees are closely tied with the operations of Remgro, first, in choosing the kind of investments made and second, in appointing directors to the various boards in Remgro's portfolio to ensure strategic direction is carried through associated firms.'[13] Additionally, the company says that Rupert is not an independent chairperson, as the King principles of good corporate governance dictate, 'but, given his knowledge of the business and his commercial experience, the Board deems this arrangement not only as appropriate but also essential for achieving the business objectives of Remgro'.[14]

The Ruperts, through their family trusts, also have control of Richemont, with almost 10% of the company's equity and 50% of the voting rights owned by the family's Swiss vehicle, Compagnie Financière Rupert, in which Rupert is the sole general managing partner.[15] Like Remgro, Richemont has been a perennial performer –

notwithstanding some headwinds in the luxury-goods market.[16]

Reinet Investments is also controlled by the Rupert family. In 2018 the value of its investment portfolio was €5.1 billion.

---···✱···---

The group may therefore be large and diversified, but there's no way a 'Steinhoff' could happen at Remgro, Durand says. 'When I hand in an expense claim, everyone knows about it. In my whole time as CEO, I've never signed a cheque on behalf of the company or signed off on a bank transfer. There is clear delegation of authority; there are checks and balances. As CEO, I'm responsible for strategic thinking, not operational functions. If anything does go wrong, there'll be questions and financial queries from a myriad of quarters. So, I'd say the chances of a Steinhoff here are zero.'

Corporate crooks will always be able to bypass the system if a company's culture is not up to scratch, Hertzog says. He believes if you want to cheat the system, there is always a way to do so, even while ticking all the right boxes. 'I studied the last Steinhoff annual report to see what they said about themselves, and looking at their audit and risk committee, with three academic doctors as members, I asked the chairperson of our audit and risk committee how I could trust them if we only have two actuaries and a chartered accountant.'

Hertzog believes these basic cultural values include honesty, transparency, teamwork and effectiveness. 'Because, at the end of the day, you have to make a profit and that is dependent on a lot of people and a lot of things working. As a senior director, you cannot cheat and you cannot disappoint, you have to be honest and you have to be able to share good and bad news. When we invested in Switzerland, we knew it could sink the company ... but we made that clear.'

Hertzog rejects the criticism that making money off the sick and infirm is in any way immoral. 'Yes, we offer specialised health services and we do so for profit, but that is the way of the world. And our offering is much more cost-effective than what the state provides, not only here but across the world. I am in favour of the free market, but I'm not blind to its faults. It however remains the better system – especially if you look at the condition of state-owned enterprises in South Africa. If you have problems with your eyesight or if you have issues with your knees, you want to be healed. People want to be healthy, and that costs money.'

He says in all his years in the private hospital industry neither the Department of Health nor government has given the private sector a helping hand. And he dismisses government's contention that the sector is partly subsidised by the state, saying individual tax relief is too small to really be considered substantial. Private healthcare takes the pressure off the public healthcare sector, he argues, and the private sector contributes billions in VAT, income tax and corporate tax to the fiscus: 'We pay 28% in tax on earnings, we create jobs in the construction of new hospitals and we provide education and training. Every year we inject newly trained nurses into the public system.' In 2016 the country's three biggest hospital groups contributed 1.3% of the country's total GDP, according to the Hospital Association of South Africa; for every R100 of private medical care delivered, the country's GDP grew by R123.[17]

Both Hertzog and Durand agree that the South African state is bloated and ineffective, that it must be downsized and that more responsibility should be given to the private sector to help with development and improving South Africans' quality of life. Why does the state not rope in big business to help with providing and improving education, healthcare or transport? 'The state's role is to create an enabling environment. It should tell the private hospital industry, for example, that if it wants to keep its accreditation it should take over the management of five or six state hospitals. So there's low-hanging fruit, which could foster trust, which really is in the doldrums now,' Durand says.

He believes government underestimates the degree to which the private sector is willing to get involved with the public sector. 'That's all we speak about when the CEOs of the big companies meet: we will help, just give us the opportunity. But nobody wants to give money any more because it gets wasted. We will help and we will make sure the money is well spent.'

To get the private sector's buy-in, Ramaphosa will have to clean up the public sector, clamp down on corruption and ensure proper project management, the Remgro CEO says. And then dialogue can start, test projects can be identified and an understanding can be established.

Big capital has a developmental role to play, he believes, because government cannot do everything. But he also says the era when business could just sit back and leave politicians to their own devices is also a thing of the past. Big business will have to be more critical of government and take a more activist role in society if the country is to succeed, Durand says. 'We have to tell government what we are willing and able to do. But we need a partner in the state. For example, if I fly to Mozambique or Zambia or Ghana or Angola, and have a meeting with a major politician, they stick to the agreement. Because they know we're big investors in their countries. But when I request a meeting with the mayor of Stellenbosch to discuss developmental projects, the meeting is cancelled 30 minutes ahead of it and we never get a meeting again. Levels of distrust are high.'

Durand has tried to engage with Stellenbosch's municipality on the issue of providing decent roads in Kayamandi, but to no avail. 'It irritates the hell out me,' he says, when the council starts to pave the affluent suburbs' roads and upgrade the sidewalks. 'We've said they should rather keep the money they're spending on us and spend it in places where it's really needed. We can look after ourselves. But the answer comes back [from the DA-led council] that they're afraid they'll lose the next election!'

Hertzog is frustrated by a government where 'profit' is considered a swearword and says he would like nothing better than to take some hot-headed politicians to countries like Venezuela or Cuba, or to show them comparisons between North and South Korea, or the former West and East Germanies.

He doesn't hold out much hope for the implementation of a well-run and effective national health insurance system. 'In Scandinavian countries, or countries like Canada and Britain, where you have the whole of the working population paying tax, it is possible to implement something like the NHI. But even in Britain, the National Health Service is becoming lumbering and cumbersome. Theresa May is going to have to pump in £20 billion because the system isn't coping and the quality of care isn't what it is supposed to be,' Hertzog says.

Can we do it here? The country's future is relatively uncertain, he believes. But Mediclinic, with 35 000 employees, has made a contribution to the country – and Stellenbosch – and if it were to disappear, it would have economic consequences for both. If you remove the private healthcare industry from the equation it will have an enormous impact, he believes.

'The public healthcare sector is sensitive because it is being exposed and shown up by the private sector. Its inefficiencies and weaknesses are glaring. We have better structures; we are more cost-effective and we have a flatter hierarchical structure than in the state system,' Hertzog says.

But South Africa remains his home, and he cannot see either himself or his family leaving. 'I was raised in a house where I knew apartheid was a disaster. Of course I cannot say that my parents never supported the National Party, because everyone hoped that one day they would do the right thing. Working overseas, in Scotland, I realised that there's no other place I want to be, and my three children feel the same way. But the way politicians are talking makes me uncomfortable. South Africa could fly, but we're barely crawling, let alone walking.'

----✲----

Durand says racial diversity in Stellenbosch is a problem and that it could benefit from more people from different backgrounds. 'It's something that we've tried to address at Remgro. Today our chief financial officer is Coloured, our chief compliance officer is female and three members of the executive are black. Ten years ago, that would not have been the case. And it happened with the encouragement of the Rupert family. If you walk around our headquarters it looks totally different in race and gender from how it did a decade ago,' Durand explains.

Stellenbosch is a town that produces young, creative spirits and the country needs them to help kick-start the economy, Hertzog says. But the economy also needs the big companies, like Remgro, Mediclinic and Distell, he insists. 'Politicians say the big companies squeeze out the little players and leave no room for entrepreneurs. I disagree. Rembrandt carried us for years. If it weren't for them, we wouldn't have been here.'

For a big company like Remgro, stability and predictability are crucial, according to Durand. There are no get-rich-quick schemes that work – 99% of success comes down to honest, hard work, long hours and a functioning relationship with the immediate environment.

Stellenbosch has struggled to come to terms with the Steinhoff bombshell. Many people lost lots of money, homes had to be sold and fortunes were lost. Jooste, once the talk of the town and Remgro's nemesis, has rarely been seen in public since. In 2018, at the Stellenbosch Academy of Sport, the Springbok Sevens rugby team trained with the Steinhoff logo blocked out with tape. 'Steinhoff used to sponsor the team, but since the crash the players have started to cover up the logo on their jerseys. Last year they received R5 million in Steinhoff shares as performance bonuses. It's all gone,' Durand says.

He adds: 'There are only ten companies left on the JSE that were listed eighty years ago. Remgro is one of them. And there's no reason why we cannot be there in a hundred years from now.' The Stellenbosch originals are still standing.

7. THE ROAR OF
THE MAROON MACHINE

'It is clear from the developments in the game that the cabal made up of SuperSport and Saru [South African Rugby Union] are pushing old white interests. The Stellenbosch mafia are also involved in the manipulation of the sport.'

– Statement by trade-union federation Cosatu, 26 June 2018

IN STELLENBOSCH the dark, wet winters revolve around rugby. The driving rain soaks playing fields from touchline to touchline while the Simonsberg and Stellenbosch mountains disappear behind ice-grey clouds, sometimes to reappear briefly to reveal the dark-blue granite cliffs and crevasses shimmering in the sun. Many diehards spend Saturday afternoons supporting the junior teams, before the first XV, or the Maties, as the university rugby club is officially known, take the field at 4 p.m.

The Stellenbosch Rugby Football Club is one of the oldest rugby clubs in the country and, according to lore, the biggest club in the world. It has produced by far the most Springbok rugby players of any club in the country, and playing in the famous maroon-and-gold jersey is considered by many an honour second only to playing for the national team. The club has produced some of the country's most revered Springboks, including Bob Skinstad, Breyton Paulse, Schalk Burger, Morné du Plessis, Paul Roos and Danie Craven.

But the club is about more than just rugby. Rubbing shoulders with the club's extended fraternity of businessmen, winemakers and former Springboks opens doors to some formidable networks. The VIP section in the grandstand of the Danie Craven Stadium, with its bar and reception areas, is a place to court the town's elite, develop new relationships and exhibit one's status. The club draws in all the town's heavyweights – except, oddly enough, Rupert.

When Jooste relocated Steinhoff to Stellenbosch, the rugby club was his entry point into the town's elite circles. He made it his mission to ingratiate himself with the club's top brass and he didn't stop until the club was officially branded the Steinhoff Maties. As we shall see, his efforts to buy himself a place among the Stellenbosch boys helped elevate the fortunes of one of the club's favourites, Jurie Roux, to the very top of South African rugby.

The Danie Craven Stadium, named after the club's greatest champion, known universally as Mr Rugby, can be cold and vast, but the main stand always sees a couple of hundred loyal supporters whenever the team plays, even when sheets of rain are pounding the field. Craven is without doubt the club's biggest personality and regarded as its greatest servant. He was a Springbok, served as administrator in the old South African Rugby Board for decades, completed three PhDs and was the first professor of human movement sciences at the University of Stellenbosch. He also coached the Maties for years and was the resident head of Wilgenhof. Craven is regarded as the sole reason why South African rugby was able to maintain a measure of contact with the outside world during the years of South Africa's sporting isolation, and he is credited with the first attempts to integrate rugby racially, saying during apartheid in 1972 that the time was ripe for a mixed-race rugby team. Craven, who detested the Broederbond and once refused a nomination to the university council because it was so dominated by broeders, angered then president PW Botha when he flew to Harare to meet with the ANC in 1987 to try to win support for the sport's return to the international fold.

Maties, so called because the team jersey in the early years was reminiscent of the colour of a *tamatie*, or tomato, has been a source of pride for the town since the club's first recorded match in

1880. It has won more Western Province league and national club championship titles than any other club, and although modern rugby has robbed supporters of the joy of watching provincial, or even international, players don the maroon jersey, Maties remains the standard against which every other university and club is measured.

The Coetzenburg Club and Die Stal are the social heartbeat of the club, where players, officials and supporters gather on Saturday evenings to replay classic matches or commiserate after a poor refereeing decision has cost the home team points. This is also where some members of the Mafia have been spotted in their maroon-coloured Maties blazers, normally reserved for first-team players, but, in certain instances, also donned by influential supporters.

The Coetzenburg Club smells of stale beer and sweat, and the wood-panelled bar has seen better days, but its walls are adorned with more than a hundred years of history. Literally hundreds of photographs of long-forgotten teams are arranged in enormous picture frames, with ties and jerseys of invitation teams providing a visual reminder of a bygone amateur era. And many hours have been spent there by current and former Maties – as well as many a Springbok – regaling one another with tales of glorious conquest and undeserved defeat.

But besides young and talented rugby players, slightly over-the-hill veterans and club officials with nowhere else to go, the Coetzenburg Club – and on occasion Die Stal – is a venue that draws the elite. Many of the club's former players have become leading businessmen, and it has become the source of close bonds, which extend from the changing room to the boardroom.

When the club wanted to publish a commemorative book in 2007, the cash-strapped project was rescued by Jannie Mouton, who commandeered the town's luminaries to support the project. The club's benefactors read like the board of a supercharged multinational. Besides Mouton, PSG's Chris Otto (then executive director) and Jaap du Toit (then non-executive director) donated money, as did Mediclinic's Hertzog, property mogul Francois Dercksen, sports-rights supremo George Rautenbach, Remgro's Gys Steyn, Naspers's Koos Bekker and Ton Vosloo, the Rand Merchant Bank trio of Laurie Dippenaar, Paul Harris and GT Ferreira (at one stage a club regular) and Capitec's Le Roux – as well as a relative newcomer in one Markus Jooste, whose company had then just embarked on a sponsorship deal brokered by club chairperson and his good friend, Jurie Roux.

Roux is a Stellenbosch blue blood. Before he was appointed CEO of the South African Rugby Union (SARU) in 2010, he had been a fixture at the university's rugby club as a player, coach and administrator, prior to becoming chairperson in 2005. After his studies, Roux worked in Stellenbosch University's finance department, and eventually rose to the position of senior director of finance. He was elected as a member of the Western Province Rugby Football Union's audit committee (2003) as well as the union's council (2004). His tenure in charge of Maties rugby between 2005 and 2010 was a busy one. The club had to adapt to the fast-changing environment of professional sport, and the club, being one of the university's crown jewels as well as a major marketing tool, had to work hard to keep up with other universities, which had started to invest more money in sport.

During this time, Roux, alongside former Springbok rugby captain Francois Pienaar and Potchefstroom rugby administrator Duitser Bosman, established the Varsity Cup. Roux served on the board from the beginning, eventually becoming chairperson in 2010. During the first years of the Varsity Cup, the team from Stellenbosch that Roux helped build dominated the competition, winning the inaugural competition in 2008, and completing a trifecta in 2010 after also claiming the 2009 title.

It was an ambitious competition, with the country's major universities competing at a national level every Monday for almost two months. Given the status of the sport at the traditional universities, such as Stellenbosch, Cape Town and Pretoria, alongside Potchefstroom, Johannesburg and Bloemfontein, the Varsity Cup quickly gained traction as a popular competition, and university rugby clubs and management soon realised the value of winning the prestigious series.

But it was also expensive, with travel costs and logistical requirements demanding huge investment. Luckily Pienaar, who was with FNB at the time, was able to secure a sponsorship. The rest of the sponsorship requirements were footed by Steinhoff. By then, Jooste had apparently become quite a supporter of the rugby club and by all accounts a good friend of Roux.

During the initial years of the Varsity Cup, then dominated by Stellenbosch, it wasn't unusual to see tycoons like Ferreira being entertained by the club's management at post-match cocktail functions. Roux was usually at the centre of such social events. A rugby man's man, he was a popular figure among players, administrators and supporters, and never shy to share a drink or buy a round. He accompanied Maties teams wherever they went, whether it was to an intervarsity in Pretoria or a jaunt to the annual Melrose Sevens tournament in Scotland, which had become a sweetener for players who showed loyalty to the club during the season.

When on 1 October 2010 Roux was appointed CEO of SARU – the most powerful position in the sport – it was a natural progression for someone who had bided his time in club structures, helped construct a successful and sexy new competition and engineered his club's lavish success. 'Jurie has a wealth of experience in rugby as well as proven business acumen and we're looking forward to his taking operational leadership of the organisation,' said Oregan Hoskins, SARU president, when Roux was appointed.[1]

Stellenbosch was again in charge of South African rugby.

----★----

In 2012, internal auditors came across a series of unexplained and odd transactions booked to four of the University of Stellenbosch's office of student fees cost centres, effectively regarded as four different accounts. When those in charge of the student fees office could not adequately explain the disbursements and expenses, the council's audit and risk committee contracted auditors KPMG to conduct a forensic audit to get to the bottom of the apparent movement and shifting of funds from some cost centres to others. What they found shocked them.

It seemed that while Roux had been treasurer and chairperson of the rugby club, as well as a senior financial manager at the university, he had for several years moved funds from the institution's reserves to benefit the rugby club, in contravention of policy and procedure.

The bomb burst about a year after the investigation had begun, when *Beeld* reported in November 2013 that the Hawks were investigating Roux. 'Although it is not claimed that Roux derived personal benefit [from the transactions], the Hawks are investigating practices where the university irregularly financed rugby players' studies, accommodation and other costs,' the newspaper reported.[2]

The Hawks admitted that they were looking into the matter but would not confirm the details of the alleged misdeeds. The university said there was 'reasonable suspicion that fraud had been committed by former employees of the university'.[3]

It later emerged that the investigation had been sparked after irregular transactions were linked to Chris de Beer, another senior official in the university's finance department and a close friend and business partner of Roux. (De Beer had succeeded Roux as chairperson of the rugby club.) Roux, who was in Ireland on official SARU business, denied all wrongdoing at the time but admitted having been interviewed by the investigators in relation to 'policy issues' around the internal transfer of funds. 'There was no indication of any personal benefit. I am not aware of any charges laid against me. As far as I know, a report about the auditors' report has been filed at the police. ... I deny any illegality,' he said.[4]

Hoskins, with whom Roux was to have a fraught relationship, also supported his CEO. 'All that I can say is that Jurie Roux is an outstanding chief executive who ensures that this organisation adheres to the highest standards of corporate management. He enjoys our full support and trust.'[5]

It later emerged that the university's audit and risk committee had appointed a special committee in August 2013 to consider a preliminary report by KPMG and to recommend any legal action. On 12 December that year, the KPMG report was handed to the Hawks' commercial crimes investigation unit 'for purposes of its criminal investigation.'[6] This was done on the advice of Werksmans Attorneys.

In August 2014, Roux's contract as CEO of SARU was extended after a unanimous decision by the body's general council, an archaic body that consists of the country's 14 member-union presidents and acts in the way a board does in a company.

Even though the Hawks were investigating Roux and his friend, De Beer, the powers that be were happy with the organisation's performance under Roux. Hoskins, who by then had started to become skittish about events that had transpired at the university under Roux, nevertheless pledged his support: 'Jurie Roux has been an outstanding CEO of SARU and we are very happy to have extended his contract with the organisation. SARU has made major progress since he was appointed in 2010 and we look forward to continuing to grow the game with Jurie as the operational head for the foreseeable future.'[7]

However, even though SARU chose to ignore the matter, the university wasn't about to do so; it lodged a civil claim in the Western Cape High Court in June 2015 in which it sought damages personally from Roux and De Beer, who had since left the employ of the university.

The claims were substantial: the university demanded of Roux R32 million and from De Beer R700 000. It accused both of having acted 'in breach of their contracts of employment' and rather cryptically explained that Roux had 'altered [the university's] unrestricted reserves' by increasing the cost centres [accounts linked to the rugby club] by millions of rands and then transferring money to various other accounts.[8]

In effect, Roux, as a senior director of finance, was one of the very few people who had access to the institution's reserves. He allegedly took advantage of this to increase allocations from those reserves to certain cost centres, or accounts, which he then seemingly transferred to other accounts, from where the funds were used to financially support the rugby club.

'These amounts were not part of the funding that the university through its council had intended to provide to Maties Sport but were made available by Roux in breach of his contract of employment ... The mechanism used by Roux to reallocate funding was unauthorised, not consistent with the university's process to apply for funds and was contrary to the university's policies and principles,' court papers read.[9]

Roux, it was further claimed, made these transactions using a computer programme that did not leave any traces of his actions. In other words, he misrepresented the university's accounting records: 'Roux's conduct ... constituted breaches of his contract of employment, more particularly breaches of the university statute, the principles of financial management, his duty to act in good faith and the fiduciary duty owed to the university.'[10]

Yet SARU was immovable and refused to entertain any queries about whether the management and control of the sport could be left in the hands of someone accused of neglecting his fiduciary duties to an institution of higher learning, a national asset funded in part by the taxpayer.

Roux's popularity among players, supporters and friends in

town allegedly came down to two things: he was a great guy, and he was always ready with an anecdote and a drink. But rugby, the preserve of a few, was now circling its wagons around Roux, the former Matie full back, and heart and soul of many a post-match social engagement in Stellenbosch.

Until the KPMG investigation started, Roux seemed to have earned his popularity in rugby circles. The findings of that investigation remained under wraps, and Roux resisted any and all attempts for it to be released. But, in September 2015, the Western Cape High Court made a finding after an application was lodged in terms of the Promotion of Access to Information Act by *Beeld*, which effectively led to KPMG's preliminary findings being released – and this ripped open the opaque world of the university's rugby club, revealing how it was managed by a son of Stellenbosch who eventually came to be in charge of South African rugby.

The voluminous report, consisting of hundreds of pages and various annexures as evidence, concluded that between 2002 and 2010, when Roux was treasurer and later chairperson of the rugby club, he provided funds totalling tens of millions of rands from the university's unrestricted reserves. He was the only person who processed and transferred the funds to the rugby club, which in an email he referred to as '*sparries*', presumably Afrikaans slang for '*spaargeld*', or savings.

'The investigation has identified that for an extended period from 2002 to 2010 two former senior finance staff [Roux and De Beer] have disguised the use of university funds to irregularly fund the rugby club and rugby players (amongst other things) totalling approximately R38 million,' KPMG found.[11]

The report painted a picture of the rugby club living large in comparison to the university's other sporting codes, which had to make do with an annual allocation of less than the club's budget of between R150 000 and R200 000.

Financial statements annexed to the KMPG report, which was

eventually released in January 2016 after Roux unsuccessfully petitioned the Supreme Court of Appeal, showed how the club had spent money to buy wine from premier estate Rust en Vrede, paid for fourballs at Pezula Golf Estate in Knysna, held a 'strategy weekend' in the renowned Arniston Hotel – in the middle of the rugby season – spent thousands on prizes at golf days and purchased golf kit.[12]

Many of these ledger entries had been requested and authorised by Roux in handwritten notes. One entry denotes R1 500 spent on a fourball and R4 000 buying a round at Pezula – all on the same day. Another entry showed R24 000 spent on eight fourballs accompanied by a handwritten note from Roux with 'transfer of golf expenses' as explanation. Adidas was paid more than R100 000 in 2010 for 'prizes and clothing for golf day'.[13]

KPMG found that R21 million had been transferred by Roux to the rugby club 'for general use'; R9 million for 'general expenses'; and R5 million for bursaries.[14]

De Beer, 'with the knowledge of Roux', approved 'bursaries' to people affiliated with the club but who weren't students at the university, including Chean Roux, then the Maties coach, who was later appointed to a senior position at SARU.

The report revealed that Roux allegedly 'misused' university reserves and created the impression that the club was financially independent from the university thanks to sponsors, such as Steinhoff. Senior club officials told KPMG that the funding of the rugby club had been seen by them as Roux's great success as chairperson, because he had led them to believe that he had secured the money through sponsorships from the likes of Steinhoff and FNB. This was partly true, but the sponsorship income was insufficient to fund all the club's lavish expenditure.[15]

De Beer admitted that the club had found additional funding after 2006 to attract and retain rugby players but that it had not applied for the money from the university. Roux accessed reserves before financial year-end and proceeded to withhold funds from the university council. He then 'manipulated' the financial systems and 'disguised' transfers to the club as sponsorship funding.

The report was devastating. Although it states that there are no indications that Roux derived personal benefit from the transactions, it found that he and De Beer had acted together in the 'concealment and/or misrepresentation' of university expenditure.

Before he left the club for the management heights of SARU, Roux not only ensured that De Beer would have money in the form of '*sparries*' to continue funding the club, but also lobbied for De Beer to take over as chairperson.

Jean Swart, a finance officer at the university, said that she thought that certain allocations to the rugby club seemed odd. 'At the time, although I thought these practices were unusual, I was made to believe that rugby players had different rules to the other students,' she said in a sworn affidavit to the forensic investigators.

Perhaps she was right, and in Stellenbosch, the rugby family was seemingly given different treatment.

Days after the KPMG report was made public, another KPMG report came to light. This report, into an alleged conflict of interest that Roux and his friend De Beer might have had, had been completed five months after the earlier report and was based on confidential information handed to Prieur du Plessis, chairperson of the university's audit and risk committee. It contained new information, including the fact that the university had laid a criminal charge against Roux and that KPMG had recommended that the university ask the police to subpoena Roux's bank records to determine whether he had derived personal benefit from his involvement with a sports management agency.

KPMG found that Roux was a director of Stellar Africa, a players' agency, and that he arranged bursaries for players represented by the company.[16] This company, in turn, was entitled to receive commission on that bursary. Hoskins in private admitted that Roux's continued position as CEO had become problematic and a furious internal battle ensued as the SARU president attempted to get to the bottom of the Roux matter.

Roux, however, had by then gained control over the most important levers of power in the sport and, as CEO, he held the provinces' purse strings. He was also influential in deciding which unions were awarded test matches, which serve as big money spinners for cash-strapped provinces. All Hoskins's efforts to have Roux explain his involvement in the alleged irregularities at Stellenbosch came to nothing, and Hoskins resigned in August 2016, leaving Roux effectively in charge of South African rugby.

Hoskins' committed to a code of omertà and signed an agreement that bound him to secrecy for two years after his departure.

In June 2016, Roux filed papers in the Western Cape High Court denying any and all allegations of irregularities at the university. He admitted that he had a duty to the university to be 'honest, loyal and to act in good faith' but denied that he had ever acted in breach of his contract of employment. He specifically denied that he at any stage caused the university to suffer damages or that he illegally transferred funds or that he misappropriated university assets.[17]

His lawyer, Frikkie Erasmus, had said reports about the KPMG investigation were nothing but attempts to sully his client's name and reputation, and to link him to events that had nothing to do with him.[18]

Roux has resolutely clung to his position at SARU since, but South African rugby's fortunes have declined. Not only did the guarantor of the sport in the country lose a series of headline sponsors, but the sport has also become unwieldy and difficult to manage, with the national team's performances at their lowest ebb ever in the modern era. The Springboks, once vying for the title of the best team in the world alongside the All Blacks, were ranked fifth in the world in May 2019.

Stellenbosch, though, remains at the pinnacle of amateur rugby in the country. The club won the 2018 and 2019 editions of the Varsity Cup, which Roux helped found with irregular contributions from Stellenbosch, KPMG alleges.

High court proceedings between the university and Roux, set down for May 2019, were postponed when both parties agreed to mediation. At the time of writing the process was closed to the media.

····✦····

When former Springbok wing Ashwin Willemse stormed off set during a live television broadcast and accused fellow rugby analysts Nick Mallett and Naas Botha of racism in June 2018, Cosatu said the episode was emblematic of the continued racism in South African rugby. The trade union federation also claimed that the sport was manipulated 'by the Stellenbosch mafia'.[19] Stellenbosch undoubtedly has an outsized influence on the sport. Rugby used to be the Afrikaners' game, the sport in which they could thumb their nose at the world and compete on an even footing with the rest of the rugby-playing universe. In the amateur, pre-1994 days, the game was indeed administered from the town by Craven.

Even though the sport is no longer run along the parochial lines of before, it is true that Stellenbosch's influence over rugby in present-day South Africa remains significant. Besides Jooste's partner in Maties rugby, Roux, there are a number of former Maties in senior positions at SARU, from the administration down to coaching structures. That in itself, of course, isn't necessarily a bad thing. But Roux's legal travails, as well as the manner in which the rugby establishment have defended him despite serious allegations of impropriety, are perhaps an illustration of how influential networks not only open doors, but provide a safety net, too.

Rugby is Stellenbosch's game. And for the well-heeled elite, to be accepted into the brotherhood of the Maties is more than just about watching the game – it's about being part of the network. So, when Jooste moved his company, Steinhoff, to Stellenbosch, there was nothing that he wanted more than to be accepted into this network and inner circle. And the rugby club was his pathway to acceptance.

8. MARKUS JOOSTE AND HIS BIG EGO

*'When Steinhoff arrived, the town's culture changed. I asked,
"But who are these people?"'*

– **Jannie Durand, CEO of Remgro.**[1]

IN EARLY 2008, the Varsity Cup, a South African inter-university rugby competition, was launched with glitz, glamour and a lot of razzmatazz. Modelled on the successful American football college tradition, it was slated not only to light up dour and depressing post-weekend Mondays with matches between the country's top university sides, but also to provide a conveyor belt of talent for the Springboks.

Steinhoff International was unveiled as one of the headline sponsors and, soon, its corporate logo – along with that of FNB – was emblazoned across university campuses all over the country. Steinhoff appeared on branding, on jerseys, on supporters' T-shirts, on the safety cushions on rugby posts; it was painted on the playing surfaces; it was the brand stamped across the chests of thousands of student supporters at rugby fields from Cape Town to Pretoria; it was everywhere.

Steinhoff had already been sponsoring residence rugby at the University of Stellenbosch since 2006. Every Friday, teams with Steinhoff brands, such as Grafton Everest, Timber City and PG Bison, on their jerseys took to the field. The team representing Wilgenhof, the university residence where Markus Jooste had lived while studying accountancy at Stellenbosch, wore the logo of Gommagomma, the furniture company that was Jooste's vehicle into Steinhoff.

Besides residence rugby, Steinhoff sponsored a touch-rugby league for female students, and the value of the sponsorship in its first year came to R100 000, which included best-player prizes after every match.[2]

It was an unusual link-up between rugby and the multinational – after all, Steinhoff, as a brand, was new to the university town, whose corporate environment was dominated by companies such as Remgro, PSG, Distell and Mediclinic. And Steinhoff certainly wasn't a household name.

'I'd wondered why they decided to sponsor rugby, so I asked Jooste and Ben la Grange [then Steinhoff's chief financial officer] the question. I mean, there's no product called "Steinhoff", so what is the point,' says Piet Mouton, CEO of the PSG Group. 'They said they wanted to market Steinhoff as the employer of choice for young graduates. I thought the answer was flimsy and unbelievable. I would have thought that Unitrans, Hi-Fi Corp or any of the other brands would be better to promote.'[3]

A senior Stellenbosch businessman, who didn't want to be named, was puzzled. 'Look, Steinhoff wasn't a brand that appeared on store fronts, so why advertise on rugby poles and sponsor a tournament? I just thought, "Shit, maybe Jooste just wants people to see." It was all a bit flash.'[4]

Remgro had earlier wanted to get involved with Stellenbosch Rugby Club, the largest of its kind in the world and a jewel in the university's crown. But they were elbowed out by Jooste and Steinhoff, Durand recalls. 'We'd invested in the Stellenbosch Academy of Sport and later on we bought the Stellenbosch United Football Club. We started talking about getting involved in the rugby club, maybe in the form of awarding bursaries … but we were literally kept away from the club by Steinhoff; they were scared of our involvement. It wasn't out in the open, but everyone knew we [Remgro and Steinhoff] didn't like each other.'[5]

Mouton thinks he knows why Steinhoff wanted to sponsor

rugby, first in Stellenbosch, and then nationally. 'It was perhaps more about their egos than anything else,' he said.[6] Given subsequent events, it seems like it was more about Jooste's ego than anyone else's.

On 15 December 2015, the SARU announced that Steinhoff would be the main sponsor of the Springbok men's and women's sevens rugby teams. The men's team had just won the World Sevens Series, and Jurie Roux, the CEO of SARU and an old friend of Jooste's from Stellenbosch University's rugby club, was mighty pleased to get Steinhoff on board.

'From personal experience with the Varsity Cup, I know how effectively Steinhoff International work at leveraging their sponsorships and I am sure the sevens team, our Women Springboks and Sevens Academy will feel the benefit of Steinhoff's involvement. It's a tribute to the power of the Springbok Sevens brand that we have attracted the attention of such a major international player as Steinhoff,' Roux said.[7]

Jooste was equally thrilled: 'The Springbok sevens team is a natural progression for Steinhoff in associating ourselves with this fast-paced sport, enthusiastic fans, and leading team [in] the global arena, where most of our businesses are also based. The attention that the sport and event [create] in cities such as Paris, Hong Kong, London, Sydney and Cape Town will enhance our corporate brand in these important retail markets for Steinhoff.'[8]

A month later, in Stellenbosch, the Springbok sevens team unveiled their new jerseys, with 'Steinhoff' emblazoned on the front. Up on stage, alongside the president of SARU, Oregan Hoskins, stood a grinning Jooste.

Jooste looked at Remgro and Rupert, and he listened to his friend Mouton and moved Steinhoff's headquarters to the town. It was a homecoming for Jooste, and symbolic of his success to relocate his company and family from Johannesburg. And he knew what he had to do to gain acceptance, or at least make an impact.

He had always wanted to be part of the Stellenbosch set and he realised the path to instant influence among the elite was rugby.

At the Danie Craven Stadium, large advertising boards were erected bearing the words: 'Steinhoff: Main sponsor of Maties Rugby.' And, now, the Springbok sevens team was also Steinhoff's. Jooste's ego was reinforced.

----✦----

By the time the University of Pretoria had beaten their rivals from Stellenbosch in the final of the 2017 FNB Varsity Cup sponsored by Steinhoff International (as the competition was officially known), sponsored by Steinhoff International, Jooste's company had become a multibillion-rand, multinational enterprise. It manufactured, distributed and sold a range of household goods in more than 32 countries under the banner of 40 brands. It had 26 manufacturing facilities, 2.5 million square metres of warehouse space and 12 000 retail outlets. It was shipping 150 000 containers each year and employed 130 000 people, of whom 50 000 worked in South Africa. It had posted revenue of €8.6 billion in 2016 and a net profit of €1.5 billion, which represented year-on-year growth of almost 12%. On the JSE, its shares traded at R50.25 on 23 May 2017, which gave Steinhoff a total market capitalisation (the total number of issued shares multiplied by the share price) of R240 billion.[9]

Steinhoff was a behemoth of a company. But it was a complicated business, with multiple subsidiaries and various partners operating in many countries under different regulatory environments. Regardless, Jooste was flying high. He had engineered the construction of Steinhoff Africa and eventually Steinhoff International, and installed himself at the top of a very large corporate pyramid. The son of a postal worker from Pretoria, who spoke highly of his father and the work ethic he had instilled, made a grand return to his old university town, Stellenbosch, where many of the titans of big business either hailed from or had their personal or corporate base.

Jooste made the town his own and ensured that Steinhoff followed suit. The company moved into an office block right next to Remgro, with the Steinhoff logo clearly visible as you drive down Adam Tas Road. The building is rather nondescript for the headquarters of a company of this size, but the entrance area makes a brash statement. The glass-and-steel reception space, running from the ground level to the third floor, has an enormous, shiny, chandelier hanging from its roof. From the outside, through the dark, tinted glass, the garish chandelier dominates the entrance hall – much as Jooste's outsize personality attempted to dominate the Stellenbosch scene.

'When Steinhoff arrived, the town's culture changed,' says Durand. 'I asked, "But who are these people?" Look, I'm a pretty senior businessman, but I had to ask around to find out exactly who they were, what they did, what they sold. The company sells furniture, but why sponsor the rugby club? Students wouldn't buy the stuff and I've never seen a Steinhoff chair.'

And then the Steinhoff money started talking: fancy cars started coming and going to and from the company's head office; employees snapped up luxury properties in De Zalze, the exclusive golf estate just outside town; Jooste and his friends bought a farm in the Jonkershoek Valley, and his enormous spend on horses became the talk of the town.

Steinhoff was shiny, its senior managers brash and the company larger than life. And everyone in town was talking about them. 'It became known that some Steinhoff employees had personal drivers, which was rather odd,' Durand says. Many young graduates pined for a job at 'Markus's company' and conversations over weekends, during lunches at hotspots, such as the Hussar Grill, or at weekend rugby revolved around how 'Steinies' – which became the jargon for Steinhoff shares – were performing.

'Did I mingle with the Steinhoff people? No. Was I invited to their parties? No. Did we see each other in restaurants? Yes, and then we just exchanged pleasantries,' Durand says. But there was a nagging uncertainty about the Steinhoff business, especially among members of the Remgro family. Durand, Rupert and Hertzog all agree it was a difficult company to understand.

'We had a look at their numbers a couple of times and did some analysis,' Durand says. 'And I couldn't understand their financials; I couldn't understand the annual statements, so I decided I couldn't be bothered to try and understand it further and that we weren't going to invest there. I didn't like the people and we didn't get along.'

----✳----

In 1964 Bruno Steinhoff, a sales agent for one of Germany's largest furniture manufacturers, decided to go it alone and launched his own furniture company, sourcing products from manufacturing companies that his brother Norbert had sold equipment to.[10]

Cheap furniture manufactured in communist East Germany, and then sold to richer West Germans, became a source of stock for Steinhoff's growing company, and he developed good contacts in the communist East. His efforts at negotiating good prices with commissars who controlled pricing paid handsome dividends, and he was soon carting back truckloads of chairs and tables manufactured at low cost behind the Iron Curtain to his network in the West. He often slept in his car on these trips.[11]

Bruno Steinhoff had a knack for selling furniture and his business soon prospered.

By 1970 Steinhoff's company had expanded rapidly, and he established an upholstery factory in West Germany to supplement what he was importing from the Eastern Bloc countries. The diversification from sourcing and import to manufacturing was in line with his vision to eventually control the whole supply chain, a characteristic that was to be a golden thread in the company to this day.[12]

After the fall of the Berlin Wall, Steinhoff took advantage of government incentives to invest in the East and soon became one of the largest manufacturers in Germany.[13]

Later, in the 1990s, high manufacturing costs forced Steinhoff to expand beyond the country's borders, and he made strategic acquisitions and investments in Poland, Hungary, Ukraine, the Netherlands, Italy, France and Austria. His business now included not only manufacturing high-quality, low-cost furniture, but also marketing and distribution networks.

----*----

After attending the Afrikaanse Hoër Seunskool in Pretoria, commonly known as Affies, Jooste received a bursary to study in Stellenbosch. His college residence, 'Willows' – as Wilgenhof is affectionately known – has produced some influential South Africans, including politician Frederik van Zyl Slabbert, Constitutional Court judge Edwin Cameron and anti-apartheid theologian Beyers Naudé. Jooste's close friend Christo Wiese, as well as Shoprite's Whitey Basson, were also residents, as were his colleagues at Steinhoff Danie van der Merwe (the chief operating officer) and Nico Boshoff (executive at Steinhoff subsidiary KAP).

Jooste completed his degree and started his articles at the Cape Town audit firm of Greenwoods Ironside, while studying for an honours degree at the University of Cape Town.

'In a way,' he told financial journalist Alec Hogg, 'I was very lucky that I was very hungry. I came out of university with R100 000 of study debt, but with a chartered accountant qualification ... when I started my articles in 1982 the first office I walked into on my first day was owned by Wiese. I always said that with everything in life the path is there for you ... There was no time, like we see today, for children to travel the world for 12 months before they start studying or working ... there was no time or money to waste.'[14]

Jooste moved on to the then department of inland revenue (the South African Revenue Service) where he worked in the tax division and helped establish special investigative units.[15] It was there that he primed his tax skills and expertise, something that would come in handy later on in his career.

In 1994, when South Africa became a democracy, Claas Daun, a friend of Bruno Steinhoff's, purchased a controlling stake in struggling Johannesburg furniture manufacturer Victoria Lewis. Daun was in charge of keeping an eye on businesses in 'intensive care' for a big bank, and he had a liking for Victoria Lewis – and South Africa.[16] A year later, Daun invested in a company called Gommagomma, which had a production outlet in Garankuwa, north of Pretoria. Gommagomma produced middle- to upmarket-range lounge suites, and its financial director was the 27-year-old Jooste.[17] 'My life changed because Claas invested in us. Then as the business grew, he introduced me to Bruno Steinhoff and our story evolved. Obviously the dream was to become successful but how, what size, and what dimension, I had no idea at all.'[18]

In 1996 Jooste conceived the idea to merge Gommagomma with Steinhoff Europe,[19] and in 1997 Steinhoff Africa was born[20] when Bruno Steinhoff bought a 35% interest in Gommagomma.[21]

A year later, Daun and Jooste made an unsuccessful bid for Afcol, one of the country's biggest furniture producers, which was owned by South African Breweries. They lost out to Pat Cornick, another furniture producer. 'At that stage, Claas was my main partner and supporter and we were bidding against another recently listed company, Pat Cornick, supported by Brait, funnily enough, now owned by Christo Wiese. The bidding reached R17 a share and they went R17.50. Claas said that's too much and we walked away. Twelve months later, ... we bought the company [Cornick Group Limited] for just R3.80 a share. That bit of luck made us a powerhouse in South Africa, it triggered the escalation of Steinhoff,' Jooste told Hogg.[22]

With Jooste now at the helm, Steinhoff Africa became one of the largest manufacturers of furniture on the JSE when it listed in 1998, with South Africa giving the group a base to produce low-cost goods.[23] Jooste told Hogg that the acquisition of Cornick, Daun's entrance into his life and the merger between Daun's and Steinhoff's businesses were some of the biggest game changers of his life. Founder Steinhoff became a member of the board and remained in Germany, leaving Jooste to his own devices.

Over the following five years, Steinhoff, consisting of two units (Steinhoff Africa and Steinhoff Europe) focused on 'establishing the base', according to Jooste. The goal was to eventually control the whole value chain of the business – manufacturing, supply, retail and logistics. According to a study of the company's annual reports of the period done by the University of Stellenbosch Business School,[24] the company achieved this by concentrating on four pillars: establishing a low-cost manufacturing base, entering the British and Australian markets, making inroads into the logistics business to ensure a supply of raw material and starting to establishing sourcing operations in Asia. Its retail operations, however, remained limited.

Following Jooste's consolidation period, the company then embarked on a 'breathtaking acquisition drive' in a period of continued, exponential growth as it set out to build the value chain and expand its forays into retail, which was the last outstanding pillar in its strategy of total domination.[25]

The two decades between 1998 and 2017 saw the group achieving substantial growth thanks to Jooste's insatiable desire for expansion. The company acquired more manufacturing facilities – in Germany, Hungary and Poland (2000); entered the British and Australian markets by acquiring a mattress and furniture manufacturer (2001); invested in and acquired further manufacturing businesses in Germany and Britain (2002 and 2003); established a sourcing headquarters in China (2005); and took charge of Unitrans in South Africa in order to control its own transport and logistics functions in the country (2006 and 2007).[26]

During this phase of expansion, it bought minority shares in various companies in Europe and the Asia Pacific region, and took 100% ownership of others. A major breakthrough came in 2011 when Steinhoff, which had earned the moniker 'the Ikea of Africa', bought Conforama, a French homeware retailer. This brought another six countries into the Steinhoff orbit.[27]

In 2015 the company's footprint was again massively enlarged when it bought Wiese's Pepkor Group, with all its subsidiary businesses in Europe and Britain in addition to Africa, a move that expanded Steinhoff's retail capabilities through the addition of 4 000 retail outlets. Steinhoff was now the second largest 'integrated household goods retailer by turnover' in the world.[28]

Jooste became known as the consummate dealmaker, a businessman who ruthlessly and methodically set out the make Steinhoff the proverbial gorilla in the room. He travelled incessantly, visiting potential investments or buy-outs around the world, flying in and out for meetings before moving on to the next target[29] – although Jooste later denied that Steinhoff was willing to acquire anything at any price.

The company raised some analysts' eyebrows when it purchased Conforama at a premium of 32% a share, and when it ventured into the United States with the acquisition of Mattress Firm at a premium of 115% per share. However, in 2016 Jooste said: 'That's never been the Steinhoff way. I've walked away from more deals in my life than I've done, but because they were all private nobody knew about them … I've gotten the most compliments for walking away than for deals we actually concluded.'[30]

Rupert says everybody in the Steinhoff environment trusted Jooste. Nevertheless, even though the company grew at an astronomic pace, he remained sceptical. 'Was the Steinhoff share price artificial and inflated? Well, if the unit in which you make acquisitions – buy companies – is shares, and not cash, then there's an automatic incentive to overvalue shares. Because the more your shares are valued, the easier it is to "buy" another company with them. That's why I'm always, always reluctant and wary of people who use shares to effect takeovers. Shares are the most expensive things under the sun: it's permanent debt, it's the most expensive way to buy something. If you can't buy it with cash, then don't. That, for me, was one of the first red flags,' Rupert says.[31]

Nevertheless, in 2016 Jooste was considered a titan of South African business. And, meanwhile, Steinhoff – despite some analysts starting to raise uncomfortable questions about the real state of the company, its cash flow and its actual underlying value – was growing and attracting investors.

'For many, Steinhoff International was the epitome of a successful, global retail business. In its short 50-odd-year history it was able to make the transition from a small-time furniture peddler ... to a truly global retail giant, boasting a fully integrated supply chain covering sourcing, manufacturing, distribution, logistics and retail. This was the result of decades of conscious decisions to expand, diversify and vertically integrate the business,' found the University of Stellenbosch Business School in its study of the company.

---✦---

The deal-making continued. The company's global executive committee, which included the CEO of every subsidiary in every country, met 'religiously' every month, according to Jooste, to consider deals and acquisitions. The video conferences – attended by Wiese and Bruno Steinhoff – would start at 2 p.m. SA time and continue late into the night. Every potential deal, once it cleared the operational report stage, was referred to the executive meeting, where it would be discussed. It would then be forwarded to the company's mergers and acquisitions team in Stellenbosch and Cheltenham, in the UK, who then conducted a due diligence on the target, before it was again sent back to the executive committee for a decision.

'It's a very sophisticated system. Every CEO around the world on that video conference that day gets a chance to say what he thinks, it's a fantastic forum of highly qualified, very diverse operational people. Add in Christo's deal-making capabilities and it's like a bank's credit committee. It's not the Markus Jooste show, as the media might sometimes suggest,' Jooste said in an interview.[32]

He wasn't a 'due diligence guy' Jooste added, saying that, 99% of the time, he could judge a deal by looking at the people he was negotiating with. If you have to count the stock, read through leases and check the title deeds, 'you should never have considered the deal in the first place'.

The critical part of Steinhoff's version of due diligence before an acquisition was considering the human element, he explained. 'Ask questions like, is the management team committed? Do they have skin in the game? Are they going to fit with the Steinhoff DNA? I am very proud to say that of all the companies we've bought in the 28 years of Steinhoff, we've never lost the entrepreneurs who joined us. They're all still with the group today. They all have shares in the company and most of them are still running the same business we bought from them. That's what we tried to create: a listed, very well-run corporate governance company in an environment where a 100 per cent full-blooded entrepreneur can live out his dreams. That, really, is our culture.'[33]

One of the people who, unlike the Remgro set, did trust Jooste and his cohorts was Jannie Mouton, who was drafted onto the Steinhoff board because of the high esteem in which he held Jooste and Bruno Steinhoff. 'Markus is a workhorse, resolute and intelligent. Whatever he tackles is a success. "Crystal clear" is a term he often uses if he understands a plan and appreciates how it can benefit shareholders.

Despite our age difference we are friends, we cultivate wine together and trust each other in much more than business deals,' Mouton said in 2011.[34]

Jooste had many friends, including Mouton, and Steinhoff was soaring.[35] But in Germany, the authorities were starting to sniff around the company's European operations, suspecting tax fraud and accounting irregularities. And, in South Africa, dissident voices were also increasingly being heard.

9. TWICKENHAM, TEST RUGBY ...
AND THE GERMANS

'There were many people there who actually had nothing to do with Stein-hoff, which was surprising. The question then arises: who pays for every-thing? I mean, the helicopters and the hunting ...'

– An anonymous guest of Markus Jooste and Steinhoff
at the 2015 Rugby World Cup.

ON 24 OCTOBER 2015, the Springboks played the All Blacks in the semi-finals of the Rugby World Cup tournament at Twickenham Stadium, London.

The World Cup, the biggest stage in the sport, had been rather dour by the standards of previous years and there weren't any real challenges to the New Zealanders' dominance of the tournament, least of all from a disjointed and poor South African team. But the Springboks were, as always, up for a scrap and narrowly lost out by 18 points to 20 to the eventual champions.

The loss, however, didn't deter Jooste and the Steinhoff party, who by then had been in the country for a while, enjoying the tour-nament on the company's dime. During the semi-final, Steinhoff occupied a couple of hospitality boxes in the iconic stadium where the company entertained their guests in some style.

And Jooste, by some accounts, appeared to be in his element, holding court in one of the main boxes, loudly regaling friends and guests with stories of conquest and triumph. And when one of South Africa's foremost international businessmen walked past the box and greeted the Steinhoff party, Jooste allegedly slammed the door shut in his face with the words: 'This is the Steinhoff box, thank you.'

The jaunt to Britain became the stuff of legend in Stellenbosch, a town dedicated to rugby as much as it is to education and business. Steinhoff took a large party (some say sixty people; others put the number at nearer a hundred) to London for three weeks to attend the tournament.

It was an all-inclusive excursion, with no expense spared, and according to one of the venerable old businessmen of Stellenbosch, it cost Steinhoff's shareholders in the region of R84 million. The group flew mostly first class to Heathrow; they were put up in the five-star May Fair Hotel, close to St James's Palace, and they were royally entertained for the duration of the tournament.

Besides the Steinhoff group's getting the best seats in the house during the three weekends of rugby, a helicopter was put at their disposal to make travel in and out of the congested city easier, while Jooste's guests were treated to hunting sorties in the country during down time. Every morning, members of the party received a printed schedule of activities on offer for the day, with fishing and hunting being particularly popular.

One of the guests who were lucky enough to have enjoyed the rugger, thanks to Steinhoff's largesse, said the group had a ball and that the May Fair's bar, sometimes packed with dozens of the Steinhoff guests for up to five hours, had a particularly busy time of it. 'I bought a whisky and soda, and a glass of red wine one evening, and it cost £50. Can you imagine what that bar bill would have looked like after all the evenings the group spent there?' an anonymous Steinhoff guest said.

One regular at the hotel bar, apparently, was Malcolm King, Jooste's mysterious British-based business partner under whose name Lanzerac Wine Estate had been bought from Jooste's mentor, Wiese. Others included FirstRand's Ferreira, André de Villiers, the owner of Coetzenburg Properties in Stellenbosch, Derek Brugman, who ran Jooste's horse-racing interests, some of Jooste's children and their friends allegedly, numerous hangers-on and, of course, 'all the Steinhoff people'.

The composition of the touring group irritated some, however, as one guest, who did not want to be named, explained: 'There were many people there who actually had nothing to do with Steinhoff, which was surprising. The question then arises: who pays for everything? I mean, the helicopters and the hunting ... You can make a case that it's fair to entertain your top management and clients, but there must be limits. And then you can't fly people when they have nothing to do with the company. Jooste took his kids and they even took friends along: who paid for that? Did Jooste pay for the rugby tickets from his own pocket, the dinners and drinks, the airfare? The lines become blurred very quickly, and it was expensive.'

Durand says the trip was a prime example of the prevailing culture at Steinhoff at the time, with wealth and means and money being flaunted openly. 'Almost everyone in town received invitations to go to England with them. We [Remgro managers and executives] said, no, we're not going on any sponsored trip because we didn't want to be compromised. It's quite something to take a hundred people, at the company's expense, on a first-class trip to go and shoot and hunt. I did go to the World Cup, but I bought six tickets, including one for my wife, and I paid for them myself.'[1]

Rupert says Durand got tickets for him through Saracens, the London-based rugby club in which the company held a stake at the time, and confirmed they weren't freebies. 'We paid for our tickets. But if a company's culture is wrong, you get millions of rands of shareholder's money being spent on friends and family to go to the World Cup, and helicopter trips to go and hunt.'[2]

----*----

On 26 November 2015, just a month after Jooste had so regally entertained his guests in London and Twickenham, German police and prosecutors raided the Steinhoff premises in Westerstede, the city where the company's founder and namesake, Bruno Steinhoff, still lives. They had in their sights four managers and executives they believed were responsible for serious accounting irregularities. They took away boxes and boxes of documents and discs from private homes and the Steinhoff premises.

The timing was terrible because Steinhoff was on the verge of moving its primary listing from Johannesburg to Frankfurt, and this type of publicity ahead of what should have been the company's high-water mark did not inspire confidence. The raids came after murmurings earlier in the year of investigations into tax schemes operated by the company and increased criticism by analysts of the company's structure and true value.

But 2015 had been a significant year in another way: it saw the Jooste and Wiese union being consummated in Steinhoff's purchase of Wiese's Pepkor – in return for shares in Steinhoff. The raid, which became public eight days later, was a turning point for Jooste, who then opted not to travel to Frankfurt to witness the listing and his crowning moment, citing neck pains as the reason.

Prosecutors were circling, and it was clear they knew what the game was. Investigators told the German media their principal focus was 'balance sheet fraud to the tune of several hundred million euros'.[3] The four managers and executives who were being investigated were suspected of 'massively overstating' sales numbers for years, which had the effect of making the company seem more valuable than it was. Prosecutors told Bloomberg the company seemed to have written up the sale of assets to companies that were part of the group as real income. This led to overstatements on the balance sheet.

The news rocked Steinhoff's share price on the JSE, and after the company issued a statement on 4 December 2015 confirming the raid, the share price fell by as much as 10%, at one stage trading at R74.50 per share compared to the previous day's closing at R83.[4] Jooste and Steinhoff were cagey in their statement explaining the mess on the eve of the Frankfurt listing. He said that German investigators were looking at the balance sheet in relation to transfers involving intangible assets between Steinhoff, certain subsidiaries and third parties. The statement made reference to adherence to arm's-length valuation and proper accounting practices. 'Steinhoff … is fully committed to support the authorities, and has begun to take immediate steps in clarifying and resolving these matters.' Management was 'of the view that on a global consolidated basis the above matters have been properly reflected in its group accounts according to international financial reporting standards', read Jooste's statement.

But although it was a shock – and a little 'awkward'[5] ahead of the Frankfurt listing, according to one analyst – another said the market was 'overreaching' and that Steinhoff was 'a great business'.[6]

Rob Rose, deputy editor of the *Financial Mail*, smelt a rat and wrote that there were major questions about the company's management of its tax affairs. In the five years up until 2015, Steinhoff had paid an average corporate tax rate of 11.2% in South Africa, while the official rate is 28%. He cited a report saying the company had for a long time benefited from an 'unusually low effective corporate tax' rate but that it was unclear how it managed to wangle concessions.

In 2013/14 Steinhoff paid just R1.3 billion in tax, or 8.1% of its R16.6 billion profit. 'Yet Pepkor paid R1-billion in tax … equal to 31% of its R3.3-billion profit. By the same measure Standard Bank paid 23.5% in direct taxes last year, MTN paid 26.1% and Richemont 21.6%. There are of course legitimate ways in which Steinhoff may be doing this, including deferring tax liabilities or making use of generous tax incentives', Rose argued.[7]

He identified transfer price agreements as one of the sources of Steinhoff's problems. Under these agreements, some of the company's subsidiaries were charged to pay royalties to its Swiss arm for the right to use certain brands under the Steinhoff umbrella.[8] 'Transfer pricing' refers to the prices companies within the same group charge for goods and services rendered. It is a controversial, if legal, practice which is strictly regulated by tax authorities because it can be used to avoid paying tax, especially if these goods and services are delivered in different regulatory environments.

Tax practice dictates that goods and services needs to be procured at arm's length, that is, in line with market prices and not at a discounted or inflated price, which could lead to tax manipulation.

'Governments don't like it much,' Rose said. 'They suspect, often rightly, that companies use "transfer mispricing" to artificially shift profits into low-tax countries.'[9]

But Steinhoff saw it coming and declared in its Frankfurt pre-listing prospectus that it was under investigation for transfer pricing irregularities in Austria, Germany and South Africa. 'The group considers the transactions among its businesses to be substantially on arm's length terms,' the prospectus declared. 'If a tax authority in any jurisdiction in which the group operates reviews any of the group's practices and determines that the transfer prices and terms that the group has applied are not appropriate, or that other income of a division of the group should be taxed in that jurisdiction, the group may incur increased tax liability, including accrued interest and penalties, which would cause the group's tax expense to increase.'[10]

On 7 December 2015, Steinhoff was officially listed on the Frankfurt Stock Exchange, with stock set at €5, which gave it a market value of about €20 billion. Despite the raid and tax investigations, the company's stock increased marginally during the course of its first day of trade, reaching €5.31 by mid-morning.

Outside the bourse, on the Börsenplatz, before the start of the day's trading, an exhibition of Steinhoff brands and products had been set up, with a fully staged living room complete with couches and coffee tables, a dining room and a big screen. 'Steinhoff: adding value to your lifestyle,' read the promotional posters and banners, with enormous white flags carrying the Steinhoff logo fluttering in the wind.

While a flash mob entertained passers-by with a routine danced to the tune of pop star Bruno Mars's *Treasure*, the Steinhoff team stood on the steps, ready for the listing, which Jooste in a company statement called 'a very exciting day in the history of Steinhoff'.

At 09:05 Bruno Steinhoff, rather tensely, symbolically sounded the opening bell in Frankfurt, signalling the start of the day's trading.[11] Outside, Wiese, Ben la Grange (chief financial officer) and Danie van der Merwe (chief operating officer) posed for photographs next to a statue of a charging bull, symbolising rampant markets. On the pictures Wiese looks pleased, holding one of the bull's horns, and Van der Merwe grabs the bull's snout, while La Grange wears a massive grin. Steinhoff, who founded the company in 1964, stands to one side, seemingly uncomfortable with the swashbuckling and freewheeling South Africans. It was only the start of the unravelling.

----✦----

Steinhoff's fortunes were tied to those of two other Stellenbosch-linked companies: Wiese's Pepkor and Mouton's PSG.

Pepkor has over the years been managed and run by a gang of Stellenbosch old boys, including Wiese, who studied there and lived in the university's Wilgenhof residence with Jooste. PSG, although founded in Johannesburg by Jannie Mouton, has been headquartered in the town for almost two decades.

In 2015 Jooste helped Steinhoff acquire Pepkor through a cash-and-shares scheme of R65 billion, which became the biggest feather in Jooste's cap, while Jooste and Wiese swapped their PSG shares for Steinhoff shares, and gave Steinhoff a 20% holding in Mouton's company.

Wiese met Jooste in 1982 when Jooste was a trainee accountant auditing one of Wiese's companies, and he was impressed by the 'energetic, well-qualified young man'. Wiese and Jooste had very little contact with each other after Jooste left Cape Town in the mid-1980s to join the revenue service and later Gommagomma.

In 2011 Wiese sold Lanzerac to Jooste and King, as well as a block of shares he owned in the PSG Group to Steinhoff, which made the latter one of the biggest shareholders in PSG. And in 2013 Wiese was appointed to the Steinhoff board, which gave him the opportunity to see how the company was managed and how corporate structures functioned.

The board then consisted of some of the most highly respected individuals in the South African business world, Wiese later told MPs when he was called before Parliament's Standing Committee on Finance, and it gave him peace of mind when he initiated the deal that saw Steinhoff take control of Pepkor in 2015.[12]

Jooste has always revered Wiese, saying he 'opened his eyes'[13] to retail, and he considered Wiese a 'fantastic mentor'[14] throughout his career. He was over the moon with the transaction, saying it must 'surely be the largest of its kind in corporate history' and that he was scared he'd 'wake up and this was a dream'.[15] Wiese received Steinhoff shares for his stake in Pepkor which made him the largest single shareholder in Jooste's company, with 850 million shares, equivalent to 20% of the company. Jooste said Wiese's decision to sell Pepkor to Steinhoff was a 'huge compliment … a massive vote of confidence and something that doesn't happen often'.[16]

Wiese was equally chuffed: 'I was very confident that it was the right move to make and happy to do it. I was happy with the management and happy with what I saw. The decision was coupled with a vision we shared with other large shareholders to build, from South Africa, what we referred to as an African champion, an internationally recognised and sizeable retail player … that was the vision. Things went well, businesses did well, we just had normal hiccups,' he told Parliament.[17]

The Pepkor acquisition was an enormous boost for Steinhoff, enabling it to enlarge its European and African footprint through Pepkor subsidiaries; it also enabled the companies to join forces in China, where both had large buying offices.

---✦---

Jooste and Mouton initially had a solid friendship. Mouton has said he will remain eternally grateful for Jooste's support when in 2002 a hostile takeover of PSG was launched from within the Absa stable, and Jooste ran to Mouton's rescue. He told the PSG founder that the company 'wasn't simply there for the taking' and started buying shares 'like mad' to ward off the attempted coup.

'[Jooste] persuaded Bruno Steinhoff to get in as well and Ferreira followed suit. I also bought whatever I could afford. Thus the takeover was averted,' said Mouton.[18]

Although Mouton served on the Steinhoff board for many years, and also held a significant number of shares in the company, the relationship seemingly soured when Steinhoff acquired a larger stake in Mouton's company through what looked to Mouton like stealth. And when two of Mouton's closest allies, Thys du Toit and Jaap du Toit, swapped their PSG shares for Steinhoff shares, allegedly without telling him, he was apparently livid.

Mouton, according to Stellenbosch insiders, considers PSG shares as almost sacred and sees their sale by close friends as virtually selling off friendship. In May 2016 Mouton sold all his shares in Steinhoff and resigned from his directorship. When quizzed about the reasons for his decision, he didn't let on about anything and gave no indication that there was any unhappiness about his and his friends' dealings with Steinhoff.

He told Radio 702's Bruce Whitfield that he had sold his shares to get his 'liquidity right' and that it had helped him set up his charitable Jannie Mouton Foundation. Try as Whitfield might, Mouton deflected all questions about his views on Steinhoff or the company's liquidity and solvency positions.[19]

At its peak, Steinhoff owned 25% of Mouton's PSG. It was to prove a handy investment.

10. THREE RED FLAGS: NORFOLK PINES, RACEHORSES AND MATTRESSES

'We have more than 100 guys all over the world with all their wealth in Steinhoff. They worry about their part of the business so that I don't have to worry about it for all of them. That's the comfort that you get, from a partner: 90 per cent of his wealth is invested with you in the same company.'

– Markus Jooste, in an interview with Alec Hogg in 2016.[1]

ON 24 AUGUST 2017, German trade publication *Manager Magazin* dropped a bombshell: Jooste was one of the Steinhoff executives being investigated for fraud.

The scoop sent shockwaves through the industry. Since the company's listing in Frankfurt two years before, and the news that the German authorities had raided Steinhoff's offices in relation to possible tax fraud and inflated earnings reports, the company had been rather quiet, giving cryptic statements to the effect that it hoped to settle the matter 'amicably', but never trying to allay lingering fears of corporate misdeeds.

But the German report, which the company denied and Wiese denounced as 'drivel', was impossible to ignore. It claimed that the Jooste–Steinhoff empire was built on 'quicksand' and that both Jooste and Wiese often sailed to the very edge of legality.[2]

It alleged that the company's balance sheets were inflated by the irregular booking of the sale of items like intangible assets to companies within the group as revenue and profit. Those transactions, it was claimed, amounted to hundreds of millions of euros. It didn't stop there either. Documents seized in the 2015 raids appeared to be contracts bearing the forged signature of a former joint-venture partner of Steinhoff, Andreas Seifert, whose company XXXLutz, a furniture retailer, was involved in an acrimonious dispute with Steinhoff.[3]

Shares were immediately hit, with stock in Frankfurt dropping by as much as 14% and in Johannesburg by almost 10%.[4] Jooste and Steinhoff were rattled. The company released a curt statement on the JSE's news service rejecting the reports and putting the blame on Seifert, whom it accused of 'abusing the press as part of the process of litigation'. The company reiterated, as it had since the Westerstede raids, that it was assisting the authorities in their investigations and refuted the allegations of dishonesty contained in the *Manager Magazin* report. In particular, the company claimed, substantial facts and allegations were wrong or misleading, tellingly adding that it had 'concluded that no evidence exists that any of the transactions raised by the investigation in terms of [German law] can give rise to any contravention of any provision of German commercial law and [they] were reflected correctly in the statement of [the] financial position of the company'.[5]

The same day the statement was released, Wiese said on 702's *The Money Show*, in a spirited defence of Jooste and Steinhoff, that the matter was 'devoid of any truth'. The Frankfurt exchange applied strict rules, he said, and irregularities would have been picked up. Seemingly deflecting the attention from Steinhoff, he argued that people use such tactics to force a better outcome for themselves.[6]

Days later, Wiese was again defending the company's honour, reiterating his 'drivel' comment in the *Sunday Times* and saying the reports were the consequence of 'misconceptions' and 'rumour mongering'.[7] He rejected allegations that the company was not forthcoming with information about the German investigation and said that those who claimed so were misinformed. Wiese's stance was that it was business as usual: the scheduled results would be announced, and the planned listing of the company's Africa operation, Steinhoff Africa Retail (or STAR, which was to include Pepkor), was going ahead.[8]

But, unlike the previous round, when analysts had given

Steinhoff the benefit of the doubt, this time it was clear that there was some apprehensiveness towards the company.

Market commentator Simon Brown said Steinhoff's silence stoked fears about a complicated balance sheet. 'Generally speaking, there are two views when it comes to Steinhoff. The first is "I don't understand its balance sheet but I trust Markus Jooste" and the second is "I don't understand its balance sheet so I'm not investing."'[9]

Charles Allen, a senior retail analyst at London-based Bloomberg Intelligence, said for a group that had been so acquisitive, it was difficult to understand what the underlying growth was. This uncertainty would be magnified by issues with its accounting. 'The implication that any suggestion with accounting may not be absolutely perfect brings you closer to the idea that the organic growth may not be organic growth,' he said.[10]

And, in a blunter comment, Commerzbank analyst Andreas Riemann said Steinhoff 'simply isn't transparent … More and more investors just don't want to entrust their money to such a company anymore.'[11]

On 20 September 2017, less than a month after the *Manager Magazin* report, Steinhoff listed STAR on the JSE, with a market capitalisation of R75 billion and with Ben la Grange at the helm.[12]

Jooste then went on what he believed was a charm offensive, granting local and international interviews in which he doubled down on criticism of his company, saying that those who wanted quick returns or didn't understand the business should look elsewhere to invest. 'I can understand that feeling, but you must always take the facts into account and forget the noise, né? It is now a big business and it's in lots of countries, so, of course, it will be complicated. I had this criticism 10 years ago, and then it goes away, and then we buy something, and it comes back, and to be honest I'm not perturbed about it at all,' he told *Business Day*'s Giulietta Talevi when quizzed about Steinhoff's complicated structures and dealings.[13]

He dismissed criticism of Steinhoff's financial reporting and basically said that people didn't know what they were talking about, and that the company and its business were an open book. You do not have to go to Harvard to understand the figures, he said. 'Quite frankly, it's spelled out line for line. So, a lot of that criticism is off-the-cuff stuff. Go to the detail, that's why we take the trouble.'[14]

In another interview with Talevi, this time for the *Financial Mail*, Jooste attempted to cast the German raids as merely a function of doing business in Germany, saying there are raids on companies there almost every day and that the criminal element comes from not paying proper taxes. The current matter did not concern him at all. The investigation, he said, was part of an effort by authorities to extract more taxes. 'At the end of the day, the authorities worldwide are looking for more tax. And you can imagine, with 32 countries, there's transfer pricing between every country ... You must remember: it's a game for money. How do you settle tax? It's either right or it's wrong. This is a normal tax investigation.'[15]

To German financial daily *Handelsblatt*, he repeated his earlier admonishment that long-term stability, as opposed to short-term wins, was his philosophy: 'I have always said: Anyone who wants to have great quarterly results and win the next quarterly competition should stay away from Steinhoff.'[16]

---*✦*---

Meanwhile, in Stellenbosch, the doubts that had hung over certain boardrooms and dinner tables were now being voiced a little louder and with a little more insistence.

Mouton Jnr says the Westerstede raids, followed two years later by the *Manager Magazin* allegations, were definite warning signs. And he believes that Wiese, whom he regards as one of the most astute investors he has encountered, made a mistake with Steinhoff. 'He insinuated that it was the third party [Seifert] that was playing games, saying it's funny that those things happened just before Steinhoff made big moves. First it was the Frankfurt listing, and then amid Wiese's efforts to bring Shoprite into the Steinhoff stable.'[17]

For Rupert, three warning signs suggested that all was not well with Jooste and, by extension, Steinhoff. Besides Remgro's corporate reluctance to do business with their neighbours, his interaction with the company's CEO left him with the distinct impression that it was best if they stayed away.

The first red flag was when Jooste chopped down some old trees to make way for his mansion in Hermanus. The second was when Rupert's wife asked him to look at the financial statements of a horse-racing business in which she and Jooste both had a stake. And the third was when an American investor asked Rupert if Steinhoff was 'moronic' for buying Mattress Firm in the United States.

'The first time he came onto my radar was when he bought the vacant property next to my father's home in Hermanus,' says Rupert. 'It was always my father's wish that one of his children would build a home next to his, so we could all spend holidays together. My father built the house and a swimming pool because he couldn't go to the beach any more – he couldn't walk thirty metres without someone wanting to speak to him. But the property remained vacant. Markus, however, bought it and immediately proceeded to cut down five old Norfolk pines that fishermen used as a beacon to navigate into the old harbour, and built his house there.'

Rupert doesn't trust people who chop down trees, but Jooste seemingly had no qualms about disfiguring his father's old property. Rupert was 'flabbergasted' and asked him what had taken hold of him because the trees were the prettiest feature of the property.[18]

If that said something to Rupert of Jooste's character, it was when his wife asked him to look at the financial statements of Cape Thoroughbred Sales that the second red flag was raised. Gaynor Rupert is one of the country's most prominent horse breeders, and her Drakenstein Stud, on the family wine estate of L'Ormarins, is considered one of the finest. In 2011 Cape Thoroughbred Sales was established to consolidate the Cape bloodstock market and to act as a vehicle to promote horse racing as a sport. Gaynor Rupert agreed to serve as director and member of the board, alongside Jooste, who had his own stud farm, Klawervlei.[19]

Jooste was the country's biggest owner of racehorses and invested millions of rands in the sport. (Since the Steinhoff crash, Jooste has liquidated most of his equine interests, including his prized stud horses.) Klawervlei, near Bonnievale in the Western Cape, the biggest stud farm in the country, was a model of efficiency and modern training techniques, and Jooste's horses competed all over the world. Jooste acquired his love for horse racing from his father, who regularly took bets on races. The young Jooste used to accompany his father on Saturdays to listen to races at the Tattersalls bookmaker, close to the post office in Bosman Street, Pretoria, where Jooste Sr worked.

'At the age of 12, I was what you call a runner, the guy who ran between bookmakers with tickets, laying off their bets with each other. With that background, my interest in the sport was stimulated, but seeing it up close didn't create a nice feeling towards the betting side. My dream was to follow people I looked up to in that part of my life, the racehorse owners like Harry Oppenheimer, Laurie Jaffee and so on.'[20]

Jooste's big break in the sport – after his financial success – was when his first racehorse, National Emblem, became a champion and sought-after stallion. Horse racing became big business for him, and it was consolidated in his private company, Mayfair Speculators, managed by his son-in-law, Stefan Potgieter (also a Wilgenhof alumnus, like Jooste). 'I've never bet and that is perhaps the difference – I participate in it as a sport,' he said.[21] When asked by an interviewer in 2015 how many horses he had, he said, 'The standard answer: too many!' He said that he runs his horse interests like a company and that his horses compete the world over, including in

Australia, Singapore, Germany, France, England and Ireland.[22]

In 2014 Jooste's horse Variety Club won the prestigious Hong Kong Mile, and was named the third best in its class in that racing year.[23] 'Racing is also my relaxation outside of my day job. If I come into a hotel room at 11 at night, I fire up my iPad and watch my horses racing all over the world. That's when I relax. I don't go to the races themselves often enough but that will come in later years,' he told Alec Hogg in a 2014 interview.[24]

In May 2017 the Steinhoff-controlled British discounter Poundland bought the naming rights to a famous viewing area at Epsom racecourse in England, where the venerable Epsom Derby is held annually. Under the terms of the deal, Epsom Hill would be renamed Poundland Hill for a decade. Jooste was mightily chuffed at the coup, saying of the deal: 'Just call me "Robin Hood of Epsom"!'[25]

British tabloid *The Sun* declared that Jooste had decided not to buy a ticket to watch his horse Douglas Macarthur compete in the Epsom Derby that year, but 'instead he bought a hill'.[26]

The deal was brokered by the derby's sponsor, Investec's Brian Kantor, who is co-owner of Jooste's stud. Jooste was without doubt the biggest spender in South African racing, dropping a cool R6 million for a colt in 2016. Mayfair Speculators paid millions snapping up horses in France and elsewhere, and going into partnerships with like-minded stud farms and owners in the United States, China and the Middle East.[27]

'He's only done good things for the sport,' said Larry Weinstein, CEO of the Racing Association of South Africa. '[Jooste] has been a massive contributor to the thoroughbred industry for many years,' added Catherine Hartley, CEO of the Thoroughbred Breeders' Association.[28]

But there have been murmurings for years about Jooste's stranglehold on the industry and his 'mafia style' of doing business. In line with his business philosophy at Steinhoff, where he wanted the company to own the whole value chain, he wanted to own it all in the horse-racing industry too, it has been claimed. News24 reported in January 2018 that the company behind one of the biggest racehorse auctions in the country (Cape Thoroughbred Sales), the biggest seller of horses (Klawervlei) and the biggest buyer (Mayfair Speculators) were 'all essentially … the same … people'.[29]

'If you essentially own the horse through the stud farm selling it, and you also buy the horse through a separate company you own, you are going to get the best price for that horse. So, the horse prices are marketed to be bigger and stronger than they might in reality be,' said an insider.[30]

Rupert said that, one day, Gaynor had asked him to examine Cape Thoroughbred Sales' financial statements. 'She was unhappy and wanted an independent opinion.' What he saw did not impress him: 'I read through it and thought, "You can't do that!" I asked PricewaterhouseCoopers [PwC] to look at it, and when Jooste heard what I'd done he threw his toys out of the cot. I then said to Gaynor she should resign from the board.'

Rupert read correspondence between Jooste and other board members, in which Jooste, whose Mayfair Speculators and Cape Thoroughbred Sales shared a registered address (in Technopark, outside of Stellenbosch),[31] made off-the-cuff suggestions that Rupert was, at the very least, uncomfortable with. He also trawled through email correspondence between Jooste and other members of the board in which Jooste proposed various tax plans that made Rupert decidedly uncomfortable. 'I told Gaynor the Companies Act might well have changed, but in my day you just couldn't do what he did,' Rupert says.

Gaynor Rupert also described to her husband how Jooste was a bombast who bullied people if he couldn't get his way and told him that many people in the industry were afraid of him.[32] In horse-racing circles, rumours abounded about Jooste's inordinately high levels of spending on horses. Some said he had spent R110 million in Australia alone, others that he had splashed out R180 million in one year. The numbers are mind-boggling, even for Rupert.

'Where does he get all that money to spend on horses? If he finances it through dividend earnings, where does it come from? It surely isn't possible. If you look at what he says his shareholding is and you look at the financials and consider what he earned [as Steinhoff's CEO] … it doesn't add up,' he says. Jooste's involvement in horse racing – and the sums of money he spent on it – were warning signals for the Remgro chairperson. 'Jooste charmed everyone, including the banks. Christo was just as charming … his and Jooste's biggest talent was their charm: how to win friends and influence people, as Dale Carnegie wrote.'

----✶----

The third alarm bell for Rupert came in 2016, soon after Steinhoff had bought Mattress Firm at a 115% premium for a whopping $3.8 billion.

The purchase price for the acquisition was met with astonishment by analysts, who were surprised that one company of seemingly questionable underlying value had bought another with the same image problem. Mattress Firm was more than $1 billion in debt and had more than $2 billion in lease liabilities. Nevertheless, Steinhoff spent just five days on the due-diligence investigation.

Mattress Firm, like Steinhoff, had undergone a period of rapid expansion, growing from 500 stores to 3 500 between 2012 and 2016. Rupert had just finished playing a round of golf at the Seminole Golf Club in Florida when a prominent investor – according to Rupert, one of the more successful in recent memory – asked him about Steinhoff. 'He asked me: "Who are these effing morons that bought Mattress Firm? Steinhoff?" I said they're not effing morons, they're effing weird!' He then said after analysis that he had come to the conclusion that Mattress Firm was worth about 20% to 25% of what Steinhoff paid. "So either I'm dumb, times ten, or something's wrong," he told me. And then he went and shorted Steinhoff,' according to Rupert. 'That was when I knew: it was goodbye Steinhoff.'

---✴---

Jooste told Hogg in a 2016 interview that he believed he had surrounded himself with the right people, and that they shared a passion for the business and agreed on the course they had to take. He could never have run the business with just one, two or three lieutenants but worked hard to cultivate a culture of partnerships. And, in the process, he had made many people very rich, which was satisfying: 'I'm very proud of all the multi-millionaires that we've made at Steinhoff and that we can all share it together, and everybody has space for each other … we have more than 100 guys all over the world with all their wealth in Steinhoff. They worry about their part of the business so that I don't have to worry about it for all of them. That's the comfort that you get from a partner: 90 per cent of his wealth is invested with you in the same company.'[33]

That 'comfort' would come crashing down on 6 December 2017.

11. THE ARTFUL DODGER: JOOSTE RUNS AWAY

'I certainly wasn't surprised that Steinhoff hit a bump in the road …
If something like that happened to Remgro or Distell or Mediclinic,
I would have said that I don't believe it, that it cannot be true.
But that wasn't the feeling with Steinhoff.'

– Anonymous Stellenbosch businessman.[1]

EARLY MONDAY evening, 4 December 2017, STAR CEO Ben la Grange was talking about ladies' wear.

The newly listed entity had just delivered solid annual results and La Grange was being interviewed about the company's prospects on CNBC Africa's *Closing Bell*. He was pleased with the results, he told presenter Fifi Peters, but agreed that brands like Ackermans and PEP were 'underrepresented in ladies' wear' and said that the two flagships were planning to improve market share. 'We are looking at opening 350 new stores in South Africa in the coming financial year,' La Grange said.[2] STAR might have been going great guns, but on that December evening Steinhoff International, where the youthful La Grange served as the richly remunerated chief financial officer, had been plunged into turmoil, and the state of ladies' wear at two of the group's retailers must surely have been the last thing on La Grange's list of priorities.

On the evening of 3 December 2017, the day before STAR announced its results, the 42-year-old chartered accountant, one of the best-paid retail executives in the country (La Grange earned R50 million in 2017), was called to Steinhoff's head office by the chairperson of the board's audit and risk committee, Steve Booysen. Deloitte was refusing to sign off on the company's financial statements, due to be released in three days' time. It had compiled a report for the audit committee in which it expressed concerns. 'I became aware of the fraud when I was called in ... at that meeting I was handed the Deloitte report and the committee asked me to comment. I was shocked at was in the report but told them we had to wait for the CEO who was then on a plane back to South Africa.' Jooste would have to comment on 'the bulk of the items in the report,' La Grange recalled later.[3]

Jooste landed in Cape Town in Steinhoff's Gulfstream G550 private jet – but never pitched up at the Monday meeting, as requested. 'I then knew something was wrong,' La Grange said.[4]

On the morning of 4 December 2017, Steinhoff issued a statement on the JSE's SENS news service, saying it would not be releasing audited financial statements, as planned, in two days' time, but would instead release its numbers in unaudited form – a remarkable turn of events for one of the country's biggest and most flamboyant companies. 'Certain matters and circumstances' still had to be properly reviewed, the terse statement read.[5]

Booysen, the respected former CEO of banking giant Absa, had been working on the ticking time bomb full-time since 14 November 2017, three weeks before, when the audit committee decided to look at the allegations published earlier in *Manager Magazin*.[6]

The auditors, Deloitte, had asked the group's management on 20 September 2017 to address a number of issues, including questions about third-party entities controlled by the group that seemed to have been used to overstate revenues and understate liabilities.[7] When the auditors reported back to Booysen, he knew the company was in trouble. On Monday, after La Grange had been confronted with the Deloitte report, the audit committee awaited the CEO's arrival. He had been asked to explain the alleged irregularities identified in the Deloitte report and, according to Booysen, 'specifically some transactions, certain ledger entries and the cash flow of some deals'.

At 9.45 a.m., Jooste sent an SMS to Booysen and other members of the company's supervisory board. The message allegedly contained the words 'goodbye' and 'sorry'. This led Booysen to conclude that the message was a 'confirmation of reporting irregularities'.[8]

At 7.45 that evening, after the audit committee had waited the whole day for Jooste to appear, he resigned by sending another SMS, this time to Wiese. The game was up. 'Normally when you're in a business, and you're responsible, you can see the problems coming, you become aware of it: sales go down, liquidity dries up, people start leaving the sinking ship and you can take corrective action. In this instance it was literally a bolt out of the blue,' Wiese said later. 'It was absolute turmoil.'[9]

---***---

On Tuesday 5 December 2017, Steinhoff employees opened their inboxes to see the following email from Jooste:

> Hi there,
>
> Firstly I would like to apologise for all the bad publicity I caused the Steinhoff company the last couple of months.
>
> Now I have caused the company further damage by not being able to finalise the year end audited numbers and I made some big mistakes and have now caused financial loss to many innocent people.
>
> It is time for me to move on and take the consequences of my behaviour like a man.
>
> Sorry that I have disappointed all of you and I never meant to cause any of you any harm.
>
> Please continue to live the Steinhoff dream and I must make it very clear none of Danie, Ben, Stehan and Mariza had anything to do with any of my mistakes.
>
> I enjoyed working with you and wish you all the best for the future.
>
> Best regards
>
> Markus.

The email was a clear attempt by Jooste to absolve his closest lieutenants in the business of any wrongdoing: La Grange, Van der Merwe (chief operating officer), Stehan Grobler (executive for group treasury and finance) and Mariza Nel (executive for corporate services, information technology and human resources).

La Grange would later be suspended during his notice period, and Grobler alongside him, while Nel would resign and Van der Merwe became interim CEO. (Van der Merwe would later also resign.) Wiese and the board accepted Jooste's resignation, and Wiese, still dumbstruck by the events over the previous 48 hours, called Jooste, pleading with him to help the company make sense of the Byzantine dealings over which the now former CEO had presided.

'I said whatever happened, happened, but could he [Jooste] please come in and help the Steinhoff people to get the accounts sorted out. He undertook to do so. But I was maybe naive. Clearly, he got other legal advice. He did not show up and until today I have not heard from him again,' Wiese told 702's Bruce Whitfield in April 2018.[10]

By the end of 5 December, Steinhoff's share price had fallen by 18% from the previous Friday's close at R55.81 to R45.65 per share.[11] At 10.45 p.m. on the same day, after the close of markets in Johannesburg and Frankfurt, Steinhoff announced that Jooste had resigned and that Wiese would temporarily fill his shoes as executive chairperson.[12]

In addition, the company announced that auditors PwC had been retained to conduct a full investigation into accounting irregularities identified by Deloitte.[13] Unfolding events were quite unbelievable, with the company announcing it would release the financials only once it was in a position to do so. It would also have to investigate whether previous years' financials had to be restated.

Meanwhile, Jooste, dealmaker extraordinaire, jet-setting global executive and Stellenbosch business baron, was gone and nowhere to be found.

---*---

Steinhoff's official SENS announcement about the previous evening's dramatic events was issued on the morning of 6 December 2017, and absolute carnage ensued when trading on the JSE began at 9 a.m. In Johannesburg the share price tanked by 61% from the previous day's closing price,[14] and more than R100 billion in the company's market capitalisation was wiped off.

Wiese's personal fortune took enormous punishment: he lost $2.3 billion in 24 hours, which, according to Forbes, left him with an estimated wealth of $1.49 billion.[15]

Just before 7 o'clock. that morning, though, an explosive and damning report was released on Twitter by an opaque and obscure group called Viceroy Research, which claimed that a number of irregularities and dodgy accounting practices were evident from Steinhoff's books. 'Steinhoff's confusing roll-up structure likely holds numerous other secrets which are yet to [be] uncover[ed]. Viceroy believes incestuous managerial transactions, lack of transparency and entirely non-independent governance make Steinhoff borderline uninvestable,' it said.

Viceroy claimed that Steinhoff used three 'off balance-sheet entities' – companies that were related to Steinhoff but did not feature on the books – to hide debt and inflate revenue. Two of those companies appeared to be controlled by Wiese, Viceroy claimed. The report led to a firestorm and a global scramble to figure out who Viceroy was and how they came to their conclusions. In the report, the researchers made a number of startling claims:[16]

- Steinhoff booked interest on loans made to related entities as revenue in its statements.
- The company disguised losses by moving non-performing loans off its balance sheet.
- Shareholder funds were used to help one of the off-balance-

sheet entities purchase an Austrian company, only for Steinhoff to buy part of the company from that entity for a substantial amount more than it had been loaned.

• Steinhoff engaged in questionable tax schemes regarding depreciation of property and equipment.

On 7 December 2017, ratings agency Moody's Investor Services downgraded Steinhoff's credit rating by four notches to junk, citing uncertainty around the group's liquidity.[17] Its share price dropped as a result by another 40%, closing at R10.

Fund managers, institutional investors and pension-fund managers were struggling to make sense of South Africa's Enron (a reference to the US company that was felled by a series of accounting scandals).

Besides Wiese, the Government Employees' Pension Fund, whose assets are managed by the Public Investment Corporation, was identified as the biggest loser. It held almost 10% of Steinhoff stock and by the end of the week the value of its investment, which weeks before had been worth around R20 billion, had fallen to just over R2 billion.

Wiese and the Government Employees' Pension Fund would be in 'good company', reported Moneyweb, who scoured Steinhoff's share register. 'Behind them sits every large asset manager in the country, including Allan Gray, Coronation, Investec, Foord, Discovery and Old Mutual. Large pension funds, including those of Eskom and Sasol, have also been hit. The implications are clear: virtually every South African with investments in the form of retirement savings via retirement annuities or provident and pension funds, will all be poorer because of what has happened to Steinhoff.'[18]

When the JSE closed at the end of the week's trading, Steinhoff's share price had fallen from R55.81 the previous Friday to a precarious and measly R6 a week later, 90% down in value. This meant that R187 billion in Steinhoff's market capitalisation had been wiped out.

Reaction to the disaster was swift and brutal, with market analysts and fund managers pilloried for not seeing the looming disaster that was Steinhoff. Magda Wierzycka, CEO of Sygnia Asset Managers, and economist Iraj Abedian led the charge on corporate South Africa, arguing that corporate governance, as well as morals and ethics, was seriously lacking. Wierzycka was ruthless in her criticism:

> The serious question to ask is how so many active asset managers in South Africa missed this. Priding themselves on meticulous research, scrutiny of balance sheets and income statements, backed by interviews with management, they should have seen what was obvious from the beginning: that this was as close to a corporate-structured Ponzi scheme as one can get. When I looked at the financials of Steinhoff … it took me exactly half an hour to figure out that the structure was obfuscated, that financial items made no sense, that the acquisition spree was not underpinned by any logic and too frenzied to be well thought out, and that debt levels were out of control.[19]

She said too many people had blind faith in Wiese and that his so-called 'Midas touch' caused many people to ignore what was obvious. 'The right questions were not asked, the corporate structures were not analysed in any great detail, earnings versus debt calculations were not done, management was taken at its word – all this against a backdrop of marketing exactly the opposite and charging savers and investors for the privilege. Hence, one can assume that marketing was at best a misrepresentation backed by incompetence, at worst a falsehood.'[20]

Some analysts didn't agree with Wierzycka. Stuart Theobald, writing in *Business Day*, said: 'While many commentators have claimed that the signs were clear, I don't agree. The usual canary-in-the-coal mine signal of accounting irregularities – the cash-flow statement – looks fine for the group. Its reported profits were more or less matched by its reported operating cash inflows, meaning it was not manipulating profits by booking noncash revenue.'[21]

But he did agree that something was seriously amiss with the company and that the hiding of losses off the balance sheet was the company's undoing.[22]

Analyst Simon Brown said the collapse was 'quick, horrible and brutal'. He said when he studied the company as a possible investment destination, he was unable to figure out how Steinhoff structured its debt while the issuing of bonds was enormously complex. 'I tried to determine the debt levels but after a couple of hours I realised I didn't understand it and I couldn't invest in something I couldn't understand.' He added that many asset and fund managers had admitted to him that they, too, didn't understand the complex structures in the business but that they 'trusted' the management.[23]

---◆---

Stellenbosch was in shock. But not many people were surprised, says an anonymous and respected business leader.

'I certainly wasn't surprised that Steinhoff hit a bump in the road ... and I never ran into someone in town who said: "Steinhoff? Impossible!" If something like that happened to Remgro or Distell or Mediclinic, I would have said that I don't believe it, that it cannot be true. But that wasn't the feeling with Steinhoff. The fact that the crash was based on dishonesty ... When he didn't pitch for the audit committee meeting, when he sent those SMSs, well, it was shocking. But I wasn't surprised that there were problems.'[24]

Piet Mouton said the complexity of the Steinhoff business must have created problems, as far as corporate governance was concerned: 'I once had a meeting with analysts about PSG and when we were done, I asked them where they were headed next. "Just down the road to Steinhoff," they replied and asked me what I thought.

I replied that I believed the business was difficult and complex, and that it must be a challenge when you operate in more than 30 countries to manage, for example, all the currency issues. So they went to Steinhoff and told the people there: "Piet says you have a complicated business." That Friday evening, I receive a call from Markus ... *en hy is die donner in* [and he is livid].'[25]

Mouton, cringing while recounting the exchange with Jooste, explained he merely meant that he understood Jooste's strategy to become the dominant player in the market, so that they could leverage their buying power, but that he thought the business was complex, operating in so many jurisdictions, different currencies, regulations, tax environments and differing consumer behaviours. 'Goodness, it was a difficult conversation.'[26]

When Steinhoff imploded over those five days in December 2017, Durand never worried that his company might find itself in a similar position, because he believes the culture is different. 'I was never scared that it might happen to us. I sleep very soundly at night, but I don't know if Jooste can. Like Johann said, shocked, but not surprised – although I didn't see it coming. My wife says she predicted it, though.'

Many people in Stellenbosch lost a lot of money in the aftermath of Jooste's deceit. Lots of big family homes were put up for sale; some early retirees had to dust off their CVs again.

Talk about Steinhoff dominated dinner-table conversation for months after the crash, said Durand. 'I haven't seen Jooste since, or Danie [van der Merwe, the former chief operating officer] whom I would see now and again. They've gone, disappeared. And all the Steinhoff advertising boards at the rugby grounds are gone.'[27]

One veteran businessperson chuckles when he talks about gossip in town. 'Yup, many people lost lots and lots of money. Some of us who knew Jooste sometimes get together and talk about what happened at Steinhoff over some drinks ... because it really is remarkable.'[28]

12. CHRISTO WIESE'S 'LITTLE MISTAKE'

'I long ago thought Markus, with all his racehorses, was a little weird. And I think if you conducted a lifestyle audit on him, the books won't balance. His income wasn't equal to his lifestyle.'

– Edwin Hertzog, chairperson of Mediclinic International.[1]

WHITEY BASSON, the Shoprite supremo considered to be one of the top businessmen of the last couple of generations, wasn't in favour of his friend and colleague Wiese selling his stake in Pepkor to Jooste and Steinhoff for R65 billion. By all accounts, Basson didn't understand the Steinhoff business and wasn't impressed by Jooste, who had charmed Wiese and other businessmen, like PSG's Jannie Mouton.

But Wiese, who made his fortune by building Pepkor into the well-run and beloved company that it is today, was confident that his relatively small investment in Steinhoff in 2011, followed by a swap of his sizeable PSG shareholding for Steinhoff shares in 2013 and his multibillion-rand sale of Pepkor in 2015 to Jooste, were the right things to do.

And even though Basson didn't like Jooste's 'style', Rupert didn't trust him and Le Roux described him as 'very shiny', Wiese took a liking to him.

'I think it's one of the better cultural fits,' Wiese told Business Day TV in 2014 when the deal between Steinhoff and Pepkor was announced. 'I'm unfortunately one of those people that don't care too much about cultural fits, I manage to live with everybody … I have come a cropper on it in the past, but in this instance there's very little chance of that ... As Pieter Erasmus [Pepkor's then CEO] says, the accents are the same – a bunch of boere.'[2]

But Jooste's great betrayal destroyed everything that Wiese had spent his life building. Not only did Steinhoff lose an estimated 85% of its value in the immediate aftermath of the crash, but Wiese's fortune was also decimated. Some calculations in December 2017 estimated his wealth as having been reduced from more than $5.7 billion to less than $800 million,[3] while Bloomberg in June 2018 put his wealth at $2.3 billion, down from $5 billion before the crash.[4]

His profile on Forbes, dated 18 January 2019, puts his personal fortune at $1.1 billion, but he doesn't feature on Forbes's Real Time Billionaires tracker, which does daily estimations of fluctuations in the fortunes of the world's richest people.[5] That means Wiese, according to Forbes, has lost his dollar-billionaire status.[6]

Since Jooste's resignation, Wiese has had to sell Shoprite stock on three separate occasions to raise cash to cover debt; his stake in Steinhoff was reduced from 20.5% to 6% after banks sold shares he had put up as collateral to secure margin loans (he pumped R25 billion into Steinhoff in 2016); and, on top of that, he has put two private jets up for sale.

And he still has debt, most of it because of Steinhoff, which some estimates put as high as R40 billion, and it has been questioned whether his Shoprite stock will be able to cover it.

But, worst of all, he lost Pepkor, the business he dedicated his life to and put all his energy into.

'Christo has lost touch with reality,' said a senior business leader in Stellenbosch, who preferred not to be named, while another, also a prominent captain of industry, said that Wiese is a 'defeated man', adding that the loss of wealth because of the sale of Pepkor to Steinhoff was 'mind-boggling'. 'Pepkor is a massive company and was valued at R65 billion. Wiese took his share of the sale and put it into Steinhoff, and now it's gone. All the value that was created – gone.'

The other business leader said he wouldn't have felt sorry for

Wiese if he had been younger, but that, because he is in his mid-70s, he won't be able to restore what he's lost. 'I feel sorry for him. His whole life was about being the richest man in the country. And he won't be able to borrow; the banks want to slaughter him. He will have to get rid of his Shoprite shares to cover his debt – unless Steinhoff recovers, which I cannot see happening.'

Wiese sued Steinhoff in April 2018 for R59 billion in an attempt to undo the Pepkor purchase, arguing that the agreement – which determined that Wiese, through his family vehicle, the Titan Group, would swap his shares for Steinhoff shares – must be cancelled.

Edwin Hertzog merely shakes his head when asked about Wiese and Steinhoff, and says: 'We [Remgro] had discussions about Steinhoff in 2015 and decided not to get involved. Whitey Basson, who worked next to Wiese for years, said don't do it; Wiese didn't listen.'[7]

A respected businessman in town, who did not want to be named because he does not want to insult Wiese, said Wiese is one of the smartest investors in the country, but that, in this case, 'he made a little mistake'.[8] He doubts whether Wiese had the energy at the age of 76 that he had when he was younger to engage with the Steinhoff business as thoroughly as he should have. 'If he was 50, maybe [Jooste] would not have gotten away by giving simple answers; he would have looked for himself. Maybe he got more trusting as he got older?'

Wiese, in various interviews he gave after Jooste had fled the Steinhoff headquarters, has denied that he knew of inflated revenues, overvalued assets and off-balance-sheet entities. He has been accessible to all who would listen to him and has explained time and again that he would never have invested almost all of his life's earnings if he had known how Jooste was seemingly cooking the books. And he gets asked the same question every single time: how could he *not* have known?

'I have a business, Pepkor, built over 50 years. I had many other options, but I chose to invest that company's proceeds in a place where the financial statements are not an accurate reflection [of the company's financial state]. But there's more: a year later I put in another R25 billion. I must be crazy! Why weren't other people aware of it? All the previous directors, my fellow directors, all the audit committees, the banks, the analysts … why were they not aware of what was going on?' Wiese told Netwerk24's Willemien Brümmer.[9]

The day after that interview, responding to the same question about how he could not have known about Steinhoff's financial position, Wiese told Hanlie Retief from *Rapport*: 'It's crazy! Steinhoff had highly sophisticated internal audit systems. There was a series of boards lower down on the chain with audit committees, component auditors, statutory auditors. Nobody knew, not even the bloody banks knew, and they lent the company R150 billion! And some now say I should have known? How on God's earth!'[10]

And when asked by Alec Hogg if there was anything that had given him cause for concern, he admitted that Whitey Basson didn't approve of the Steinhoff 'style' or of 'that sort of culture'. Basson, he said, was referring to things like going to world cups. 'So, yes, there was criticism of style, but in the few years that I worked with Jooste, never once, the slightest indication of anything shady, trying to cut a corner. What I saw was a very hard-working guy, with a very strong team. They knew the regulations, the exchange control set-ups, etcetera, very impressive, very professional.'[11]

Although he denies it, Wiese seems to fear for his legacy, and has said he would like to be remembered for his career in its totality, and not for the Steinhoff mess. 'I hope people will look at me in a balanced way, a guy that worked for 53 years and gave 200 000 people jobs, who helped create prosperity and who made a contribution here and there.'[12]

Wiese, who told Business Day TV in 2014 that he wasn't worried about a cultural fit between companies, admitted in various interviews that he had been warned about Jooste's 'style' but that nobody ever said anything about irregularities or illegal activities, real or imagined.

'Whitey expressed his views very openly, to his credit, but never a suggestion of a lack of integrity, never. He just didn't like those businesses, because Shoprite and Pepkor, if I may say so in all humility, are fantastic businesses. Cash generative, defensive businesses. So, yes, Whitey, we have a furniture business in Shoprite but we acquired it, in a sense, by accident. So, I ascribed Whitey's resistance, *inter alia*, to the fact that he didn't like those businesses [and] he's perfectly entitled to that view.'[13]

----✦----

The Steinhoff implosion sent shockwaves through South African business and led to enormous wealth destruction: almost nobody with a pension or provident fund was left unaffected. Investigations were launched by the JSE, the Financial Services Board, the Department of Trade and Industry, and the Companies and Intellectual Property Commission. German and Dutch authorities intensified their investigations into the company, while lawsuits from investors in Europe and South Africa were pending.

The Steinhoff Group went into something akin to cardiac arrest in a human as access to cash to fund its European operations dried up, and the interim management, led by new chairman Heather Sonn (Wiese resigned on 14 December 2017), scurried to stop the bleeding and stabilise the company.

Analysts started picking amid the wreckage in an attempt to understand what had gone wrong. Soon everything started to make sense. A week after the crash, the *Financial Mail* wrote there was a critical mass of analysts who had never liked Steinhoff: 'Complaints were many: it was positively promiscuous in issuing shares, it paid too little tax, its profits were "low quality" and its accounting was too aggressive.'[14]

Susan Gawith, a respected portfolio manager at boutique investment manager Melville Douglas, said Steinhoff was reminiscent of American company Enron, which had gone bust because of accounting fraud. 'There were lots of warning signs over the years, but everybody was making too much money to take notice.'[15]

Adrian Saville, CEO of Cannon Asset Managers, said it was clear that criminal and civil suits were going to follow: 'Steinhoff has issued a whole lot of equity on the back of numbers that are manufactured. The board would have been aware of these structures and they were issuing equity and raising debt on the back of numbers that were simply not true. And that's criminal.'[16]

Jooste, however, wasn't there to face the music. The flamboyant CEO 'with the ladies' man appeal', as *Business Day*'s Talevi once described him, had disappeared. There were rumours in the days following his resignation that Jooste was hiding at his stud farm; there were even reports that he had fled the country. But it seems more likely that Jooste was hiding in plain sight because he was spotted in Hermanus having lunch at a favourite restaurant, he was seen in and around Stellenbosch and there are unconfirmed reports of him hanging around at the Victoria and Alfred Waterfront in Cape Town.

His main properties in the Western Cape consist of a mansion in Hermanus, near Voëlklip Beach, and a farm in the Jonkershoek Valley called Jonkersdrift (originally named Bengale), which he bought in 2003 together with two colleagues, Van der Merwe and Frikkie Nel. Bengale was purchased for R25.6 million, Nellie Brand-Jonker and Nadine Theron from Netwerk24 reported in May 2018.

Van der Merwe and Nel were close friends and colleagues of Jooste at Steinhoff and constructed their three lavish family mansions on the property, separated by vineyards and dirt roads, and protected by a wrought-iron perimeter fence and a fancy guardhouse in Cape Dutch style at the entrance. From the outside, Jonkersdrift looks every bit like a luxury housing development or an exclusive lifestyle estate – but in actual fact it belongs to just three men and their families.

Their closest neighbour is Jannie Mouton, who lives on the wine estate Klein Gustrouw. That is where Mouton and Jooste 'extended their longstanding friendship' in the making of wine, according to their advertising material. A couple of hundred metres down the road is the historic Lanzerac Estate, which Wiese sold to Jooste and his business partner Malcolm King. Everything and everyone close together.

Van der Merwe and Nel claimed that even though they shared an address with their former CEO, neither had seen Jooste for six months after the Steinhoff disaster. Van der Merwe was appointed acting CEO after Wiese left, and Nel still serves on various Steinhoff-related boards. But, even though both are involved in attempting to save the company and trying to make sense of the labyrinthine accounting structure devised by Jooste, and even though they both wake up every day not more than a couple of hundred metres from the man who allegedly is responsible for business fraud and damages to the tune of billions of rands, they say they don't see him. 'I still live on the farm but I don't know where Markus lives. I haven't spoken to him since the crisis,' Van der Merwe told Netwerk24. 'Steinhoff is demanding all of my attention ... Since Markus's resignation as CEO of Steinhoff in December 2017 I have not in any way had any contact with him,' he added.[17]

Nel's response was much the same; he reiterated that he did not know where Jooste was living: 'I communicate with Jooste via SMS about the farm's administration.'[18]

Jooste's Hermanus home is an enormous property about a hundred metres from Voëlklip Beach. But not content with the luxury setting, he started elaborate excavations and construction at a site called Kwaaiwater, next to Voëlklip, and was planning to build a new house right on the water's edge.[19]

But within days of his resignation and in anticipation of possible legal action against him, he ordered the contractors to vacate the empty plot of land and all construction was halted. The construction company was left in the lurch because it had turned down other projects to focus on Jooste's house.[20]

And on 28 December 2017, Jooste awoke to find the words 'thief' and 'con artist' spray-painted on the pristine white walls of his home on Eighth Avenue.[21] According to Stellenbosch insiders, some furious investors beat a path to Jooste's Hermanus house after the crash and demanded an explanation from him – apparently he spoke to some, including a former Western Province rugby player, who lost north of R30 million, but others were turned away.

----*----

On the face of it, Steinhoff, with its registered office in Amsterdam, its head office in Stellenbosch, and listings in Frankfurt and Johannesburg, complied with all the demands set out in those countries' regulatory environments. Its annual and integrated reports claim that the company adheres to the highest standards of ethical and good corporate conduct and that it subscribes to all policies and regulations guiding its conduct. It is, however, common knowledge that Steinhoff's reporting structures failed. So, how could Jooste not have been found out?

Perhaps because, according to some accounts, Jooste was a revered figure, serving on many other boards of directors. 'How does one prevent another Steinhoff happening? Look, I've known Markus Jooste for a long time. He served on our board. I can categorically state that he was one of the best PSG directors,' said Piet Mouton. 'He always thoroughly read his board packs [documents containing critical information distributed to directors before board meetings]. He made incisive comments during meetings. He never applied pressure on PSG to do business with Steinhoff or its associated companies. He was hands-off and understood how to keep a reasonable distance. He was an effective director, showed good insight, which we appreciated because he did business all over the world. He was aggressive, but being aggressive doesn't necessarily mean you're crooked. Look at Steve Jobs. By all accounts he was aggressive and self-centred, but he was brilliant.'[22]

A respected businessman, who has been at the forefront of his industry for many years but who does not want to be named, says Jooste is one of 'cleverest, smartest' guys he has met. He served with Jooste on company boards and believes him to be one of the best directors he's ever worked with. Jooste understood the complexity of business, according to the businessman, and was able to quickly and efficiently identify issues that may be lurking. While the rest of the directors might still be fulminating over how clients might react or what the South African Reserve Bank might say, Jooste would nail the problem.[23]

It's clear that corporate governance failed at Steinhoff, with Jooste at the helm. Its critics say the company followed a 'tick-box' approach, which means that it merely went through the motions of sticking to good corporate governance frameworks and business ethics, even though it was subject to Dutch and German regulations and the King Code of Governance Principles.

A study of Steinhoff by the University of Stellenbosch Business School warned that various risks are associated with tick-box compliance systems when they are 'not underpinned by an ethical commitment to respect and abide by relevant rules and regulations'.[24]

Wiese, appearing in Parliament in January 2018, told dumbstruck legislators that he had been caught unawares and that smarter people than the Steinhoff board have been duped by people committing fraud: 'I can only refer to many instances around the world of companies of a similar or bigger size where this has happened … To detect fraud in a company is an extremely difficult, if not impossible, task and it becomes more difficult when, as is alleged in this case, the CEO is directly involved.'[25]

When La Grange, Jooste's chief financial officer, appeared in Parliament on 28 August 2018 (and proceeded to throw his mentor,

Jooste, under the bus), he described a complex reporting structure, with no single auditor or auditing firm having sight of the company's finances as a whole. Every layer of the business, every unit or bucket, had its own auditors, and these financial results were simply reported up the chain of command, until they reached Stellenbosch, where they were merely checked for major anomalies.

La Grange spoke of inflated profits, loans converted into revenue and assets acquired for inflated prices all finding their way onto the balance sheets. If this was done by stealth, La Grange said, nobody would be able to pick it up. 'That's because [looking at the financial statements] nothing jumps right up at you. It's a practice that started a long time ago. Nobody will notice it if it's done little by little every year.'[26]

Mouton, who is in charge of a R53 billion company, argues that if a company's executive management wilfully lies to the board, there's not much that the board can do. Trust is crucial. 'I think the problems at Steinhoff partly lie with the rest of the management, whom I like on a personal level – Danie (van der Merwe), Frikkie (Nel), Ben (la Grange), Stehan (Grobler): they've been with Markus for too long. If you work alongside somebody for twenty, thirty years and he's made everyone rich ... I'm sure they didn't challenge him enough and trusted him too much. Perhaps he even played people off against each other. I don't know.'

Mouton seemingly doesn't believe La Grange was up for the job as Steinhoff's chief financial officer because he was 'reared by Jooste'. 'I have to add that Ben is a very smart and capable person, but the power dynamics were all wrong in this instance. I think Jooste may have intimidated him and even played him off against his European counterpart, I've heard stories about that,' Mouton said. The board failed in that respect, Mouton said, because it should have ensured that a headstrong personality like Jooste was surrounded by equally strong colleagues who could act as counterweight and question him on a daily basis.[27]

The problem with the board is compounded by the fact that because the company is registered in the Netherlands, it is structured according to Dutch company law, which means it has a two-tiered board system and not a unitary board, as is the case in South Africa. In this system, the non-executive directors sit on the supervisory board and the executive team on the management board. Unlike the South African structure, the non-executives and the executives don't always sit around a table together, which means that the management board always knows more about the business than the supervisory board does.

The upside, according to academics, is that the supervisory board has a strong theoretical oversight role precisely because it doesn't sit jointly with the management team.[28] The Steinhoff supervisory board had some stellar talents as members: accountant Len Konar, who served on various boards as well as being chairman of the external audit committee of the International Monetary Fund, former Absa CEO Steve Booysen and Johan van Zyl, chairman of Sanlam.

Were the supervisory board members, the non-executive directors, sufficiently independent to fulfil their oversight role? Jooste was proud of the composition of the board, which included Wiese (the biggest individual shareholder in the company), Bruno Steinhoff (the founder) and Claas Daun (his original mentor), and called it 'a club of friendship and trust'.[29]

'It is interesting to note that when Franklin Sonn resigned as an independent director in 2013, his daughter, Heather Sonn, was appointed. In a similar vein, the appointment in 2016 of the son of Christo Wiese, Jacob Wiese, appears to be questionable in the light of the need to foster independence and diversity. The appointment of family members to the board is reminiscent of a family business and "club culture", as alluded to by Markus Jooste,' said the University of Stellenbosch Business School authors in their case study.[30]

If the executive management had been stronger and not so close to Jooste, irregularities could have been identified earlier, Mouton believes. 'Everyone was paid such huge salaries and bonuses for doing deals that I believe they were conditioned not to ask the hard questions of Markus. If there were strong, independent voices on the management team, then Markus would have been challenged on the numbers when he came with "trust me". The board is the wrong place to look for answers [about what happened at Steinhoff]. Management should keep management accountable.'

The complexity of the Steinhoff business – to which Jooste took such offence when Mouton mentioned it in passing to a group of analysts – clearly was a problem because of the disparate corporate cultures in existence.

Mouton said that when one company buys another, it takes years to sort out synergies if they aren't exactly aligned from the beginning, and even though Steinhoff's strategy was clear – leverage buying power in the market by becoming the largest – it must have led to tension. 'Steinhoff made so many acquisitions that I couldn't see them creating a uniform culture. Look at the Tekkie Town debacle, the PEP story. Every acquisition was bigger than the one before. It is a red flag if companies do too many acquisitions ... but, then again, it's no reason to say it's wrong.'

The senior, anonymous business leader agrees and, like almost every other executive in Stellenbosch, says that he did not understand the Steinhoff business model either. He argues that there are major differences in running a business involved in retail and one involved in wholesale, and that they require different skill sets. Steinhoff wanted to be both, and he believes it was therefore destined to fail. 'They straddled two different worlds. The word "furniture" might appear on both sides, but a manufacturer needs to think about wood supply, factories and trade unions, while the retail side needs to consider many other things – it's a different world,' he said, adding that he could never understand how the same management team could run businesses that are so vastly different.

He says he used to bump into senior Steinhoff executives like Van der Merwe and thought he looked like a 'good, competent guy', but that he could never understand how he (Van der Merwe) could be COO of a manufacturing business and then COO [chief operating officer] of an international retail business.'[31]

Van der Merwe resigned in December 2018.

···✦···

Days after Jooste's resignation, details of the ex-Steinhoff CEO's 'style' – which Basson and others had expressed so much concern about – emerged when it was reported that the married father of three had allegedly been having an extramarital affair.

If he had known about the affair he would not have done business with Jooste, Wiese later said.[32]

According to Stellenbosch insiders, Jooste had been consorting and cavorting with a young, blonde, muscular polo player, Berdine Odendaal. She had been put up in a luxury apartment in Bantry Bay managed by Jooste's son-in-law, Stefan Potgieter, and she owned several properties at the exclusive Val de Vie polo estate in Paarl, where Jooste also owns property.

Odendaal, a socialite and prominent figure in the world of champagne and horses, doesn't appear to work and, according to the deeds registry, shared a postal address with Jooste in Pretoria and another in Somerset West with Jooste and his wife, Ingrid.

The interesting link in this liaison seems to be Potgieter, who is married to Jooste's daughter, Andrea. Potgieter was put in charge of Jooste's Mayfair Speculators, a vehicle that housed his private interests, including property and horses. He was registered as a director of Coy's Properties, which managed the Bantry Bay property that Odendaal, according to her Facebook page, which is peppered with images of her in the infinity pool on the balcony, all but considers her home.

But Potgieter has claimed never to have met his father-in-law's mistress, or to have been aware of the goings-on in the luxury apartment. 'I only make sure that the asset [the apartment] is taken care of and that Coy's Properties, on behalf of owner Malcolm King, receives rental income. The arrangements around the apartment [are] Jooste's private business,' he said.[33]

Jooste's affair was apparently an 'open secret' in Stellenbosch, and Odendaal's jet-setting lifestyle – including flying to polo tournaments in Plettenberg Bay courtesy of Jooste – the talk of the town.

Potgieter seems to have been left in the lurch by his father-in-law as the single director of Mayfair Speculators, which was sued by Absa for committing 'naked fraud' after Jooste resigned as director. Before the crash, Potgieter was flying high, managing his father-in-law's significant private affairs and earning a good living. He had also just bought an expensive property in Jonkershoek Avenue, in the old-money suburb of Mostertsdrift in Stellenbosch, where he tore down an old house to the great chagrin of well-heeled neighbours, who felt that 'Jooste's boy' just wanted to flaunt his money.

But the new property was sold within days after the crash, fetching R10 million rands, according to a local real-estate agent. 'I feel sorry for Potgieter,' Rupert says. 'He is in an invidious position: he is going to choose between his father-in-law and his wife, but, either way, he is going to be in trouble.' Friends of his say Potgieter was devastated by his father-in-law's betrayal and the crisis that he left the family in. Potgieter still lives in Stellenbosch with his young family, but is seldom seen, except when walking a newborn baby. 'He's a good guy. I don't think he knew everything that Jooste did,' one friend said. 'He was suckered into it.'

---***---

On 5 September 2018, Markus Jooste made his first public appearance, ten months to the day after his ignominious resignation from Steinhoff, when he appeared in front of a joint parliamentary committee in Cape Town. This followed a legal tussle and the exchange of numerous letters in which he sought to avoid talking to legislators, which was settled only on condition that Parliament would agree to certain parameters within which MPs were allowed to question him.

Looking healthy and fit, sporting neatly cropped hair, square-rimmed glasses and a charcoal suit, Jooste proceeded to admit nothing and deny everything. The answers thousands of South Africans had been waiting for were never given, as Jooste, accompanied by a heavyweight legal team of two senior counsel and two lawyers, navigated the potentially choppy waters with aplomb.

The agreement between the parties limiting the scope of the questioning, combined with MPs' lack of detailed knowledge about the issue, scuppered any chance of getting a meaningful probe into Jooste's actions.

As it turned out, Jooste blamed Andreas Seifert, his Austrian partner in Conforama, for the ills that had befallen the company. He claimed that his frantic letter to colleagues, saying he had 'made big mistakes' and that he would have to face the consequences 'like a man', merely referred to his having made a bad choice in Seifert as a business partner.

Jooste proceeded to blame the collapse of the company's share price on the board's decision to authorise a new investigation into irregularities, saying that when the decision was taken, he was tired of dealing with the allegations and had resigned for that reason.

He neglected, interestingly, to mention that, in its announcement to the JSE, Steinhoff had said it had received information regarding 'accounting irregularities' and was launching an investigation. The natural consequence of this would have been the delay in signing off on the financials and, from Jooste's own account in Parliament, he seems to have tried to strong-arm the board into dismissing Deloitte and appointing new auditors.

'On 29 November 2017 the chairpersons of the board and audit committee met with three representatives from the auditors, after which it was decided that a new investigation was not necessary any more and that they could focus on finalising the audit. However, on 30 November 2017 Deloitte sent a letter to Booysen and the board requesting that it commission a new investigation by a firm appointed and approved by Deloitte,' was how Jooste related the events to the MPs.[34]

'Wiese, however, explained to them that an investigation was done in Germany by two reputable firms, that it took two years to complete and that a new investigation won't be finalised in time for the financial statements to be signed off on.'

The gist of Jooste's narrative in Parliament was that he had attempted to safeguard the interests of the company at all times and that the auditors were being unnecessarily obstinate. 'This [Deloitte's position] was not acceptable to us because it put the entire group at risk and would have impacted on our banking relationships, issued bonds and investor expectations,' he said.

A square-jawed Jooste then explained that he had shared his concerns with Wiese, who, he said, agreed with him – a claim that the former chairman of Steinhoff has never alluded to, either in the many interviews he has given since or when he appeared in Parliament.

'My personal view was: terminate the Deloitte mandate with immediate effect, appoint new auditors and announce the unaudited results, which were 90% complete. Deloitte had lost all independence in the matter ... we had to announce the results by 31 January 2018 if we were to prevent a disaster.'

But then, according to Jooste, Wiese made an about-turn – as Deloitte had done – and decided that an investigation was necessary after all. Jooste left Steinhoff in decent nick, he explained, and said that he had not been 'aware of any accounting irregularity'.

Jooste's performance was astonishing: he showed no remorse, never felt compelled to take any blame for what had happened to the company and deftly batted away any feeble attempts to extract anything resembling culpability from him. Afterwards, hemmed in by a throng of photographers and journalists, he marched out into a lift and disappeared.

---*---

After Steinhoff's demise, Stellenbosch took some time to adjust.

The university and the Springbok sevens rugby team removed all the Steinhoff signage and branding. The sevens team, having won the world series in 2017, were also hit in their pockets: they had received Steinhoff shares as part of an incentive scheme, but those had become almost worthless after the crash.

Suddenly a slew of exclusive Stellenbosch houses went on the market, with an initial tally of forty homes rumoured to have been put up for sale in the immediate aftermath, including in the De Zalze estate, where several Steinhoff executives used to have their homes.

In the aftermath of the storm, a number of Stellenbosch business leaders reflected on Jooste and the events at Steinhoff, and most were disarmingly honest about their distrust of Jooste and the company he had destroyed. Schadenfreude? Perhaps. But Jooste also rubbed people up the wrong way.

'I never bought shares in Steinhoff,' says Hertzog. 'I long ago thought Markus, with all his racehorses, was a little weird. And I think if you conducted a lifestyle audit on him, the books won't balance. His income wasn't equal to his lifestyle. The financial and annual statements were muddled and I couldn't understand it.'[35]

Rupert was never taken by Steinhoff mania. 'But when I did look at the statements and saw what was going on there, I said to whomever was asking that a guy who structures a business like that I don't trust a hundred per cent. And then GT Ferreira, Thys du Toit and Jaap du Toit swapped their shares in PSG for Steinhoff shares, allegedly without telling Jannie Mouton [PSG's founder], their best chum, and suddenly Jooste owned 25 per cent of PSG.

'When Wiese sold Lanzerac to Jooste, I started wondering who these people were and what was going on. I had a look [at Steinhoff] and immediately realised there's something funny. And I thought something was wrong with Jooste when he and Wiese started becoming best friends,' Rupert says.[36]

Today, the aftershock is still palpable in Stellenbosch. There's almost nothing left of the flashy cars, raucous parties and big deals that were once associated with the Steinhoff *inkommers*. Yet, more than a year after the collapse, nobody had been held accountable or charged with any crimes relating to the alleged large-scale fraud at Steinhoff. And the result of the much-vaunted investigation by auditors PwC into the debacle was so weak it gave the public almost no insight into events at Steinhoff whatsoever. A summary of the report told the country what everyone already knew: that fraud on an industrial scale had taken place. Yet it doesn't mention Jooste or his cronies, adding that former executives would be 'invited' to comment. Writing on Fin24, Ferial Haffajee called the report a 'whitewash', 'mealy-mouthed' and 'laced with white privilege'.[37]

'I find it a distasteful summary that lacks respect for the public and for the many, many hardworking ordinary working people who save and trust that companies are what they say they are. It is the kind of treatment that an untransformed business community is used to meting out to a public that too often is indulgent of outdated business practices that would not be countenanced in many parts of the world,' Haffajee said.[38]

More than 18 months after the crash, there still was no clarity on the state of the Hawks' investigation, and the South African Institute of Chartered Accountants had also taken no action against

Jooste, or anyone else. Printed in bold red letters across every page of Steinhoff's 2016 annual report, a disclaimer read: 'Information can no longer be relied on.'

In January 2019 Pepkor published statements that showed that Jooste had been paid R122 million in his last full financial year in charge of Steinhoff. He received R5 million in the last two months of his employment with the company.

Jooste has kept a low profile since the events at Steinhoff, and he wasn't seen or heard from after his appearance in Parliament.

Wiese and Jooste were as close as business partners could be, and the former invested his life's work in the latter's enterprise. However, the two had no contact after Jooste deserted his mentor, his colleagues and his company, opting to flee to the safety of his luxurious Hermanus and Jonkershoek properties, safe behind high walls and a firewall of expensive lawyers.

The former Pepkor boss has maintained that he knew nothing of Jooste's creative accounting and management practices, arguing that if he had known, he would never have invested so extensively in Steinhoff. Besides, the story goes, Wiese was hands-off with Shoprite, preferring to leave the heavy lifting to the trustworthy Basson. It was the same at Steinhoff. In Stellenbosch, however, many, including some regulars at the Decameron lunches, question this, arguing that Wiese would have been intimately involved, given the scale of his investment. And what if it were all just part of a scheme to move money out of the country?

Wiese is fighting back, though, lodging a claim and instituting a suit asking the court to declare his original investment null and void because Steinhoff had misled investors about the true state of the company's finances.

Some Stellenbosch heavyweights, including those who wouldn't begrudge the Clifton-based former billionaire his misfortune, believe Wiese is done for and that he won't be able to recover what has been lost in the Steinhoff fire. And there's wide agreement that he will probably have to sell some Shoprite stock to partly repair damage to his fortune. Asked in February 2019 whether he had had any contact with Jooste, Wiese replied: 'Not a word.'[39]

At Magica Roma, an old family-owned Italian restaurant in the Cape Town suburb of Pinelands, Wiese's regular corner table is now empty. The owner doesn't want to say much. And the gregarious Wiese, who used to hold court there with friends and confidants over bottles of Italian wine and traditional Roman fare, doesn't go there quite as often as he used to. Now in his eighth decade, he is fighting to get his money back from Steinhoff … if there's anything left.

13. TURNING NEW MONEY INTO OLD

'The reality is that Remgro has its roots here, and the rest moved down from Johannesburg ... Steinhoff, their head office was here ... Of the rest ... Distell and Mediclinic, and, out of our group, Capitec [are] here; the heart of our business [PSG Group] is here too'

– Piet Mouton, CEO of the PSG Group.[1]

IF THOSE IN ORBIT around the old Rembrandt Group and the Rupert family represent 'old' Stellenbosch money, and the wreckage that is Steinhoff serves as an ominous warning of what could happen to 'new' money, then PSG and Capitec are the perfect combination of the two: new money gracefully turning old.

Stellenbosch has become the redoubt of some of the country's top banking and financial entrepreneurs, with most of them returning to the town they called home when they were students or schoolboys.

Rand Merchant Bank's Ferreira studied at the University of Stellenbosch; he and Jannie Mouton attended the same university residence, Simonsberg. One of their protégés, Michael Jordaan, the FNB wunderkind, moved back to the town of his youth after his very profitable and productive spell as CEO of the bank concluded in 2013 at the age of 46 (he was just 36 when he took the helm).

Capitec's founder Michiel le Roux started out in the Rembrandt stable, at the erstwhile Distillers Corporation, before he and fellow Distillers man Riaan Stassen, another Paul Roos Gymnasium old boy, helped found Capitec Bank.

But, even though the links between the groups, companies and individuals are indisputable, there is no Stellenbosch Mafia, says

Le Roux (estimated net worth: $1.2 billion[2]) with a wry smile. He was recruited into PSG by Chris Otto as a consultant to explore the micro-lending business, and became the driving force behind Capitec. 'Stellenbosch is a nice little town,' he says. 'There are good people here, and I guess the fact that many Afrikaans businesspeople have decided to make it their base can be put down to the influence Anton Rupert has had. He established a business community here.'[3]

The bright, sunny boardroom of the PSG Group's head office is bedecked with works by some of the country's finest artists: Maggie Laubser, Irma Stern, JH Pierneef and Adriaan Boshoff, to name but a few. The value of the various oil-on-canvas country scenes, renditions of seaside holidays or mountain vistas must run into the millions. But the room, and the suite of offices, are anything but ostentatious and the atmosphere is much more relaxed than, for example, the heavy-carpeted corridors of Anglo American's pre-war edifice in Main Street, Johannesburg.

Piet Mouton, who succeed his father as chief executive of the PSG Group in 2010, grins at the thought of the Mafia, and says the only thing the alleged members of the group have in common is the fact that many of them studied at Stellenbosch. 'GT made his money in Johannesburg, where Rand Merchant Bank started, and he returned to Stellenbosch after being shot[4]... PSG also started out in Johannesburg and moved down only after the business was decentralised. GT told Jannie [as Mouton refers to his dad] that he had bought this building, doesn't he want to move down, Jannie will even furnish offices for him,'[5] Mouton recalls.

He points out that Steinhoff also used to have their head office in Johannesburg before Jooste uprooted the company to move to the Boland. 'I think it's a mere coincidence that so many of us live and work in Stellenbosch. People like the place; it's a nice town and many of us studied here. It has become a little bit of a hotbed for business to take root, I suppose like Zug in Switzerland [without the tax benefits], which is also home to some big European companies.

Look, we're exposed to high-level interaction with senior business-people here, so it's very, very stimulating,' says Mouton, who took PSG's reins at the age of 32. 'But I can tell you one thing: the town is infinitely more pleasurable when the students are away.'

'It's certainly not out of the ordinary that these people all know each other, the South African business community is small. But, having said that, I meet people every day who I did not know and who have been doing remarkable things for ten or twenty years. The idea of the Mafia though is a daft one. I look at it as a bit of tongue in cheek,' Mouton says. 'And I haven't been invited ...'

Yet it sounds as if he has a good grasp of the so-called Mafia's inner workings. 'We laugh about it. Of course, the Mafia has some serious issues now after what has happened at Steinhoff. Jannie and GT were in the same residence and we actually compete very strongly with each other. FNB and Capitec vie for the same clientele; they grew up together and have great respect for each other. Some of the big Mafia figures are – allegedly – Johann and Christo, but they seemingly don't like each other, which makes the whole Stellenbosch Mafia thesis laughable. And Whitey and Markus never liked each other. And Christo actually lives in Clifton and Johann technically lives in Somerset West, but he's abroad most of the time.'

'The reality is that Remgro has its roots here, and the rest moved down from Johannesburg. If you run a big business, then you have to be in Joburg ... take Steinhoff, their head office was here but the engine room was there. Of the rest: Remgro is here, Distell and Mediclinic, and, out of our group, Capitec is here; the heart of our business [PSG Group] is here too. But very few businesses don't have larger operations elsewhere.'

···✱···

Rembrandt, and later Remgro, dominated the business scene in Stellenbosch for decades. Thanks to Anton Rupert, the company established itself as one of the town's major institutions, alongside the university and some schools. But the coming of democracy saw the creation of new companies, with some choosing to make Stellenbosch their base. They include PSG and Capitec, the former a product of Johannesburg, and the latter the brainchild of former Rupert employees.

PSG was conceived after Jannie Mouton was asked to resign from his stockbroking firm just shy of his 50th birthday in 1995, and he had to start from scratch. A prickly man, his colleagues believed him to be difficult to work with, and Mouton says he took time while recovering from the shock to take stock of his life and evaluate his weaknesses and strong points. The result was the establishment of a company with a market capitalisation of more than R50 billion.

Today the PSG Group is, like its Stellenbosch stablemate Remgro, an investment holding company with interests in a number of ventures, but one of its biggest investments has been in Capitec Bank, which started life as an amalgamation of a number of micro-lending businesses that were spun out into the Business Bank. It was eventually renamed and Capitec was established in March 2001, with the company listing on the JSE in 2002.

Capitec has grown in leaps and bounds and today operates 826 branches and can lay claim to 9.9 million clients, of which 46% are primary banking clients (i.e. Capitec is their main service provider).[6]

'The bank has been successful because we all came from the liquor trade, and in the liquor trade you learn how to market products so that consumers really want to buy them,' explains Le Roux. 'For example, vodka is heavily regulated. It is a colourless, tasteless spirit with 43% alcohol. According to law, there's no difference between a bottle that costs R340 and one that costs R89. But if you have better branding and marketing, you can sell it.'

When Le Roux and Stassen arrived in the world of banking, they realised two things: firstly, there are real and palpable differences between banking products; and, secondly, banks ignored their clients. Banks created complicated products and then called in their marketers to sell them to the market. Capitec did it the other way around: they first went to their market to ascertain what its needs were, and then they built a bank around those needs. 'It's not rocket science, but it's light years removed from what Absa did,' Le Roux says.

A bank's biggest concern is risk management, and its clients pose the biggest risk. Le Roux says the whole structure and organisation of banking is geared towards minimising that risk, which means there is an inherent suspicion about clients, which those clients sense and feel. There is no experience as frustrating, or one that makes a young client as angry, as when he applies for his first credit card and is treated as if he wants to steal money, Le Roux says.

'A Capitec client's first experience of a bank is far removed from that of a young, white professional in his first job. It might be a dirty factory worker who walks in: shoes dirty, hands dirty, underdressed, and the whole environment, the whole atmosphere says: "What are you doing here?" Banks will deny it, but many have been built to make people feel unwelcome.'

When Otto poached Le Roux to investigate the microlending business, he visited branches of lenders that PSG had stakes in, and what he saw impressed him no end. PSG made lots of money from lending to mainly working class customers who often paid R300 interest on a loan of R1 000. But because the micro-lenders knew that their clients were good business, they were treated well. A worker might make one or two transfers from his bank account a month, which does not mean a lot for the bank's bottom line. But micro-lenders made good money from the same market.

'So I walked into one of these micro-lending businesses and I saw the white Afrikaans manager drinking a cup of tea with a working class client. And we realised: one reason why these businesses, which many wanted closed down because they were said to be exploiting the working class, were doing so well was because customers walk in, sit down and drink tea with the manager, and walk out feeling like a human being ... with R1 000 in their pockets. And not one of these banks, which look down on the micro-lenders, would even consider lending to that market,' Le Roux says.

When Capitec was formed a couple of years after the micro-lending epiphany, treating people with dignity in an environment that, for most people, is intimidating became a cornerstone of the business. It also became their calling card and did much more for the Capitec brand than any above-the-line marketing campaign ever did. And the same principle applied not only to the working-class or lower-middle-class clients, Le Roux says: the same goes for the higher end of the market. 'A top businessman once lamented that he needed to renegotiate his lines of credit with his bank and that it was causing him sleepless nights, preparing to go and see the bank manager. I just told him, "Goodness, pal, do you know how important your business is to the bank? It is a disgrace that it is you who is feeling under pressure! The bankers are the ones who should be struggling to sleep, fearful that they might lose your account!" Banks have this attitude that they're doing you a favour, that they don't really trust you.'

When developing the Capitec model, Stassen, Le Roux and their colleagues took great care to ensure that a visit to one of their branches would be as pleasurable an experience as possible, especially for potential clients who in the past had been made to feel unwelcome in banks. Managers, tellers and staff were trained to communicate in such a way that clients could see that they were welcome. The dynamic between the teller and the client changes when they sit down together, he explains. 'All our clients are made to sit down; they don't stand when we serve them. That is very important to me, because if you sit down and the consultant or staff member looks at you, it means you can't be rushed. But if you stand, the consultant, halfway through the transaction, starts to look across your shoulder at whoever is behind you. And, often, the client, sometimes standing there at the booth reading though a document, senses that the teller wants to move on and then either doesn't understand the transaction, or decides to leave and come back later,' Le Roux says.

Capitec also had the idea of turning the teller's computer screen at an angle, so the client can follow the transaction. 'There's nothing worse than a teller grimacing or whistling at a screen that you can't see ... a client must be able to see what's on the screen and if, for example, he wants his name in capital or small letters, he can ask for it.' Capitec staff are trained to make sure the last questions are: 'Are you satisfied? Do you understand everything? Is there anything else?'

Capitec was not, as is the common perception, targeting the unbanked or black working class when it was established. It did, however, emerge from the micro-lending business, in which most of the clients were black; nevertheless, all had bank accounts. 'My idea was to keep it simple and focus on that market. But Riaan said I mustn't be daft and that if we were to build a bank, we needed to build it for everyone, not just a specific segment,' Le Roux recalls.

Although the client base was initially made up of mainly black salary earners, it quickly changed. It remains a complicated business with many customers borrowing from Capitec but banking elsewhere. People's relationships and decision-making processes with money are sophisticated and complicated, Le Roux says. 'Decisions are often emotional and I believe conservative. For example, some always put their wallets in the same drawer or transact at the same ATM; people are careful with their money. That's why we regard it as an absolute triumph that we managed to get millions of people to change their banks.'

···✦···

With the downfall of Steinhoff in December 2017, rumours began circulating that Viceroy, the obscure outfit that specialises in short-selling, and which had helped lay bare Jooste's schemes, was now targeting another South African company – Capitec. When it issued a report reminiscent of the job it did on Steinhoff, accusing the bank of hiding unrecoverable loans and calling it a 'loan-shark', the bank reacted strongly, denying Viceroy's allegations and rejecting its conclusion that the bank was 'uninvestable'.

Capitec's CEO, Gerrie Fourie, addressed numerous press conferences explaining why the bank dismissed Viceroy's statements; he made himself available to any analyst or journalist who wanted to question the company's financials. It also helped Capitec that the governor of the South African Reserve Bank pledged his support to the bank, saying that Capitec was adequately capitalised to cover deposits. Le Roux says it later became clear that Viceroy, which was later exposed as being led by a former social worker with a patchy history, was looking to take down another company in the Steinhoff environment.

'We became the target,' says Le Roux. 'Steinhoff held 25% of PSG, and PSG is our largest shareholder, so we weren't exactly detached from Steinhoff. A bank, by definition, is always exposed, and the fear that you cannot cover your bad debt always lingers.'

'Capitec was a good target, but [Viceroy] never actually had anything on us.' Rumours about banks' liquidity abound every year, Le Roux said, including the biggest banks in the country. 'It's unsettling because a depositor has nothing to gain if he stays with a bank that could seemingly go bust. And, as a new bank, we did get asked questions about sustainability – look at Saambou and African Bank. Banks are conceived amid serious questions about credibility, financials and capital.'

Transparency is a bank's most important currency. When Capitec started out, Le Roux even considered posting the bank's financials on the walls in every branch, so customers could see for themselves that the bank had 'billions in capitalisation'. Rumours about Capitec, Le Roux believes, originated from its competitors. 'If you were to attack Distell or Remgro in that fashion it won't work. But, as a bank, we're always in the firing line,' he says.

----✹----

Mouton is proud of what 'Jannie' built at PSG and that the culture established by his father is one of challenging and questioning, and that approach has stood the company in good stead over the years.

'My dad and I have had fights where either he or I have left the boardroom; we've really clashed over stuff. The culture is such that everyone knows that to say "amen" to everything really helps no one.'

Mouton doesn't want to be drawn on the inner workings of Steinhoff, which he, like most businesspeople in Stellenbosch, didn't fully understand. But he does believe that corporate governance was a problem at the company – although not because it wasn't adhered to. With the King Code of Good Governance and how companies manage it, he says, there's a lot of red tape, and that makes running a business so much harder. Information about a business should be readily available for the board to assess and there needs to be honesty about the state of play. Mouton argues that the 'tick-box' method of corporate governance – partly the result of the King Code – prevents a board from properly engaging with the innards of a business and that it leads to cover-ups, especially when someone, like a chief executive, is wilfully dishonest. 'The hours spent doing all the governance checks misses the point: you could make King ten times as strict as it is now, yet it won't prevent another Steinhoff because the focus is on the wrong things,' he says.

In Steinhoff's case, if the (disengaged) board's questions were answered to their relative satisfaction, then there is not much you can do if it turns out that those answers were lies.

PSG never invests in a company unless it can appoint a senior executive, like the chief financial officer or the financial director, says Mouton. 'It's the first thing we write into the contract. We need to be able to trust the person in that position; the person needs to be in the middle of things and needs to be able to report to us. That is a non-negotiable and I think it's the only thing that can prevent [a Steinhoff].'

PSG did have a look at the company's internal processes, culture and protocols after the Steinhoff scandal, but, as Mouton says, if people in senior positions are dishonest, then it's rather difficult to smoke them out. For Mouton, what is the biggest lesson in executive management that came out of the messiest corporate meltdown South Africa has seen? 'Ensure proper checks and balances.'

And opulence. When a company starts to spend money on entertainment and other vanities, it should raise red flags, he says. 'Leaders genuinely need to respect shareholders' money.'

Mouton doesn't approve of executives billing their companies for their entertainment expenses. 'If I was to pay R50 000 for a shirt worn by Dale Steyn at a corporate event, and afterwards tell my financial director he needs to pay for it, he'd laugh at me in my face.'

It's become commonplace, he says, to justify expenses such as holidays with friends and business partners, and bill your company for the cost. 'But,' he says, 'it's misuse of shareholders' money.' To commit large-scale fraud at PSG would be 'almost impossible', even for Mouton – because he doesn't control the purse strings: 'I sign big instructions, yes, but after I have signed it, there's a long way to go before it is executed. If I wanted to commit fraud, I'd have to get the financial director and others in the finance department on board, which would mean that they would have to move the money and I'd have to explain it.'

---*---

Le Roux served as chairman of the board at Capitec until 2016; he now spends his time managing the well-endowed Millennium Trust, funded by his personal fortune, which is estimated at $1.1 billion.[7]

Sitting in the boardroom of the trust's offices in Devonshire

House, Stellenbosch, Le Roux is reluctant to talk about the funding and activities of the organisation, which, according to some estimates, has a war chest of more than a billion rands. He says its goal is to 'make South Africa a better place' and, with that objective, it supports and invests in organisations that he feels help achieve that.

The trust funds investigative-journalism unit amaBhungane, the scourge of rent-seekers everywhere and one of the original publishers of the leaked Gupta emails, which served as a catalyst to resist state capture and corruption. It also supports retired judge of the Constitutional Court Johann Kriegler's organisation Freedom Under Law, which, among other law suits, has defended Pravin Gordhan in court, as well as Corruption Watch, another non-governmental organisation fighting graft.

Given that these organisations, which were so deeply involved in exposing state capture, are supported by a billionaire from Stellenbosch, it is not beyond the bounds of reason to see how conspiracy theorists and defenders of grand corruption can construct the narrative of the Stellenbosch Mafia. When Ramaphosa's project to clean up and reform the state began in earnest with the rescue operation at Eskom, those who resisted once again pointed fingers at Stellenbosch as supposedly being behind attempts to take control of the state.

Le Roux rubbishes conspiracies and says the trust supports only viable and transparent organisations. 'We don't do charity; we're not a secret organisation; we have wonderful trustees, and staff who help identify projects that we believe can make the country a better place. AmaBhungane is such a project because you can literally see how the investment is helping the country. They know what they're doing. It's a worthwhile investment.'

---✷---

Mouton says even though South Africa has found itself in choppy economic and political waters following Zuma's ousting, PSG still sees immense opportunity in the country. 'It's difficult here, but I think it's difficult everywhere. We're a South African company and this is where our skills set lies. The more companies go and waste their time overseas, the less competitive it becomes here, and that's good for us. When you go to a place like Britain, there are a hundred guys cleverer than you are, with more contacts and more money. There will always be opportunities locally.' Mouton lived in England for a number of years before joining 'Jannie's' firm. He does not believe he will emigrate.

As with all the investments PSG makes, Mouton is thinking long-term and says he is firmly of the view that Ramaphosa is committed to leaving a Mandela-like legacy. But the only way to do that is to put the economy front and centre of government's plans, with job creation as the engine of growth. 'If Ramaphosa really wants to kick-start the economy, he needs to take his lead from Margaret Thatcher and break the hold of the unions. My biggest problem with them is that they don't act in the interests of their constituents,' he says. Unionised teachers have an enormously detrimental impact on children's education because there is no accountability, says the man who keeps a beady eye on PSG investment in its Curro private schools.

PSG is very much a South African company. It was started in 1995 and made its money in the new South Africa. 'We built businesses from the ground up, with strong management teams at PSG and Capitec and invested in Curro in 1998 when they had three schools; now we have 140. Ours are new South African companies, which were started with relatively little capital . It's not old money, it's new. We tried new things and we built companies that weren't there before.'

Stellenbosch has traditionally been dominated by old money and old networks, with *inkommers*, like Jooste, who barged in and left in disgrace. But some, like the Moutons from Johannesburg, have adapted to the town and become part of the firmament. And while Capitec was started by townsfolk, it is also an *inkommer* among the established corporations that have called Stellenbosch HQ for many years.

A mafia refers to a gang, an organised group of criminals who run protection rackets, smuggle contraband, extort money and take out rivals. There isn't a mafia of that sort in Stellenbosch, and the only alleged illegal dealings involve an *inkommer* – Jooste – who has departed the scene in disgrace (although, at the time of writing, he's still to face the music).

But there most certainly is an intricate network of a connected and privileged few, a network with access to vast reservoirs of human and financial capital and a network that looks inward before it ventures outside of the Bubble.

'Stellenbosch Mafia' has become a political insult, a racial epithet and a reference to rich, old white men. It may not exist formally and it may not be involved in crime or illegal dealings. But there are few networks more influential or affluent than the one consisting of the business heavyweights and snappy entrepreneurs of the Boland town by the banks of the Eerste River.

NOTES

1. A powerful elite, out of touch and out of reach

1 Given Mkhari, Calling on those locked in the world of apartheid to imagine a different future, *Sunday Times*, 9 December 2018.

2 Ferial Haffajee, So a really rich white guy said really dumb things, and you're surprised?, Fin24, 5 December 2018, https://www.fin24.com/Opinion/ferial-haffajee-so-a-really-rich-white-guy-said-really-dumb-things-and-youre-surprised-20181205-2.

3 Eusebius McKaiser, The messenger does matter, Talk Radio 702, 6 December 2018, http://www.702.co.za/articles/329826/eusebius-on-black-wealth-the-messenger-does-matter.

4 EFF lashes out at 'president of whites' Johann Rupert following radio interview, News24, 5 December 2018, https://www.news24.com/SouthAfrica/News/eff-lashes-out-at-president-of-whites-johann-rupert-following-radio-interview-20181205.

5 Alec Hogg, Moneyweb market report (transcript), Moneyweb, 7 January 2003, https://www.courtneycapital.co.za/david-shapiro-jse-report-3/.

6 Jan Cronjé, 'Stellenbosch mafia' controls SA – Malema, *Weekend Argus*, 16 March 2014, https://www.iol.co.za/news/stellenbosch-Mafia-controls-sa-malema-1662015.

7 Karabo Ngoepe, Zuma is not our enemy – Malema, News24, 16 April 2016, https://www.news24.com/SouthAfrica/News/zuma-is-not-our-enemy-malema-20160416.

8 Jenni Evans, BLF faces Rupert company interdict against 'unlawful land invasion', News24, 14 February 2018, https://www.news24.com/SouthAfrica/News/blf-faces-rupert-company-interdict-against-unlawful-land-invasion-20180214.

9 Iavan Pijoos, WATCH – 'You kill one black person, we kill five white people' – BLF president, SowetanLive, 10 December 2018, https://www.sowetanlive.co.za/news/south-africa/2018-12-10-watch--you-kill-one-black-person-we-kill-five-white-people-blf-president/.

10 *African Communist*, The Guptas aren't the only threat to our NDR – just the most obvious, 7 April 2016, http://www.sacp.org.za/pubs/acommunist/2016/issue191.pdf.

11 Ibid.

12 Ibid.

13 Gareth van Zyl, Stop lying about me, Johann Rupert tells Julius Malema, News24, 10 November 2016, https://www.fin24.com/Economy/stop-lying-about-me-johann-rupert-tells-julius-malema-20161110.

14 News24Wire, Rupert has never challenged me – Malema, 21 June 2017, http://www.polity.org.za/article/rupert-has-never-challenged-me---malema-2017-06-21.

15 Eric Naki, Ramaphosa acting like Zuma with jobs for pals, Malema says, *The Citizen*, 5 February 2018, https://citizen.co.za/news/south-africa/1807509/ramaphosa-acting-

like-zuma-with-jobs-for-pals-in-state-organs-says-malema/.

16 Nkosinathi Shazi, Malema trashes Ramaphosa, demands no-confidence debate before Sona, Huffington Post South Africa, 6 February 2018, https://www.huffington-post.co.za/2018/02/06/malema-trashes-ramaphosa-demands-no-confidence-debate-before-sona_a_23353831/.

17 Deon Wiggett, The Afrikaner privilege machine, News24, 17 December 2017, https://www.news24.com/SouthAfrica/News/the-afrikaner-privilege-machine-20171216.

18 Christopher Rutledge, The seagull's name was Markus Jooste: Steinhoff and the 'Stellenbosch Mafia', Huffington Post South Africa, 12 December 2017, https://www.huffing-tonpost.co.za/christopher-rutledge/the-seagulls-name-was-markus-how-a-patriarchal-culture-at-steinhoff-allowed-it-to-hide-the-losses_a_23303325/.

19 Franz Wild, Janice Kew and Ruth David, How investors bought into the Steinhoff success story despite the red flags, Bloomberg, 18 December 2017, https://www.businesslive.co.za/bd/companies/retail-and-consumer/2017-12-18-how-investors-bought-into-the-steinhoff-success-story-despite-the-red-flags/.

20 Alec Hogg, David Shapiro: Market report, Moneyweb, 7 January 2003, http://www.courtneycapital.co.za/david-shapiro-jse-report-3/.

21 Jana Marais, South Africa's Stellenbosch Mafia, The Africa Report, 5 December 2014, http://www.theafricareport.com/Southern-Africa/south-africas-stellenbosch-Mafia.html.

22 Khaya Koko, Steinhoff scandal is clear mismanagement, corruption at its best, *The Star*, 8 December 2017, https://www.iol.co.za/news/south-africa/gauteng/steinhoff-scandal-is-clear-mismanagement-corruption-at-its-best-12311546.

23 Justin Brown, Steinhoff hits junk as R282bn in value is lost, *City Press*, 10 December 2017, https://www.fin24.com/Companies/Retail/steinhoff-hits-junk-as-r282bn-in-value-is-lost-20171210.

24 Raeesa Pather, Supercool Jooste stays untouched, *Mail & Guardian*, 7 September 2018.

25 Interview with the author, 21 June 2018.

26 Ibid.

27 Sharenet, Top 100 companies by market capital, 29 June 2018, http://www.sharenet.co.za/index.phtml?content=/free/topco.phtml.

28 The World Bank, Overcoming poverty and inequality in South Africa, March 2018, http://documents.worldbank.org/curated/en/530481521735906534/pdf/124521-REV-OUO-South-Africa-Poverty-and-Inequality-Assessment-Report-2018-FINAL-WEB.pdf.

29 African National Congress, Strategy and tactics document, 26 March 2017, http://www.anc.org.za/sites/default/files/2017_Strategy_Tactics.pdf.

30 Malema was leader of the ANC Youth League before he was suspended and eventually ejected from the party in 2012.

31 *African Communist*, The Guptas aren't the only threat to our NDR – just the most obvious, 7 April 2016, http://www.sacp.org.za/pubs/acommunist/2016/issue191.pdf.

32 Interview with the author, 22 August 2018.

2. Stellenbosch: Life in the Bubble

1 Address by Nelson Mandela at Paul Roos Gymnasium, Stellenbosch, 20 March 2002, http://www.mandela.gov.za/mandela_speeches/2002/020320_paulroos.htm.

2 See Wilbur Smith, *Rage*. London: Heinemann, 1987.

3 Gustav Thiel, Politicians and business leaders laud Daling, Independent Online, 6 February 2002, https://www.iol.co.za/news/south-africa/politicians-and-business-leaders-laud-daling-78918.

4 Hermann Giliomee, *The Afrikaners*. Cape Town: Tafelberg, 2003.

5 Ibid.

6 Ibid.

7 Ibid.

8 Ebbe Dommisse, *Anton Rupert: A Biography*. Cape Town: Tafelberg, 2005.

9 Ibid.

10 Clem Sunter, The economic liberation of Afrikaners, News24, 24 March 2010, https://www.news24.com/Columnists/ClemSunter/The-economic-liberation-of-Afrikaners-20100324.

11 Adriaan Basson and Pieter du Toit, *Enemy of the People: How Jacob Zuma Stole South Africa and how the People Fought Back*. Cape Town: Jonathan Ball Publishers, 2017.

12 Ebbe Dommisse, *Anton Rupert: A Biography*. Cape Town: Tafelberg, 2005.

13 Mpumelelo Mkhabela, Rupert's interview provides hard lessons for those willing to hear them, News24, 6 December 2018, https://www.news24.com/Columnists/Mpumelelo_Mkhabela/ruperts-interview-provides-hard-lessons-to-those-willing-listen-20181206.

14 Hermann Giliomee, *Die Laaste Afrikanerleiers*. Cape Town: Tafelberg, 2012.

15 Hermann Giliomee, *The Afrikaners*. Cape Town: Tafelberg, 2003.

16 HB Thom, *D.F. Malan*. Cape Town: Tafelberg, 1980.

17 Lindie Koorts, *D.F. Malan and the Rise of Afrikaner Nationalism*. Cape Town: Tafelberg, 2014.

18 CFJ Muller, *Sonop in die Suide: Geboorte en Groei van die Nasionale Pers*, 1915–1948. Nasionale Boekhandel, 1990.

19 Ibid.

20 Henry Kenney, *Verwoerd, Architect of Apartheid*. Cape Town: Jonathan Ball Publishers, 2016.

21 Ibid.

22 Ibid.

23 Hermann Giliomee, The war against Afrikaans at Stellenbosch, Politicsweb, 28 April 2016, http://www.politicsweb.co.za/opinion/the-war-against-afrikaans-at-stellenbosch.

24 Marelize Barnard, Engels maak deure oop, sê De Villiers, Netwerk24, 25 March 2018, https://www.netwerk24.com/Nuus/Onderwys/engels-maak-deure-oop-se-de-villiers-20180325.

25 Statistics South Africa, Quarterly Labour Force Survey, 30 October 2018, http://www. statssa.gov.za/publications/P0211/P02113rdQuarter2018.pdf.

26 Stellenbosch Heritage Foundation, Spatial development framework, June 2014.

27 The South Africa Wealth Report, AfrAsia Bank and New World Wealth, March 2018, https://www.afrasiabank.com/media/2770/south-africa-2018.pdf.

28 Ibid.

29 Mark Swilling, Sustainable Stellenbosch: Opening dialogues, SunMedia, 2012.

30 Stellenbosch Heritage Foundation, Spatial development framework, June 2014.

31 Simon Nicks, Sustainable Stellenbosch: Opening dialogues, SunMedia, 2012.

32 Ronnie Donaldson, The production of quartered spaces in Stellenbosch, inaugural address, University of Stellenbosch, Department of Geography and Environmental Studies, 4 September 2014, http://www.stellenboschheritage.co.za/wp-content/uploads/intreerede-final-email.pdf.

3. *The white monopoly capitalist*

1 The author interviewed Johann Rupert at his family home on 21 June and 22 August 2018. This chapter draws from those interviews.

2 SABC Digital News, Jack Ma addresses the inaugural SA Investment Summit dinner, YouTube, 26 October 2018, https://www.youtube.com/watch?v=dMKvxQKfn3k.

3 Alec Hogg, Ramaphosa: SA's entrepreneurs need to be treated like heroes, BizNews, 26 October 2018, https://www.biznews.com/undictated/2018/10/29/ramaphosa-sa-entrepreneurs-treated-heroes.

4 Author's notes from an EFF press conference where Julius Malema addressed the media in Braamfontein, Johannesburg, 16 October 2018.

5 Jenni Evans, EFF sent Ruperts packing, says Malema, News24, 2 February 2019, https://www.news24.com/SouthAfrica/News/eff-sent-ruperts-packing-says-malema-20190202.

6 Correspondence between the author and Floyd Shivambu, 4 February 2019.

7 South African Heritage Resources Agency, http://www.sahra.org.za/sahris/sites/920830002.

8 In 2018 the Hermanus suburbs of Zwelihle and Hawston were plagued by incidents of violence caused by anger about the allocation of houses.

9 Ebbe Dommisse, *Anton Rupert: A Biography*. Cape Town: Tafelberg, 2006.

10 Ibid.

11 Pieter du Toit, How Rupert was warned about Bell Pottinger, Huffington Post South Africa, 25 January 2017.

12 Marc Hasenfuss, Johann Rupert vexed by 'spin campaign', *Business Day*, 2 December 2016.

13 Ed Caesar, The reputation-laundering firm that ruined its own reputation, *The New Yorker*, 25 June 2018, https://www.newyorker.com/magazine/2018/06/25/the-reputation-laundering-firm-that-ruined-its-own-reputation.

14 Ibid.

15 Ibid.

16 The Guptas' news channel was discontinued by DStv in August 2018.

17 According to Forbes, on 13 April 2019, https://www.forbes.com/profile/johann-rupert/#1c42cb974922.

18 The Appeal of Conscience Award was presented by the foundation of the same name on 26 September 2018. His co-recipient was Christine Lagarde, the managing director of the International Monetary Fund.

19 Communication from Johann Rupert to the author, September 2018.

4. The first Afrikaner businessman

1 Dirk and Johanna de Villiers, *Paul Sauer*, Tafelberg Publishers, 1977.

2 This is calculated on the basis of the exchange rate of R13.23 against the dollar on 25 July 2018.

3 Staff writer, Nicky Oppenheimer overtakes Johann Rupert as five South Africans are dollar billionaires, BusinessLive, 8 March 2018, https://www.businesslive.co.za/bd/national/2018-03-08-nicky-oppenheimer-overtakes-johann-rupert-as-five-south-africans-are-dollar-billionaires/. The City Press Wealth Index, published on 29 July 2018, put Rupert down as the eighth richest South African, with an estimated wealth of R13.2 billion. The Oppenheimer family did not feature, while Ivan Glasenberg from Glencore came it at no.1 with a fortune of R71.8 billion.

4 According to Forbes.com, accessed on 25 July 2018, https://www.forbes.com/profile/nicky-oppenheimer/#c06ea943b93d

5 Ibid.

6 Corinne Gretler and Dylan Griffiths, South Africa's richest man calls Zuma's policy theft, Bloomberg, 13 September 2017, https://www.bloomberg.com/news/articles/2017-09-13/south-africa-s-richest-man-calls-president-zuma-s-policy-theft.

7 Pieter du Toit, Rupert: 'Injustices in SA need to be corrected', Huffington Post South Africa, 14 September 2017, https://www.huffingtonpost.co.za/2017/09/13/rupert-injustices-in-sa-need-to-be-corrected_a_23207963/.

8 ANC statement on Johan Rupert's remarks on radical economic transformation, 14 September 2017, http://www.anc.org.za/content/anc-statement-johan-ruperts-remarks-radical-economic-transformation.

9 Thami Mazwai, Rupert's theft claim is a kick in the teeth for black South Africans, Business Report, 19 September 2017.

10 Edna Molewa, Radical transformation the only way to halt monopoly grip on the economy, *Business Day*, 29 September 2017.

11 Tim Cohen, Afrikaner plan a far cry from ANC looting, *Business Day*, 2 October 2017.

12 Ibid.

13 Report of the Truth and Reconciliation Commission, Volume Four, Institutional

hearing: Business and labour, http://www.justice.gov.za/trc/report/finalreport/ Volume%204.pdf.

14 Hermann Giliomee, *The Afrikaners*, Tafelberg, 2003.

15 Ibid.

16 Henry Kenney, *Verwoerd: Architect of Apartheid*, Jonathan Ball Publishers, 1980.

17 Hermann Giliomee, *The Afrikaners*, Tafelberg, 2003.

18 Ebbe Dommisse, *Anton Rupert: A Biography*, Tafelberg, 2005.

19 Ibid.

20 Ibid.

21 Ibid.

22 Interview by the author with Michiel le Roux, 1 August 2018.

23 Ebbe Dommisse, *Anton Rupert: A Biography*, Tafelberg, 2005.

24 Rupert decided on the name Rembrandt for his company after dreaming about it one night. It is named after the Dutch master, and according to him had no negative branding connotations, writes Rupert's biographer, Ebbe Dommisse.

25 Anton Rupert obituary, *The Scotsman*, 24 January 2006, https://www.scotsman.com/ news/obituaries/anton-rupert-1-689447.

26 Ebbe Dommisse, *Anton Rupert: A Biography*, Tafelberg, 2005.

27 Ibid.

28 Ibid.

29 Ibid.

30 Ibid.

31 Interview by the author with Michiel le Roux, 1 August 2018.

32 Ibid.

5. *Making money during apartheid*

1 Interview by the author with Johann Rupert, 22 August 2018.

2 Ebbe Dommisse, *Anton Rupert: A Biography*. Cape Town: Tafelberg, 2005.

3 Hermann Giliomee, *The Afrikaners*. Cape Town: Tafelberg, 2003.

4 Ibid.

5 Ebbe Dommisse, *Anton Rupert: A Biography*. Cape Town: Tafelberg, 2005.

6 Henry Kenney, *Verwoerd: Architect of Apartheid*. Johannesburg and Cape Town: Jonathan Ball Publishers, 1980.

7 Ebbe Dommisse, *Anton Rupert: A Biography*. Cape Town: Tafelberg, 2005.

8 Ibid.

9 Ibid.

10 Ibid.

11 Jopie Fourie was an Afrikaner military officer who was executed by the Louis Botha

government after the rebellion of 1914. He subsequently became a martyr and an almost mythological Afrikaner figure.

12 Ebbe Dommisse, *Anton Rupert: A Biography*. Cape Town: Tafelberg, 2005.

13 Ibid.

14 Ibid.

15 Allen Drury, *A Very Strange Society: A Journey to the Heart of South Africa*. New York: Trident Press, 1967.

16 The author interviewed Johann Rupert on 16 and 22 August 2018; this section draws from those interviews.

17 Andringa Street is one of the main thoroughfares in Stellenbosch. It was declared part of white Stellenbosch in terms of the Group Areas Act and all Coloured people were removed from their homes there.

18 Truth and Reconciliation Commission, Special hearing: business, 12 November 1997, http://www.justice.gov.za/trc/special/business/busin2.htm.

19 Ibid.

20 Ibid.

21 Ibid.

22 Ibid.

23 Ibid.

24 Ibid.

25 Ibid.

26 Truth and Reconciliation Commission, Final Report, Volume 4, 1998, http://www.justice.gov.za/trc/report/index.htm.

27 Ibid.

28 Ibid.

29 Ibid.

30 Ibid.

31 Ibid.

32 Ibid.

33 Hennie van Vuuren, *Apartheid, Guns and Money*. Jacana Publishers, 2017.

6. *Old money and the Stellenbosch originals*

1 The author interviewed Edwin Hertzog on 21 June 2018, from which material is taken for this chapter.

2 The author interviewed Jannie Durand on 22 June and 3 August 2018, from which material is taken for this chapter.

3 Durand's father, Professor Jaap Durand, was a theologian and the first vice chancellor of the University of the Western Cape. He is credited with leading the institution from

being a so-called 'bush college' to becoming a fully fledged university. He was lauded for building the university in the face of apartheid regulations, opting to 'lead demonstrations, face rubber bullets and teargas' according to Professor Stanley Ridge, and was also the target of apartheid dirty tricks. During his time at the university, the institution challenged apartheid from a Black Consciousness perspective, and his long service in churches frequented by black congregants gained him acceptance among black staff members. Mandela praised Professor Durand's activism during a speech at the university in 1996.

4 On 27 August 2018, according to Sharenet. As for South Africa's other private hospital groups, Netcare was valued at R43 billion and Life Healthcare at R40 billion.

5 Author's interview with Edwin Hertzog on 21 June 2018.

6 Leopard Creek Estate, in Malelane, on the edge of the Kruger National Park, is Johann Rupert's exclusive members-only golf estate.

7 Otto is one of the founders of Capitec Bank; Schoeman is a stockbroker.

8 Daan Hoogenhout was one of the original Rembrandt partners, alongside Rupert and Hertzog.

9 Ebbe Dommisse, *Anton Rupert: A Biography*. Cape Town: Tafelberg, 2005.

10 Cape Business News, Proud days for the Ruperts, 22 September 2008.

11 Teboho Bosiu, et al, Growth and strategies of large and leading firms: Remgro Limited company assessment, Centre for Competition, Regulation and Economic Development, University of Johannesburg, November 2017.

12 Ibid.

13 Ibid.

14 See Remgro governance framework, https://remgro.com/governance-and-sustainability/governance-framework.

15 See Richemont, group structure, https://www.richemont.com/group/corporate-governance/group-structure.html.

16 Bloomberg, 17 August 2018, https://www.bloomberg.com/quote/CFR:SJ.

17 Tamar Kahn, SA's private hospitals provide R55bn GDP injection, study finds, *Business Day*, 26 September 2016, https://www.businesslive.co.za/bd/economy/2017-09-26-sas-private-hospitals-provide-r55bn-gdp-injection-study-finds.

7. The roar of the maroon machine

1 South African Press Association, Roux elected new Saru CEO, News24, 30 July 2010, https://www.sport24.co.za/Rugby/Roux-elected-new-SARU-CEO-20100730.

2 Adriaan Basson, Pieter du Toit and Pauli van Wyk, Valke bekyk rugbybaas, *Beeld*, 21 November 2013.

3 Ibid.

4 Ibid.

5 Ibid.

6 Answering affidavit by Professor Leopoldt van Huyssteen, in the matter between Pieter

du Toit, Media24 and Stellenbosch University, case no. 10332/14.

7 Sport24, Saru approves extension of Saru CEO's contract, 14 August 2014, News24, https://www.news24.com/Archives/Witness/Saru-approves-extension-of-CEO-Rouxs-contract-20150430.

8 Founding and supplementary papers, in the civil matter between Stellenbosch University and Jurie Roux, Western Cape Division of the High Court.

9 Ibid.

10 Ibid.

11 KPMG, Report on Stellenbosch University Rugby Club and student fees office, 12 December 2013.

12 Ibid.

13 Ibid.

14 Ibid.

15 Ibid.

16 KPMG, Supplementary report on Stellenbosch University Rugby Club and fees office investigation, 27 March 2014.

17 George Germishuys, Jurie Roux ontken enige skuld, Netwerk24, 8 June 2016, https://www.netwerk24.com/Nuus/Hof/jurie-roux-ontken-enige-skuld-20160608.

18 Adriaan Basson and Pieter du Toit, Jurie baat by sparries, Netwerk24, 5 February 2016, https://www.pressreader.com/south-africa/beeld/20160205/281479275452048.

19 Cosatu, Western Cape, Statement on Springbok rugby, 26 June 2018.

8. Markus Jooste and his big ego

1 Interview by the author with Jannie Durand, 22 June 2018.

2 Isabelle Huys, A history of 'koshuisrugby' at Stellenbosch, Master's dissertation, University of Stellenbosch, March 2008.

3 Interview by the author with Piet Mouton, 3 August 2018.

4 Interview by the author with an anonymous Stellenbosch businessman, 1 August 2018.

5 Interview by the author with Jannie Durand, 22 June 2018.

6 Interview by the author with Piet Mouton, 3 August 2018.

7 Sponsorship boost for Blitzboks, News 24, 12 December 2015, https://www.sport24.co.za/Rugby/Sevens/sponsor-boost-for-blitzboks-20151215.

8 Ibid.

9 Piet Naudé et al, Business perspectives on the Steinhoff saga, University of Stellenbosch Business School, June 2018, https://www.usb.ac.za/wp-content/uploads/2018/06/Steinhoff_Revision_28_06_2018_websmall.pdf.

10 Steinhoff International Holdings prospectus, 1998.

11 Alec Hogg, The Steinhoff story: Revisiting the roots of today's R260-billion giant, BizNews, March 2006, https://www.biznews.com/sa-investing/2015/06/19/the-steinhoff-

story-revisiting-humble-roots-of-a-r260bn-giant; Piet Naudé et al, Business perspectives on the Steinhoff saga, University of Stellenbosch Business School, June 2018, https://www.usb.ac.za/wp-content/uploads/2018/06/Steinhoff_Revision_28_06_2018_web-small.pdf.

12 Ibid.

13 Ibid.

14 Alec Hogg, Meet Markus Jooste: Our in-depth interview with the Steinhoff CEO, BizNews, June 2016, https://www.biznews.com/undictated/2017/12/14/markus-jooste-former-steinhoff-ceo.

15 James-Brent Styan, *Steinhoff en die Stellenbosse Boys*. Pretoria: LAPA Publishers, 2018.

16 Alec Hogg, The Steinhoff story: Revisiting the roots of today's R260-billion giant, BizNews, March 2006, https://www.biznews.com/sa-investing/2015/06/19/the-steinhoff-story-revisiting-humble-roots-of-a-r260bn-giant.

17 Steinhoff International Holdings prospectus, 1998.

18 Alec Hogg, Meet Markus Jooste: Our in-depth interview with the Steinhoff CEO, BizNews, June 2016, https://www.biznews.com/undictated/2017/12/14/markus-jooste-former-steinhoff-ceo.

19 Piet Naudé et al, Business perspectives on the Steinhoff saga, University of Stellenbosch Business School, June 2018, https://www.usb.ac.za/wp-content/uploads/2018/06/Steinhoff_Revision_28_06_2018_websmall.pdf.

20 Steinhoff International Holdings prospectus, 1998.

21 Ibid.

22 Alec Hogg, Meet Markus Jooste: Our in-depth interview with the Steinhoff CEO, BizNews, June 2016, https://www.biznews.com/undictated/2017/12/14/markus-jooste-former-steinhoff-ceo.

23 Piet Naudé et al, Business perspectives on the Steinhoff saga, University of Stellenbosch Business School, June 2018, https://www.usb.ac.za/wp-content/uploads/2018/06/Steinhoff_Revision_28_06_2018_websmall.pdf.

24 Ibid.

25 Ibid.

26 Steinhoff International Holdings N.V. prospectus, 19 November 2015.

27 Matthew Davies, Steinhoff: The Ikea of Africa?, BBC, 13 July 2016, https://www.bbc.com/news/business-36781821.

28 Steinhoff International Holdings N.V., Frankfurt pre-listing prospectus, 19 November 2015.

29 Alec Hogg, Meet Markus Jooste: Our in-depth interview with the Steinhoff CEO, BizNews, June 2016, https://www.biznews.com/undictated/2017/12/14/markus-jooste-former-steinhoff-ceo.

30 Alec Hogg, Markus Jooste – On losing bids, building Steinhoff and drawing inspiration, BizNews, 3 June 2016, https://www.biznews.com/entrepreneur/2016/06/03/markus-jooste-on-losing-bids-building-steinhoff-and-drawing-inspiration.

31 Interview by the author with Johann Rupert, 22 August 2018.

32 Alec Hogg, Meet Markus Jooste: Our in-depth interview with the Steinhoff CEO, BizNews, June 2016, https://www.biznews.com/undictated/2017/12/14/markus-jooste-former-steinhoff-ceo.

33 Ibid.

34 Alec Hogg, Special report podcast: Jannie Mouton – executive chairman, PSG Group, Moneyweb, 18 April 2011, https://www.moneyweb.co.za/archive/special-report-podcast-jannie-mouton-executive-ch/.

35 Jannie Mouton with Carié Maas, *And Then They Fired Me*. Cape Town: Tafelberg Publishers, 2011.

9. Twickenham, test rugby ... and the Germans

1 Interview by the author with Jannie Durand, 22 June 2018.

2 Interview by the author with Johann Rupert, 22 August 2018.

3 Andreas Dörnfelder, Gertrud Hussla and Peter Köhler, Police raid overshadows Steinhoff IPO, *Handelsblatt*, 7 December 2015, https://global.handelsblatt.com/companies/police-raid-overshadows-public-listing-388392.

4 Mark Allix, Tax raid ricks Steinhoff subsidiary, *Business Day*, 7 December 2015, https://www.pressreader.com/south-africa/business-day/20151207/281513635085668.

5 Ibid.

6 Andries Mahlangu, German tax probe hits Steinhoff on the JSE, *Sunday Times*, 6 December 2015, https://www.pressreader.com/south-africa/sunday-times/20151206/282394103380134.

7 Rob Rose, Steinhoff's tax headache, *Financial Mail*, 11 December 2015, https://www.pressreader.com/south-africa/financial-mail/20151211.

8 Ibid.

9 Ibid.

10 Steinhoff International Holdings N.V., Frankfurt pre-listing prospectus, 19 November 2015.

11 Andreas Dörnfelder, Gertrud Hussla and Peter Köhler, Police raid overshadows Steinhoff IPO, *Handelsblatt*, 7 December 2015, https://global.handelsblatt.com/companies/police-raid-overshadows-public-listing-388392.

12 Christo Wiese's testimony before the Standing Committee on Finance, Parliament, Parliamentary Monitoring Group, 31 January 2018, https://pmg.org.za/committee-meeting/25753/.

13 Alec Hogg, Meet Markus Jooste: Our in-depth interview with the Steinhoff CEO, BizNews, June 2016, https://www.biznews.com/undictated/2017/12/14/markus-jooste-former-steinhoff-ceo.

14 Alec Hogg, Markus Jooste on Steinhoff's history-making deal, BizNews, 25 November 2014,

https://www.biznews.com/sa-investing/2014/11/25/markus-jooste-todays-history-making-deal-r200bn-steinhoff-ready-take-world.

15 https://www.biznews.com/sa-investing/2014/11/25/markus-jooste-todays-history-making-deal-r200bn-steinhoff-ready-take-world

16 Alec Hogg, Markus Jooste: After today's history-making deal, R200bn Steinhoff ready to take on the world, BizNews, 25 November 2014, https://www.biznews.com/sa-investing/2014/11/25/markus-jooste-todays-history-making-deal-r200bn-steinhoff-ready-take-world.

17 Christo Wiese's testimony before the Standing Committee on Finance, Parliament, Parliamentary Monitoring Group, 31 January 2018, https://pmg.org.za/committee-meeting/25753/.

18 Jannie Mouton, with Carié Maas, *And Then They Fired Me*. Cape Town: Tafelberg, 2011.

19 Bruce Whitfield, PSG chair Jannie Mouton opens up (kind of) about Steinhoff, 702, 12 December 2017, http://www.702.co.za/articles/284417/psg-chair-jannie-mouton-opens-up-about-steinhoff.

10. Three red flags: Norfolk pines, racehorses and mattresses

1 Alec Hogg, Markus Jooste – On losing bids, building Steinhoff and drawing inspiration, BizNews, 3 June 2016, https://www.biznews.com/entrepreneur/2016/06/03/markus-jooste-on-losing-bids-building-steinhoff-and-drawing-inspiration.

2 Ursula Schwarzer and Sven Clausen, Chef des Möbelherstellers Steinhoff im Visier der Justiz, Manager Magazin, 24 August 2017, http://www.manager-magazin.de/unternehmen/artikel/steinhoff-ermittlungen-gegen-markus-jooste-wegen-bilanzfael-schung-a-1164191.html.

3 Ibid.

4 Alexander Kell, Janice Kew and Karen Matussek, Investors dump Steinhoff on CEO fraud report, Bloomberg, 24 August 2017, https://www.fin24.com/Companies/Retail/steinhoff-slumps-on-report-ceo-is-being-probed-in-fraud-case-20170824.

5 Steinhoff International Holdings N.V., Response to press statement published by *Manager Magazin*, SENS announcement, 24 August 2017, https://www.moneyweb.co.za/mny_sens/steinhoff-international-holdings-n-v-response-to-press-statement-published-by-manager-magazin/.

6 Bruce Whitfield, German prosecutors probing Steinhoff CEO Markus Jooste (for accounting fraud), 702, 24 August 2017, http://www.702.co.za/articles/269785/german-prosecutors-investigating-steinhoff-ceo-markus-jooste-for-accounting-fraud.

7 Palesa Tshandu, Wiese quashed 'rumour-mongers', *Sunday Times*, 27 August 2017, https://www.businesslive.co.za/bt/business-and-economy/2017-08-27-wiese-quashes-rumour-mongers/.

8 Ibid.

9 Prinesha Naidoo, Steinhoff slams German fraud allegations, Moneyweb, 25 August 2017, https://www.moneyweb.co.za/news/companies-and-deals/steinhoff-slams-german-fraud-allegations/.

10 Palesa Tshandu, Wiese quashed 'rumour-mongers', *Sunday Times*, 27 August 2017, https://www.businesslive.co.za/bt/business-and-economy/2017-08-27-wiese-quashes-rumour-mongers/.

11 Wolfgang Dreschler and Gertrud Hussla, Pulling back the curtain on furniture-maker Steinhoff, *Handelsblatt Global*, 27 November 2017, https://global.handelsblatt.com/companies/pulling-back-the-curtain-on-furniture-maker-steinhoff-south-africa-germany-858122.

12 Sandile Mchunu, Analysis: Steinhoff makes STAR debut on JSE, Business Report, 21 September 2017, https://www.iol.co.za/business-report/analysis-steinhoff-makes-star-debut-on-the-jse-11296871.

13 Giulietta Talevi, Steinhoff is not Christo Wiese's parking place, says Markus Jooste, *Business Day*, 22 September 2017, https://www.businesslive.co.za/bd/companies/2017-09-22-steinhoff-not-christo-wieses-parking-place-for-assets/.

14 Ibid.

15 Giulietta Talevi, Inside the mind of Markus Jooste, *Financial Mail*, 12 October 2017, https://www.businesslive.co.za/fm/features/2017-10-12-inside-the-mind-of-markus-jooste/.

16 Wolfgang Dreschler and Gertrud Hussla, Pulling back the curtain on furniture-maker Steinhoff, *Handelsblatt Global*, 27 November 2017, https://global.handelsblatt.com/companies/pulling-back-the-curtain-on-furniture-maker-steinhoff-south-africa-germany-858122.

17 Interview by the author with Piet Mouton, 3 August 2018.

18 Interview by the author with Johann Rupert, 22 August 2018.

19 New sales company announcement, *Sporting Post*, 2 September 2011, https://www.sportingpost.co.za/2011/09/new-sales-company-announcement/.

20 Alec Hogg, Meet Markus Jooste: Our in-depth interview with the Steinhoff CEO, BizNews, June 2016, https://www.biznews.com/undictated/2017/12/14/markus-jooste-former-steinhoff-ceo.

21 Ibid.

22 Interview mit Markus Jooste, SportWeltTV, 13 February 2015, https://www.youtube.com/watch?v=_SBA3KTAsYc&list=PLT40dekSvvOM0ydPresb8ruMiP0qmWfkm.

23 Ibid.

24 Alec Hogg, Meet Markus Jooste: Our in-depth interview with the Steinhoff CEO, BizNews, June 2016, https://www.biznews.com/undictated/2017/12/14/markus-jooste-former-steinhoff-ceo.

25 Greg Wood, Epsom to feature 'Poundland Hill' as part of Derby Festival sponsorship, *The Guardian*, 11 May 2017, https://www.theguardian.com/sport/2017/may/11/epsom-rename-famous-derby-festival-area-poundland-hill-sponsorship-horse-racing.

26 Harriet Fuller, 'I've got a hill! Poundland Hill!' Markus Jooste buys a hill to watch his horse Douglas Macarthur run in the Epsom Derby, *The Sun*, 12 May 2017, https://www.thesun.co.uk/sport/horseracing/3538915/poundland-hill-markus-jooste-buys-a-hill-to-watch-his-horse-douglas-macarthur-run-in-the-epsom-derby/.

27 Stafford Thomas, Jooste's horses: Shutting the stable door …', *Financial Mail*, 21 December 2017, https://www.businesslive.co.za/fm/money-and-investing/2017-12-21-joostes-horses-shutting-the-stable-door-/#.

28 Ibid.

29 Angelique Serrao, How the Markus Jooste scandal may impact SA's biggest horse racing auction, News24, 19 January 2018, https://www.fin24.com/Companies/Agribusiness/how-the-markus-jooste-scandal-may-impact-sas-biggest-horse-racing-auction-20180119.

30 Ibid.

31 Ibid.

32 Interview by the author with Johann Rupert, 22 August 2018.

33 Alec Hogg, Meet Markus Jooste: Our in-depth interview with the Steinhoff CEO, BizNews, June 2016, https://www.biznews.com/undictated/2017/12/14/markus-jooste-former-steinhoff-ceo.

11. *The artful dodger: Jooste runs away*

1 Interview by the author with an anonymous Stellenbosch businessman, 1 August 2018.

2 Africa retail giant STAR reveals expansion plans, CNBC Africa, 4 December 2017, https://www.cnbcafrica.com/videos/2017/12/04/african-retail-giant-stars-ceo-reveals-expansion-plans/.

3 Joint meeting of the Parliamentary Standing Committee on Finance, the Standing Committee on Public Accounts and the Select Committee on Finance, 29 August 2018.

4 Ibid.

5 Steinhoff International Holdings NV, Announcement of 2017 results and update on the 2017 audit process, SENS announcement, 4 December 2017, http://www.steinhoffinternational.com/downloads/2017/1-Steinhoff-Announcement-update-on-audit-process-JSE-FY17-4-December-2017.pdf.

6 Linda Ensor, Steinhoff director spills the beans about accounting irregularities and Jooste's disappearing act, BusinessLive, 31 January 2018, https://www.businesslive.co.za/bd/companies/retail-and-consumer/2018-01-31-steinhoff-director-spills-the-beans-about-accounting-irregularities-and-joostes-disappearing-act/#.

7 Giulietta Talevi, No bottom in sight for Steinhoff, *Financial Mail*, 21 December 2017, https://www.businesslive.co.za/fm/money-and-investing/2017-12-21-corporate-governance-no-bottom-in-sight-for-steinhoff/.

8 Nellie Brand-Jonker, Jooste bly weg – en toe die SMS …, Netwerk24, 31 January 2018, https://www.netwerk24.com/Sake/Maatskappye/jooste-bly-weg-en-toe-die-sms-20180131.

9 Joint Meeting of the Parliamentary Standing Committee on Finance, Standing Committee on Public Accounts and the Portfolio Committee on Public Service and Administration, Parliamentary Monitoring Group, 31 January 2018, https://pmg.org.za/committee-meeting/25753/.

10 James-Brent Styan, *Steinhoff en die Stellenbosse Boys*, LAPA Publishers, 2018.

11 Robert Laing, Steinhoff shares plunge 60% as CEO Markus Jooste quits, BusinessLive, 6 December 2017, https://www.businesslive.co.za/bd/companies/retail-and-consumer/2017-12-06-markus-jooste-quits-as-steinhoff-ceo/.

12 Ibid.

13 Ray Mahlaka, Steinhoff shares plunge after CEO Markus Jooste quits, Moneyweb, 6 December 2017, https://www.moneyweb.co.za/news/companies-and-deals/steinhoff-ceo-markus-jooste-quits/.

14 Sandile Mchunu, Dark days as Steinhoff loses R100-billion, *Business Report*, 7 December 2017, https://www.iol.co.za/business-report/dark-days-as-steinhoff-loses-r100-billion-12298121; in Frankfurt, shares fell by 52% to €1.42 per share, while STAR's share price dropped by almost 30% to R17.55 per share.

15 Abram Brown, South African billionaire's fortune plunges more than $2-billion in a day amid accounting scandal, Forbes, 6 December 2017, https://www.forbes.com/sites/abrambrown/2017/12/06/steinhoff-christo-wiese-accounting-scandal/#5d604bdd7dbf.

16 Hanna Ziady, Claims against Steinhoff uncover revolving tangle of dodgy deals, *Business Day*, 14 December 2017, https://www.businesslive.co.za/bd/companies/retail-and-consumer/2017-12-14-claims-against-steinhoff-uncover-revolving-tangle-of-dodgy-deals/#.

17 Jessica Dye, Moody's slash Steinhoff rating amid accounts probe, *Financial Times*, 7 December 2017, https://www.ft.com/content/69c0fbc2-fd17-3f88-a228-e3a3a15b42ba.

18 Warren Thompson, Collateral damage: Who owns Steinhoff?, Moneyweb, 6 December 2017, https://www.moneyweb.co.za/news/economy/collateral-damage-who-owns-steinhoff/; see also Eugenie du Preez, Steinhoff fallout: Fedusa, PIC to discuss pension damage control, Fin24, 11 December 2017, https://www.fin24.com/Companies/Retail/steinhoff-fallout-fedusa-pic-to-discuss-pension-damage-control-20171211.

19 Magda Wierzycka, Hard questions about Steinhoff and asset managers, Fin24, 7 December 2017, https://www.fin24.com/Opinion/magda-wierzycka-asks-hard-questions-about-steinhoff-and-asset-managers-20171207.

20 Ibid.

21 Stuart Theobald, Steinhoff catastrophe biggest yet in SA and ranks among notorious global collapses, 11 December 2017, https://www.businesslive.co.za/bd/opinion/columnists/2017-12-11-stuart-theobald-steinhoff-catastrophe-biggest-yet-in-sa-and-ranks-among-notorious-global-collapses/.

22 Ibid.

23 Aldi Schoeman and Riana de Lange, Steinhoff: Wiese skuld?, *Rapport*, 10 December 2017, https://www.netwerk24.com/Sake/Maatskappye/steinhoff-wiese-skuld-is-dit-20171210.

24 Interview by the author with an anonymous Stellenbosch businessman, 1 August 2018.

25 Interview by the author with Piet Mouton, 3 August 2018.

26 Ibid.

27 Interview by the author with Jannie Durand, 22 June 2018.

28 Interview by the author with an anonymous Stellenbosch businessman, 1 August 2018.

12. Christo Wiese's 'little mistake'

1 Interview by the author with Edwin Hertzog, 21 June 2018.

2 Business Day TV, Steinhoff snaps up 92% stake in Pepkor for R63bn, 25 November 2014, https://www.youtube.com/watch?v=0YBGtBBpu2E.

3 BusinessTech, Wiese loses billionaire status as Steinhoff continues massive sell-off, 8 December 2017, https://businesstech.co.za/news/wealth/215497/wiese-loses-billion-aire-status-as-steinhoff-continues-massive-sell-off/.

4 Janice Kew, Billionaire Wiese takes blow as Brait struggles with losses, Bloomberg, 19 June 2018, https://www.moneyweb.co.za/news/companies-and-deals/billionaire-wiese-takes-blow-as-brait-struggles-with-losses/.

5 As of 4 September 2018. Five South Africans feature on the list: Nicky Oppenheimer, Johann Rupert, Koos Bekker, Stephen Saad and Patrice Motsepe.

6 See Forbes Real Time Billionaires, https://www.forbes.com/billionaires/list/45/#version:-realtime.

7 Interview by the author with Edwin Hertzog, 21 June 2018.

8 Interview by the author with Piet Mouton, 3 August 2018.

9 Willemien Brümmer, Ek sou Jooste wou vra: 'Hoekom?', Netwerk24, 27 April 2018, https://www.netwerk24.com/Nuus/Algemeen/christo-wiese-praat-met-willemien-brummer-ek-sou-jooste-wou-vra-hoekom-20180427.

10 Hanlie Retief, Hanlie Retief gesels met Christo Wiese, Rapport, 29 April 2018, https://www.netwerk24.com/Stemme/Menings/hanlie-retief-gesels-met-christo-wiese-20180429-2.

11 Alec Hogg, Christo Wiese: Insider view on Steinhoff CEO Jooste's corporate crime of the century, BizNews, 28 April 2018, https://www.biznews.com/premium/2018/04/28/christo-wiese-jooste-suing-steinhoff.

12 Willemien Brümmer, Ek sou Jooste wou vra: 'Hoekom?', Netwerk24, 27 April 2018, https://www.netwerk24.com/Nuus/Algemeen/christo-wiese-praat-met-willemien-brummer-ek-sou-jooste-wou-vra-hoekom-20180427.

13 Alec Hogg, Christo Wiese: Insider view on Steinhoff CEO Jooste's corporate crime of the century, BizNews, 28 April 2018, https://www.biznews.com/premium/2018/04/28/christo-wiese-jooste-suing-steinhoff.

14 Rob Rose, Giulietta Talevi and Adele Shevel, Inside Steinhoff's house of cards, *Financial Mail*, 14 December 2017.

15 Franz Wild, Janice Kew and Ruth David, Five decades to build Steinhoff, two days to kill its share price, Bloomberg, 18 December 2017, https://www.biznews.com/wealth-building/2017/12/18/steinhoff-fraud-wiese-jooste.

16 Patrick Cairns, Steinhoff: We didn't believe the numbers, Moneyweb, 8 December 2017, https://www.moneyweb.co.za/news/companies-and-deals/steinhoff-we-didnt-believe-the-numbers/.

17 Nellie Brand-Jonker and Nadine Theron, Steinhoff brand wyl base knus langs Markus woon, Netwerk24, 5 May 2018, https://www.netwerk24.com/Nuus/Algemeen/steinhoff-brand-wyl-base-knus-langs-markus-woon-20180504.

18 Ibid.

19 Pieter du Toit, Markus Jooste might be finished but his Hermanus home ain't, Huffington Post South Africa, 7 December 2017.

20 Garreth van Niekerk, Builders left jobless as construction of Markus Jooste's holiday home stops, Huffington Post South Africa, 8 December 2017, https://www.huffingtonpost.co.za/2017/12/08/builders-left-jobless-as-construction-on-markus-joostes-holiday-home-stops_a_23301048/.

21 Garreth van Niekerk, Markus Jooste's home tagged with insulting graffiti, Huffington Post South Africa, 28 December 2018, https://www.huffingtonpost.co.za/2017/12/28/markus-joostes-home-tagged-with-insulting-graffiti_a_23318423/.

22 Interview by the author with Piet Mouton, 3 August 2018.

23 Interview by the author with an anonymous Stellenbosch businessman, 1 August 2018.

24 Piet Naudé, Brett Hamilton, Marius Ungerer, Daniel Malan and Mias de Klerk, Business perspectives on the Steinhoff saga, University of Stellenbosch Business School, June 2018, https://www.usb.ac.za/wp-content/uploads/2018/06/Steinhoff_Revision_28_06_2018_websmall.pdf.

25 Parliamentary Monitoring Group, meeting of the standing committee on finance, 31 January 2018, http://pmg-assets.s3-website-eu-west-1.amazonaws.com/180131joint-finance1.mp3.

26 Testimony of Ben la Grange before the Parliamentary Standing Committee on Finance, 29 August 2018, Parliamentary Monitoring Group, https://pmg.org.za/committee-meeting/26960/.

27 Interview by the author with Piet Mouton, 3 August 2018.

28 Piet Naudé, Brett Hamilton, Marius Ungerer, Daniel Malan and Mias de Klerk, Business perspectives on the Steinhoff saga, University of Stellenbosch Business School, June 2018, https://www.usb.ac.za/wp-content/uploads/2018/06/Steinhoff_Revision_28_06_2018_websmall.pdf.

29 Giulietta Talevi, Inside the mind of Markus Jooste, *Financial Mail*, 12 October 2017, https://www.businesslive.co.za/fm/features/2017-10-12-inside-the-mind-of-markus-jooste/.

30 Piet Naudé, Brett Hamilton, Marius Ungerer, Daniel Malan, Mias de Klerk, Business perspectives on the Steinhoff saga, University of Stellenbosch Business School, June 2018, https://www.usb.ac.za/wp-content/uploads/2018/06/Steinhoff_Revision_28_06_2018_websmall.pdf.

31 Interview by the author with an anonymous Stellenbosch businessman, 1 August 2018.

32 Hanlie Retief, Hanlie Retief gesels met Christo Wiese, *Rapport*, 29 April 2018, https://www.netwerk24.com/Stemme/Menings/hanlie-retief-gesels-met-christo-wiese-20180429-2.

33 Angelique Serrao and Pieter du Toit, Markus Jooste, the blonde and the Bantry Bay flat, Huffington Post South Africa, https://www.huffingtonpost.co.za/2017/12/12/exclusive-markus-jooste-the-blonde-and-the-bantry-bay-flat_a_23305215/.

34 Testimony by Markus Jooste before the Parliamentary Standing Committee on Finance, 5 September 2018, Parliamentary Monitoring Group, https://pmg.org.za/committee-meeting/27013/.

35 Interview by the author with Edwin Hertzog, 21 June 2018.

36 Interview by the author with Johann Rupert, 22 August 2018.

37 Ferial Haffajee, PwC's Steinhoff report is a whitewash laced with white privilege, Fin24, 22 March 2019, https://www.fin24.com/Opinion/ferial-haffajee-pwcs-steinhoff-report-is-a-whitewash-laced-with-white-privilege-20190320.

38 Ibid.

39 Correspondence between the author and Wiese, 18 February 2019.

13. Turning new money into old

1 Interview by the author with Piet Mouton, 3 August 2018.

2 According to Forbes, as at 10 January 2018.

3 All references to Capitec and quotes by Le Roux in this chapter are based on an interview conducted by the author with Le Roux in Stellenbosch on 3 August 2018.

4 Ferreira was shot in the chest in a botched hijacking in 1992 and retired three years later.

5 All references to PSG and quotes by Piet Mouton are based on an interview conducted by the author with Mouton in Stellenbosch on 1 August 2018.

6 See Capitec Bank Holdings annual report 2018, https://resources.capitecbank.co.za/capitec_bank_integrated_annual_report_2018.pdf.

7 According to Forbes Africa's Billionaires, 21 February 2019, https://www.forbes.com/africa-billionaires/list/.

ACKNOWLEDGEMENTS

Writing a book is at once thrilling and daunting, exciting and excruciating, and even more so when you have a full-time job at Media24, the country's foremost media company, in an era of enormous political and social upheaval. You don't want to miss a thing, but you also have a deadline to make!

This effort isn't mine alone, but the result of my family, employer and publisher giving me the time, space and encouragement to finish a book about a subject that used to be nothing more than a conversation starter.

Love, thanks and respect to my wife, Janetha, who kept body and soul together while I disappeared for days, weeks and months into the darkness that my study became. And to my boys, Schalk and Lukas, for providing much needed levity in times of despair and frustration. *Pappa is nou terug, ek belowe.*

In an era of job cuts and an assault on quality journalism, Media24, my employer, remains a beacon of hope on the South African newscape. The company continues to invest in the right places and encourages its journalists and editors to write books: a rare privilege. Thanks to my bosses, past and present, for allowing me to do this: Esmaré Weideman, Andreij Horn, Charlene Beukes and Ishmet Davidson.

I have written a book with Adriaan Basson, but if it weren't for his encouragement and comradeship, I wouldn't have done one on my own. Thanks, bro.

This book would not have been published without the support of the excellent team at Jonathan Ball Publishers. CEO Eugene Ashton not only persuaded me that Stellenbosch was a story to tell, but didn't let up when I told him I had my doubts. Jeremy Boraine, the patient publishing director, along with wordsmith

Mark Ronan, salvaged the first draft, and the book is better for their stoic efforts. And thanks to Ceri Prenter, who took care to make the book as visually appealing as the content would allow. Caren van Houwelingen's patience with the final text was exemplary.

Much of the material contained in the book is based on other journalists' excellent work. Without that body of work (for example, Alec Hogg's treasure trove of interviews with Markus Jooste), *The Stellenbosch Mafia* would have been poorer. Thank you to all.

I am from Stellenbosch. I went to school and university there. I love the place. A number of people I write about here I know personally, and many of the anecdotes in the book I heard from friends and acquaintances I have known for decades. The inevitable mistakes are my own.

Many of the people I interviewed for this book, like Johann Rupert, gave freely of their time, not knowing exactly what the end result would be. I appreciate the trust they showed me and hope they accept that I have attempted to write an honest and colourful story about an oft-maligned but much-loved town.

Pieter du Toit

INDEX

CPSIA information can be obtained
at www.ICGtesting.com
Printed in the USA
BVHW041334240719
554170BV00029B/346/P